MW00387625

CompTIA
Network+
Exam: N10-007

Technology Workbook

Document Control

Proposal Name	:	CompTIA Network+ Certification Exam
Document Version	:	Version 2
Document Release Date	:	10 Jan 2020
Reference	:	CompTIA

Feedback:

If you have any comments regarding the quality of this book, or otherwise alter it to better suit your needs, you can contact us through email at info@ipspecialist.net

Please make sure to include the book's title and ISBN in your message

About IPSpecialist

IPSPECIALIST LTD. IS COMMITTED TO EXCELLENCE AND DEDICATED TO YOUR SUCCESS.

Our philosophy is to treat our customers like family. We want you to succeed, and we are willing to do everything possible to help you make it happen. We have the proof to back up our claims. We strive to accelerate billions of careers with great courses, accessibility, and affordability. We believe that continuous learning and knowledge evolution are the most important things to keep re-skilling and up-skilling the world.

Planning and creating a specific goal is where IPSpecialist helps. We can create a career track that suits your visions as well as develop the competencies you need to become a professional Network Engineer. We can also assist you with the execution and evaluation of your proficiency level, based on the career track you choose, as they are customized to fit your specific goals.

We help you STAND OUT from the crowd through our detailed IP training content packages.

Course Features:

❖ Self-Paced learning
  - Learn at your own pace and in your own time
❖ Covers Complete Exam Blueprint
  - Prep-up for the exam with confidence
❖ Case Study Based Learning
  - Relate the content with real life scenarios
❖ Subscriptions that suits you
  - Get more and pay less with IPS subscriptions
❖ Career Advisory Services
  - Let the industry experts plan your career journey
❖ Virtual Labs to test your skills
  - With IPS vRacks, you can evaluate your exam preparations
❖ Practice Questions
  - Practice questions to measure your preparation standards
❖ On Request Digital Certification
  - On request digital certification from IPSpecialist LTD

About the Authors:

This book has been compiled with the help of multiple professional engineers. These engineers specialize in different fields e.g. Networking, Security, Cloud, Big Data, IoT etc. Each engineer develops content in his/her own specialized field that is compiled to form a comprehensive certification guide.

About the Technical Reviewers:

Nouman Ahmed Khan

AWS-Architect, CCDE, CCIEX5 (R&S, SP, Security, DC, Wireless), CISSP, CISA, CISM, Nouman Ahmed Khan is a Solution Architect working with a major telecommunication provider in Qatar. He works with enterprises, mega-projects, and service providers to help them select the best-fit technology solutions. He also works as a consultant to understand customer business processes and helps select an appropriate technology strategy to support business goals. He has more than 14 years of experience working in Pakistan/Middle-East & UK. He holds a Bachelor of Engineering Degree from NED University, Pakistan, and M.Sc. in Computer Networks from the UK.

Abubakar Saeed

Abubakar Saeed has more than twenty-five years of experience, managing, consulting, designing, and implementing large-scale technology projects, extensive experience heading ISP operations, solutions integration, heading Product Development, Pre-sales, and Solution Design. Emphasizing on adhering to Project timelines and delivering as per customer expectations, he always leads the project in the right direction with his innovative ideas and excellent management skills.

Uzair Ahmed

Uzair Ahmed is a professional technical content writer holding a Bachelor's Degree in Computer Science from PAF-KIET University. He has sound knowledge and industry experience in SIEM implementation, .NET development, Machine learning, Artificial intelligence, Python and other programming and development platforms like React.JS Angular JS Laravel.

Afreen Moin

Afreen Moin is a professional Technical Content Developer. She holds a degree in Bachelor of Engineering in Telecommunications from Dawood University of Engineering and Technology. She has a great knowledge of computer networking and cybersecurity. She became a part of several networking training programs. She possesses a keen interest in research and develop contents related to computer networking and cybersecurity that boost her professional career.

Heba Dorazahi

Heba Dorazahi is a Technical Content writer. She has completed her bachelor's degree with a major in Telecommunication Engineering from Sir Syed University of Engineering & Technology. Throughout her academic studies, she gained extensive research and writing skills. She has done online courses of network security and cryptography to develop her expertise.

Free Resources:

With each purchased workbook, IPSpecialist offers free resources to our valuable customers.

Once you buy this book you will have to contact us at info@ipspecialist.net or tweet @ipspecialistnet to get this limited time offer without any extra charges.

Free Resources Include:

Exam Practice Questions in Quiz Simulation: IP Specialists' Practice Questions have been developed keeping in mind the certification exam perspective. The collection of these questions from our technology workbooks is prepared keeping the exam blueprint in mind, covering not only important but necessary topics as well. It is an ideal document to practice and revise your certification.

Career Report: This report is a step by step guide for a novice who wants to develop his/her career in the field of computer networks. It answers the following queries:

- Current scenarios and future prospects.

- Is this industry moving towards saturation or are new opportunities knocking at the door?
- What will the monetary benefits be?
- Why to get certified?
- How to plan and when will I complete the certifications if I start today?
- Is there any career track that I can follow to accomplish specialization level?

Furthermore, this guide provides a comprehensive career path towards being a specialist in the field of networking and also highlights the tracks needed to obtain certification.

IPS Personalized Technical Support for Customers: Good customer service means helping customers efficiently, in a friendly manner. It is essential to be able to handle issues for customers and do your best to ensure they are satisfied. Providing good service is one of the most important things that can set our business apart from the others of its kind.

Great customer service will result in attracting more customers and attain maximum customer retention.

IPS is offering personalized TECH support to its customers to provide better value for money. If you have any queries related to technology and labs you can simply ask our technical team for assistance via Live Chat or Email.

Become an Author & Earn with Us

If you are interested in becoming an author and start earning passive income, IPSpecialist offers "Earn with us" program. We all consume, develop and create content during our learning process, certification exam preparations, and during searching, developing and refining our professional careers. That content, notes, guides, worksheets and flip cards among other material is normally for our own reference without any defined structure or special considerations required for formal publishing.

IPSpecialist can help you craft this 'draft' content into a fine product with the help of our global team of experts. We sell your content via different channels as:

1. Amazon – Kindle
2. eBay
3. LuLu
4. Kobo
5. Google Books
6. Udemy and many 3rd party publishers and resellers

Our Products

Technology Workbooks

IPSpecialist Technology workbooks are the ideal guides to developing the hands-on skills necessary to pass the exam. Our workbook covers official exam blueprint and explains the technology with real life case study based labs. The content covered in each workbook consists of individually focused technology topics presented in an easy-to-follow, goal-oriented, step-by-step approach. Every scenario features detailed breakdowns and thorough verifications to help you completely understand the task and associated technology.

We extensively used mind maps in our workbooks to visually explain the technology. Our workbooks have become a widely used tool to learn and remember the information effectively.

vRacks

Our highly scalable and innovative virtualized lab platforms let you practice the IP Specialist Technology Workbook at your own time and your own place as per your convenience.

Quick Reference Sheets

Our quick reference sheets are a concise bundling of condensed notes of the complete exam blueprint. It is an ideal and handy document to help you remember the most important technology concepts related to the certification exam.

Practice Questions

IP Specialists' Practice Questions are dedicatedly designed from a certification exam perspective. The collection of these questions from our technology workbooks are prepared keeping the exam blueprint in mind covering not only important but necessary topics as well. It's an ideal document to practice and revise your certification.

Content at a glance

Table of Contents

About this Workbook

This workbook covers all the necessary information you need to pass the CompTIA Network+ Certification Exam Objectives N10-007 exam. The workbook is designed to take a practical approach of learning with real life scenarios and case studies.

> ➤ Covers complete CompTIA Network+ N10-007 blueprint
> ➤ Summarized content
> ➤ Case Study based approach
> ➤ Ready to practice labs on Virtualized Environment
> ➤ 100% pass guarantee
> ➤ Mind maps

CompTIA Certifications

CompTIA certification program is a vendor-neutral certification program that recognizes the best certifications in IT world. From the beginning till now CompTIA launched more than two million certifications.

The CompTIA Cloud Essentials certification focuses on the real-world issues and practical solutions of cloud computing in business and IT. It's the preferred cloud certification for business professionals and non-IT staff. Although it is not a challenging technical certification, but it's concept based on the principles of cloud computing.

CompTIA certifications are grouped by skill set. Currently, CompTIA certs fall info four areas: Core, Infrastructure, Cybersecurity and Additional Professional certifications. The certification of CompTIA cloud essentials lies in the Additional Professional area.

Figure 1. . CompTIA offering Certification Programs

How does CompTIA certifications help?

CompTIA certifications are a de facto standard in networking industry, which helps you boost your career in the following ways:

1. Gets your foot in the door by launching your IT career
2. Boosts your confidence level
3. Proves knowledge which helps improve employment opportunities

As for companies, CompTIA certifications is a way to:

1. Screen job applicants
2. Validate the technical skills of the candidate

3. Ensure quality, competency, and relevancy
4. Improve organization credibility and customer's loyalty
5. Meet the requirement in maintaining organization partnership level with OEMs
6. Helps in Job retention and promotion

CompTIA Certification Tracks

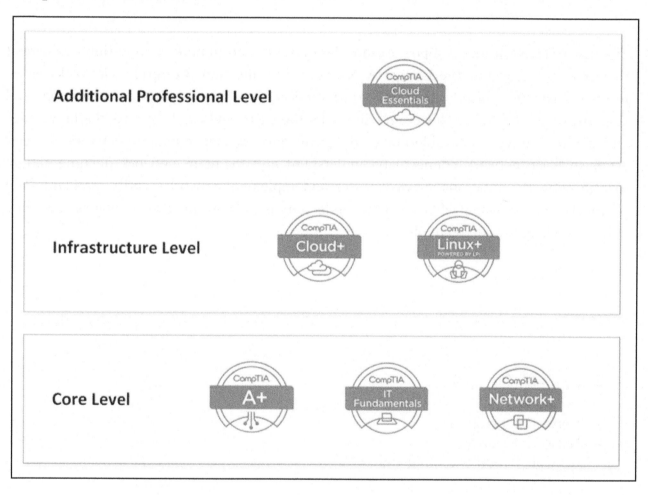

Figure 2. CompTIA Certification Tracks

About the CompTIA Exam

➤ **Required Exam:**   CompTIA Network+ N10-007
➤ **Number of Questions**:   Maximum of 90
➤ **Duration:**   90 minutes

> **Recommended Experience:** • CompTIA A+ Certified, or equivalent
> • Minimum of 9 months of experience in network
>   support or administration; or academic training

> **Passing Score**:   720 (on a scale of 100–900)
> **Exam Registration:**   Pearson VUE

The CompTIA Network+ composite exam (N10-007) is a 90-minute, 90 question assessment that is associated with the CompTIA Network+ certification. CompTIA Network+ is an internationally recognized validation of the technical knowledge required of foundation-level IT network practitioners. This exam will certify the successful candidate has the knowledge and skills required to troubleshoot, configure, and manage common network devices; establish basic network connectivity; understand and maintain network documentation; identify network limitations and weaknesses; and implement network security, standards, and protocols. The candidate will have a basic understanding of enterprise technologies, including cloud and virtualization technologies.

The following topics are general guidelines for the content likely to be included on the exam

> ➢ Networking Concepts   23%
> ➢ Infrastructure   18%
> ➢ Network Operations   17%
> ➢ Network Security   20%
> ➢ Network Troubleshooting and Tools   22%

How to become CompTIA Cloud Essential Certified?

Step 1: Pre-requisites

The CompTIA Network+ certification is an internationally recognized validation of the technical knowledge required of foundation-level IT network practitioners.

CompTIA Network+ candidates are recommended to have the following:

• CompTIA A+ certification or equivalent knowledge, although CompTIA A+ certification is not required

• At least 9 to 12 months of work experience in IT networking

Step2: Prepare for the CompTIA Exam

Exam preparation can be accomplished through self-study with textbooks, ebooks, practice exams, and on-site classroom trainings.

IPSpecialist provides full support to the candidates in order for them to pass the exam.

Step 3: Register for the exam

When you are ready to take your CompTIA certification exam, you can schedule your test on the Pearson VUE website.

Follow these three steps:

1. Create a Pearson VUE testing account

You will need a Pearson VUE testing account to register for your certification exam and store your testing information with the testing center.

2. Find a Pearson VUE test center

All CompTIA certification exam testing is provided by our global testing partner, Pearson VUE. When you are ready to take your exam, visit Pearson VUE's website to find an authorized Pearson VUE test center near you to schedule your test. You will be able to select the testing center of your choice when scheduling your exam.

3. Schedule your exam

Sign in to your Pearson VUE account to find a testing center, as well as schedule, reschedule or cancel an exam appointment. You can buy a voucher through CompTIA or on the Pearson VUE website.

4. Save your exam appointment confirmation

Once your exam date is scheduled, you will receive a confirmation email with registration information as well as additional information that you may need to provide to your testing center. Make sure to kept this information safely. Certain information that you provide during

the registration will be required to sign in to your certification account once you have passed your certification exam.

How much does an exam cost?

Computer-based certification exam prices (written exam) depend on scope and exam length. You may refer to the " Exam Pricing" link on the CompTIA website for complete details.

Step 4: Getting the Results

After you complete an exam at an authorized testing centre, you will get immediate, online notification of your pass or fail status, a printed examination score report that indicates your pass or fail status, and your exam results by section.

Congratulations! You are now CompTIA Network+ Certified.

Chapter 01: Networking Concept

Technology Brief

Generating a network from the ground up needs a large number of hardware and software technologies to operate together to obtain the information from one machine to another: In essence, there is sets of rules on what a network should do and how it should be done.

These sets of rules and the software written to follow these rules are broken down into individual rules known as protocol. When a series of protocols are specifically designed to operate together, they are called a protocol suite. These protocol suites invariably are named with some form of protocol name/protocol name format.

Purposes and Uses of Ports and Protocols

The TCP/IP suite is a set of protocols used on today's computer networks specifically on the Internet. It provides end-to-end connectivity by specifying that the data should be packetized, addressed, transmitted, routed and received on a TCP/IP network. This functionality is arranged into four consideration layers, and each protocol in the suite operates in a particular layer. This section will focus only on three protocols- ICMP, TCP, and UDP.

Protocols and Ports

Many protocols run on the different layers of the OSI model and their port numbers identifies those protocols. This section will discuss the importance of protocols and ports associated with them.

SSH 22

Secure Shell (SSH) has replaced an unsecure protocol Telnet. SSH involves SSH servers that use Public Key Infrastructure (PKI) in the form of an RSA key. When a client tries to log into an SSH server, the server sends its public key to the client first then the client receives this key. It creates a session ID and encrypts it using the public key, and sends it back to the server. The server decrypts this session key ID and uses to forward all data. It is secure therefore only the client, and the server knows this session ID. SSH uses port 22 and TCP for connections.

DNS 53

Domain Name System (DNS) translates the human-readable domain names to IP addresses. A DNS server is a special type of server that directs, holds and processes internet domain names and their related records. The DNS uses TCP port 53.

SMTP 25

Simple Mail Transfer Protocol (SMTP) defines the process of email transferring between the hosts on a network. SMTP works at the Application layer of the OSI model and uses TCP to guarantee error-free delivery of messages, to hosts using port 25.

SFTP 22

SFTP (SSH File Transfer Protocol) is a secure alternate of File Transfer Protocol (FTP). It runs over the SSH protocol. SFTP offers security and authentication of SSH to secure the communication channel. SSH port 22 is the SFTP port number.

SFTP has replaced the FTP providing more security against password sniffing and man-in-the-middle attacks and more reliability (it protects the integrity of the data using encryption) with ease of configuration. There is no reason to use the vulnerable file transferring protocols any more.

FTP 20 and 21

File Transfer Protocol (FTP) is the most common way of sending and receiving files between two computers. FTP is not very secure because data transfers are not encrypted by default, so add usernames and passwords to prevent all but the most severe hackers from accessing your FTP server. The old active FTP used TCP ports 21 and 20 by default, although passive FTP only uses port 21 for a default.

Real World Scenario

Background

FTP is an application layer protocol within the TCP/IP protocol suite that enables transfer of information primarily via ports 20 and 21. Port 21 is the FTP control port, while port 20 is the data port.

Although FTP is widely used, several vulnerabilities should be addressed to ensure security. FTP authentication is sent as clear-text, making it easy for an individual to view usernames and passwords with a packet sniffer. Because hackers and malicious software can be used to get this data quite easily, when traffic does not need to cross firewalls or routers on a network, it is essential to block ports 20 and 21.

Challenges

Healthcare data is the most coveted data type for hackers and cyber criminals, far more than credit card data. The FBI alerted medical and dental facilities about a new cybercrime threat that involves the active targeting of anonymous FTP servers in order to gain access to Protected Health Information (PHI) and Personally Identifiable Information (PII).

The anonymous extension of FTP "allows a user to be authenticated to the FTP server with a common username such as 'anonymous' or 'ftp' without submitting a password or by submitting a generic password or email address".

As a result, hackers continuously launch cyberattacks on businesses that use anonymous FTP within the medical and dental industries attempting to compromise sensitive PHI and PII data with the "purposes of intimidating, harassing, and blackmailing" business owners.

Solution

Here are three steps to help eliminate the risk:

1. **Do a Systems Audit:** Performing a systems audit will help to identify any systems that might be running on anonymous.

2. **Stop Using Anonymous FTP:** An outdated protocol carries more risks than rewards.

3. **Start Using a Secure Managed File Transfer (MFT) Solution:** A quality Managed File Transfer (MFT) solution not only offers a variety of secure protocols like FTPS, HTTPS, and SFTP, but also provides other security features,

> such as multi-factor authentication, resource controls with permission groups, password complexity, expiring inactive accounts, and of course, encryption.
>
> **Conclusion**
>
> FTP is same as Telnet where credentials and information are sent in clear-text so that, if captured through a passive attack such as sniffing, the data could be exploited to provide unauthorized access. Although FTP is a popular protocol to use for transmitting data, the fact that it transfers the authentication data in a cleartext format also makes it extremely insecure.

TFTP 69

Trivial File Transfer Protocol (TFTP) has similar functionality as FTP that both allows the transfer of files within a network. Although FTP allows for the browsing of files and folders on a server, TFTP requires to know the exact name of the file users want to transfer and the exact location of where to find the file. In addition, whereas FTP uses the connection-oriented TCP, TFTP uses the connectionless UDP. TFTP is most often used for simple downloads such as transferring firmware to a network device (router or switch). Data transfer through TFTP is usually initiated through port 69.

TELNET 23

It is a terminal emulation that enables a user to connect to a remote host or device using a telnet client. Telnet is measured insecure because it transfers all data in clear text. Users who want secure transmission of data consider SSH as opposed to telnet. The port associated with Telnet is 23.

DHCP 67 and 68

Dynamic Host Configuration Protocol (DHCP) is a dynamic IP addressing protocol working on client-server based model, which allows the network devices to request and the DHCP server to allocate the IP address to this host automatically. It helps to reduce the workload of a network administrator to manually assign an IP address to each device. DHCP uses User Datagram Protocol (UDP) port 67 for the server and UDP port 68 for the client.

DHCP provides the following benefits:

- Reliable IP address configuration
- Reduced network administration

HTTP 80

Hypertext Transfer Protocol (HTTP) is the protocol to browse the World Wide Web via port no 80. HTTP clients use a browser to make special requests from an HTTP server that contains the files they require. The files on the HTTP server are formatted in web languages such as Hypertext Markup Language (HTML) and are located using a Uniform Resource Locator (URL). The URL contains the type of request being generated (http://, for example), the DNS name of the server to which the request is being processed, and optionally, the path to the file on the server.

HTTPS 443

Hypertext Transfer Protocol Secure (HTTPS) provides a more secure solution that uses a Secure Sockets Layer (SSL) to encrypt information that is sent between the client and the server. For HTTPS to operate, both the client and the server must support it. While browsing through HTTPS, you need to fill out forms, sign in, authenticate, and encrypt an HTTP message when users make a reservation or buy something online. HTTPS uses port 443.

SNMP 161

Simple Network Management Protocol (SNMP) is a tool that can help in identifying devices called agents in the network such as routers, and switches. It also determines the status and configuration of these devices. SNMP uses UDP ports 161 and 162 for non-secure communication. The Network Management Station (NMS) receives/listens on port 162. The agent receives/listens on port 161.

RDP 3389

Remote Desktop Protocol (RDP) is a proprietary protocol used by computers running the MS Operating Systems, although clients exist that allow Linux and Unix systems to connect to MS computers using RDP. It can be used to connect to a computer and take control of the system remotely. Every MS client since Windows XP has RDP software built-in. For security means, it is not initially enabled. To connect to a computer remotely, users must enable the software and configure the appropriate authentication. By default, the server listens on TCP port 3389 and UDP port 3389.

RTP 5004 and 5005

RTP defines a standardized packet format for delivering audio and video over the Internet. It is frequently used in streaming, video conferencing, and push-to-talk applications. RTP typically runs over User Datagram Protocol (UDP).

- 5004 UDP port is used for delivering data packets to clients that are streaming by using Real Time Streaming Protocol UDP (RTSPU)
- 5005 UDP port is used for receiving packet loss information from clients and providing synchronization information to clients that are streaming by using RTSPU

NTP 123

Network Time Protocol (NTP) provides time synchronization to all our network devices. In simple words, NTP synchronizes clocks of computer systems over packet-switched, variable-latency data networks. The current protocol is version 4 (NTPv4), which is a proposed standard as documented in RFC 5905. It sends and receives timestamps using the User Datagram Protocol (UDP) on port number 123.

Typically, users will have an NTP server that connects through the Internet to an atomic clock. This time can then be synchronized through the network to keep all routers, switches, servers, etc. receiving the same time information.

Correct network time within the network is important:

- Tracking of events in the network is possible with correct time
- Clock synchronization is critical for the correct interpretation of events within the syslog data
- Clock synchronization is critical for digital certificates

SIP 5060 and 5061

Session Initiation Protocol (SIP) is an incredibly popular signaling protocol used to build up and break down multimedia communication sessions, for many things like voice and video calls, video conferencing, streaming multimedia distribution, instant messaging, presence information, and online games over the internet. It also enables IP telephony networks to utilize advanced call features such as SS7. SIP clients typically use TCP or UDP on port numbers 5060 or 5061 for SIP traffic to servers and other endpoints. Port 5060 is commonly used for non-encrypted signaling traffic whereas, port 5061 is typically used for traffic encrypted with Transport Layer Security (TLS).

SMB 445

Server Message Block (SMB) is a legacy protocol that is used to provide shared access to files, folders, printers, and so on over a computer network. It has been substituted by other

more efficient and more secure protocols. SMB Protocol can also be used without a separate transport protocol directly over TCP, port 445.

POP 110

Post Office Protocol (POP) gives us a storage facility for incoming mail, and the latest version is called POP3. POP3 is one of the protocols that is used to retrieve emails from SMTP servers. Using POP3, clients connect to the server, authenticate, and then download their email. Once they have downloaded their email, they can read it. Normally, the email is then deleted from the server, although some systems hold a copy of the email for a period of time specified by an administrator. One of the drawbacks of POP3 authentication is that it is generally performs in clear text. This means that an attacker could sniff the POP3 password from the network as users enter it. POP protocol uses port number 110.

IMAP 143

Internet Message Access Protocol (IMAP) version-4 is another protocol that is used to retrieve email from SMTP servers, but IMAPv4 offers some advantages over POP3. IMAPv4 provides a more flexible method of handling email through port 143. Users can read the email on the email server and then determine whether they to want to download this email to the PC. Since the email can stay in the mailbox on the server, users can retrieve it from any computer that they want to use. Google Gmail is a good example of an IMAPv4 type of service. Users can access Gmail account from any browser. Users can then read, answer, and forward email without downloading the messages to the computer.

LDAP 389

The Lightweight Directory Access Protocol LDAP is an open standard, application protocol. LDAP is for accessing and maintaining distributed directory information services. A directory service plays an important role by allowing the sharing of information like user, system, network, service, etc. throughout the network. LDAP provides a central place to store usernames and passwords. Applications and Services connect to the LDAP server to validate users. LDAP functions by default on TCP and UDP port 389.

LDAPS 636

LDAPS (LDAP over SSL). LDAPS is the non-standardized "LDAP over SSL" protocol in contrast with StartTLS (LDAP with TLS). LDAPS functions by default on port 636.

H.323 1720

H.323 is a protocol that provides a standard for video on an IP network that defines how real-time audio, video, and data information is transmitted. This standard provides signaling, multimedia, and bandwidth control solution. H.323 uses the RTP standard for

communication. H.323 is also used for multimedia communications on mobile phones and other portable devices. H.323 uses TCP port number 1720.

MGCP 2427

Media Gateway Control Protocol (MGCP) is a standard protocol for handling the signaling and session management necessary during a multimedia conference such as Voice over IP (VoIP) telecommunication systems. The protocol defines a means of communication between a media gateway, which converts data from the required format for a circuit-switched network to that required format for a packet-switched network. MGCP can be used to set up, maintain, and terminate calls between multiple endpoints. The architecture of the MGCP and its methodologies and programming interfaces are described in RFC 2805. Media gateways use the UDP port number 2427, and call agents use 2727 by default.

NetBIOS

NetBIOS is a legacy protocol that was used by computers, running Microsoft operating systems as a name-resolution tool. It has been superseded now by DNS. There is still an implementation of NetBIOS over TCP/IP on newer operating systems, if a legacy application requires it. NetBIOS protocol uses port number 137-139.

- UDP port 137 (name services)
- UDP port 138 (datagram services)
- TCP port 139 (session services)

Types of Protocol

Several types of protocols are discussed below.

ICMP

Internet Control Message Protocol (ICMP) works at the Network layer of the OSI model and the internet layer of the TCP/IP suite. ICMP provides error checking and reporting functionality. Additionally, ICMP provides many functions; the most commonly known is its ping utility. The ping utility is most often used for troubleshooting. In a typical ping scenario, an administrator uses a host's command line, and the ping utility, to send a stream of packets, called an echo request to another host. When the destination host receives the packets, ICMP sends back a stream of packets referred to as an echo reply. This confirms that the connection between the two hosts is configured properly, and that TCP/IP is operational.

UDP

User Datagram Protocol (UDP) also operates at the Transport layer of the OSI model and uses IP as its transport protocol, but it is a connectionless protocol, which means it does not guarantee the delivery of packets because UDP does not establish a session. However,

UDP is quite demanding unlike TCP because of its advantage of low overhead regarding bandwidth and processing effort. Whereas a TCP header has 11 fields of information that have to be processed, a UDP header has only 4 fields. Applications that can handle their own acknowledgments and that do not require the additional features of TCP, might use UDP to take advantage of the lower overhead. Services such as the Domain Name System (DNS) service also take advantage of the lower overhead provided by UDP.

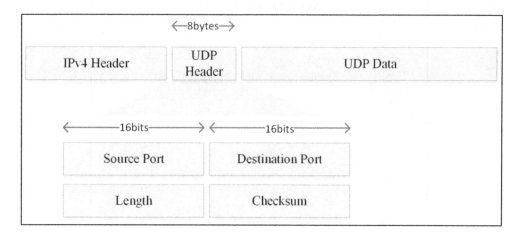

Figure 1-01: UDP Segment Format

TCP

Transmission Control Protocol (TCP) is a connection-oriented protocol that works at the Transport layer of the OSI model. It uses IP as its transport protocol and assists IP by providing a guaranteed mechanism for delivery. TCP requires establishing a session first between two computers, before communicating. Additionally, TCP also includes features such as flow control, sequencing, and error detection and correction. TCP works by a process referred to as a three-way handshake.

The TCP three-way handshake works as follows:

1. TCP sends a short message called an SYN to the target host
2. The target host opens a connection for the request and sends back an acknowledgment message called a SYN ACK
3. The host that originated the request, sends back another acknowledgment, called an ACK, confirming that it has received the SYN ACK message and that the session is ready to be used to transfer data

A similar process is used to close the session when the data exchange is complete. If a packet is not acknowledged within the timeout period, the packet is resent automatically

by TCP. The only disadvantage of a connection-oriented protocol, is that the large overhead associated with the acknowledgments, inclines to slow it down.

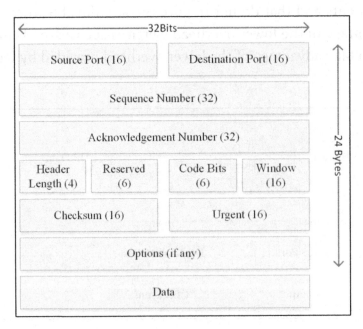

Figure 1-02: TCP Segment Format

IP

Internet Protocol (IP) is a layer 3 protocol containing address information as well as control information of the packet. This control information helps the packet to be routed. IP is documented in RFC 791. This protocol is called on by host-to-host protocols in an internet environment. Being the primary network layer protocol in the internet protocol suit, IP has two primary responsibilities:

1. Addressing
2. Fragmentation

The internet protocol uses four key mechanisms in providing its service:

1. **Type of Service:** Indicates the quality of the service.
2. **Time to Live:** An indication of an upper bound on the lifetime of an internet datagram.
3. **Options:** The options include provisions for timestamps, security, and special routing.
4. **Header Checksum:** Provides a verification that the information used in processing internet datagram has been transmitted correctly.

Connectionless Vs Connection Oriented

Following table shows the difference of connectionless and connection oriented protocols with respect to connection, reliability and usage:

	Connection-Oriented	Connectionless
Connection	Prior connection establishment required	No prior connection establishment
Resource Allocation	Prior resources allocation	No prior resources allocation
Reliability	Reliable data transfer	Best effort delivery
Congestion	No congestion	Congestion may occur
Transfer Mode	Circuit switching or Virtual Circuits	Packet Switching
Retransmission	Retransmission of data lost in communication	No retransmission of lost bits in communication
Suitability		
Signaling	Signaling for connection establishment	No signaling concept
Packet Travel	Sequential packet receiving at destination	Random packet receiving at destination
Delay	Delay due to connection establishment	No delay of connection establishment
Application	TCP, ATM, Frame Relay, MPLS	IP, UDP, ICMP, DNS etc.

Table 1-01: Difference of Connectionless and Connection-Oriented Protocols

Exam Tip

Be able to describe protocols and ports for the exam objective. Know different types of protocols such as ICMP, UDP, TCP and IP.

Mind Map of Ports and Protocols

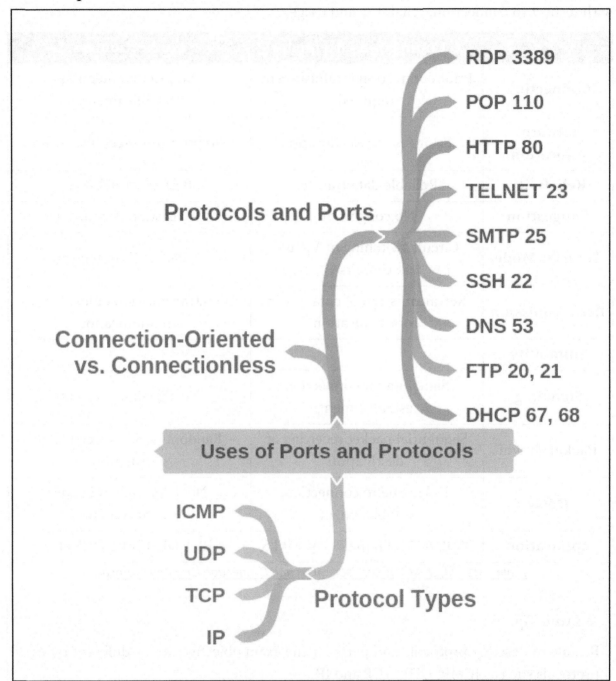

Figure 1-03: Mind Map of Purposes and Uses of Ports and Protocols

Devices, Applications, Protocols and Services at their Appropriate OSI Layers

The Open Standards Interconnection (OSI) model was developed by the International Organization for Standardization (ISO) in the 1980's. The purpose of the model was to allow developers to focus on only the layers that applied to them and only on the protocols at those layers. OSI provides a means of relating the components and their functions to each other, and a way of standardizing components and protocols.

The seven layers and their function in the OSI model are as follows:

Layer 1 – Physical

The Physical layer (Layer-1) controls the signalling and transferring of raw bits onto the physical medium. The Physical layer is closely related to the Data-Link layer, as many technologies such as Ethernet, contain both data-link and physical functions. The Physical layer provides specifications for a variety of hardware:

- Cabling
- Connectors and Transceivers
- Network Interface Cards (NICs)
- Hubs

Layer 2 – Data Link

The Data-Link layer (Layer-2) is responsible for transporting data within a network. The Data-Link layer consists of two sublayers:

Logical Link Control (LLC) Sublayer: The LLC sublayer serves as the midway between the physical link and all higher layer protocols. It ensures that protocols like IP can function irrespective of what type of physical technology is being used. Additionally, the LLC sublayer can perform flow-control and error-checking.

Media Access Control (MAC) Sublayer: The MAC sublayer controls access to the physical medium, serving as a mediator. If multiple devices are competing for the same physical link, Data-Link layer technologies have various methods of doing this. Ethernet uses Carrier Sense Multiple Access with Collision Detection (CSMA/CD), and Token Ring utilizes a token.

The Data-Link layer packages the higher-layer data into frames so that the data can be put onto the physical layer. This packaging process is referred to as framing or encapsulation. The encapsulation type will vary depending on the fundamental technology.

Common Data-Link layer technologies include the following:

- Ethernet – the most common LAN data-link technology

- Token Ring – almost entirely deprecated
- FDDI (Fiber Distributed Data Interface)
- 802.11 Wireless
- Frame-Relay
- ATM (Asynchronous Transfer Mode)

Layer 3 – Network

The Network layer (Layer-3) controls the internetworking of communication and has two key responsibilities:

Logical Addressing: Provides a unique address that identifies both the host, and the network that host exists on.

Routing: Determines the best path to a particular destination network and then routes data accordingly.

Two of the most common Network layer protocols are:

- Internet Protocol (IP)
- Novell's Internetwork Packet Exchange (IPX)

Layer 4 – Transport

The Transport layer (Layer-4) is responsible for the reliable transfer of data, by ensuring that data arrives at its destination, error-free, and in order.

Transport layer communication falls into two categories:

Connection-Oriented: Requires a connection establishment with specific collaborated parameters before sending data.

Connectionless: Requires no connection before data is sent.

Connection-oriented protocols provide several important services:

- **Segmentation and Sequencing** – Data is segmented into smaller parts for transport. Each segment is assigned a sequence number so that the receiving device can reassemble the data on arrival
- **Connection Establishment** – Connections are established, maintained, and ultimately terminated between devices
- **Acknowledgments** – Receipt of data is confirmed through the use of acknowledgments. Otherwise, data is retransmitted
- **Flow Control (or windowing)** – Data transfer rate is exchanged, to prevent congestion

The TCP/IP protocol suite incorporates two Transport layer protocols:

- **Transmission Control Protocol (TCP)** – connection-oriented

- **User Datagram Protocol (UDP)** - connectionless

Layer 5 – Session

The Session layer (Layer-5) is responsible for establishing, maintaining, and ultimately terminating sessions between devices. If a session is broken, this layer can attempt to recover the session.

Sessions communication falls under one of three categories:

- **Full-Duplex** – simultaneous two-way communication
- **Half-Duplex** – two-way communication, but not simultaneous
- **Simplex** – one-way communication

Many modern protocol suites, such as TCP/IP, do not implement Session layer protocols. Lower layers, such as the Transport layer, often control connection management.

Layer 6 – Presentation

The Presentation layer (Layer-6) controls the formatting and syntax of user data for the application layer. This ensures that data from the sending application can be known by the receiving application.

Standards have been developed for the formatting of data types, such as text, images, audio, and video.

Examples of Presentation-layer formats include:

- **Text** - RTF, ASCII, EBCDIC
- **Images** - GIF, JPG, TIF • Audio - MIDI, MP3, WAV
- **Movies** - MPEG, AVI, MOV

If two devices do not support the same format or syntax, the Presentation layer can provide conversion or translation services to assist communication.

Moreover, the Presentation layer can perform encryption and compression of data, as required.

Layer 7 – Application

The Application layer (Layer-7) provides the interface between the user application and the network. A web browser and an email client are examples of user applications. The user application itself does not present at the Application layer, but the protocol does. The user interacts with the application through application layer protocol.

Examples of Application layer protocols include:

- **FTP** by an FTP client
- **HTTP** by a web browser
- **POP3 and SMTP** by an email client
- **Telnet**

The Application layer provides a variety of functions:

- Identifies communication partners
- Determines resource availability
- Synchronizes communication

Exam Tip

The CompTIA Network+ exam expects you to know the layers by name, how they function in relation to each other, and what they represent.

Mind Map of OSI Layers

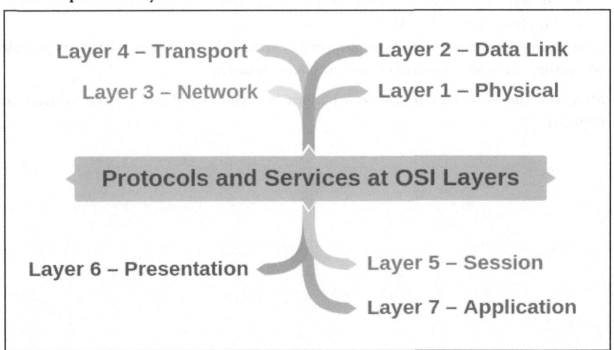

Figure 1-04: Mind Map of OSI Layers Protocols and Servicesa

The Concepts and Characteristics of Routing and Switching

Routing allows users to interconnect individual LANs into WANs. Routers, the magic boxes that act as the interconnection points, have all the built-in smarts to inspect incoming packets and forward them toward their eventual LAN destination.

Properties of Network Traffic

Network traffic can be identified by certain properties. For example, what happens before sending the message and who hears the message. Let's explore these concepts in greater detail.

Multicast vs. Unicast vs. Broadcast

Three major types of addressing schemes are used on IPv4 networks. These are unicast, multicast, and broadcast. Unicast addressing has one source address and one destination address. Multicast addressing can be much more complex than unicast. With multicast addressing, there is still only one source address, but there can be multiple destination addresses.

Every IPv4 network or subnet has a broadcast address, which is the last numerical address before the next network. In the binary form of a broadcast address, you will notice that all the host bits are 1s. For example, the broadcast address of the network 192.168.1.0/27 is 192.168.1.31.

Broadcast Domains vs. Collision Domains

Collision domains occur when network devices share the same transmission medium, and their packets can collide. Collisions increase as the number of devices in a collision domain increases.

Broadcast domain occurs in the network where computers can receive frame-level broadcasts from their neighbors. Increasing devices on a network segment increases broadcast traffic on a segment.

Device	Collision Domain	Broadcast Domain
Hub	All devices connected to the hub are in the same collision domain	All devices are in the same broadcast domain
Bridge or Switch	All devices connected to a single port are in the same collision domain; each port is its collision domain	All devices connected to the bridge or the switch are in the same broadcast domain

	All devices connected to a single interface are in the same collision domain	All devices accessible through an interface (network) are in the same broadcast domain. Each interface represents its broadcast domain if the router is configured to not forward broadcast packets
Router		

Table 1-02: Broadcast Vs. Collision Domain

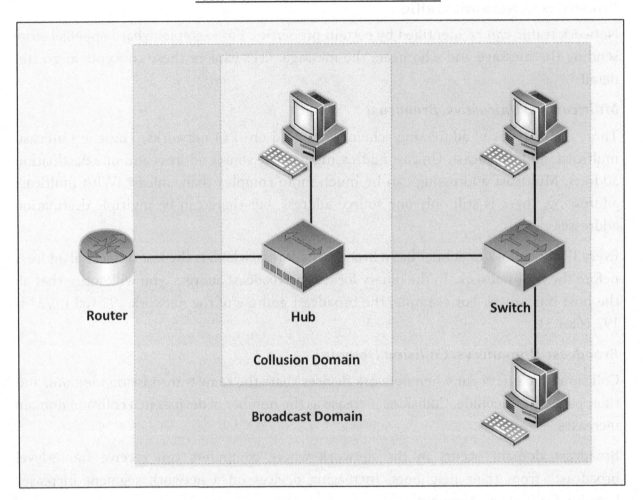

Figure 1-05: Broadcast Domain Vs. Collision Domain

CSMA/CD

In the past, networks had contained devices called hubs. These hubs created a shared network, which meant that each computer connected to the network had equal access to the same electrical paths as the others. Since the paths were baseband and therefore could carry only one communication at a time, the computers had to take turns accessing the wire. A protocol called Carrier Sense Multiple Access with Collision Detection (CSMA/CD) was developed to sense the wire that determines whether current is fluctuating and

therefore whether some other computer is using it. If another computer has the wire, then the first computer must wait until the wire is not in use before it can send its data. Once the collision is detected by the protocol, each computer will be given a set time to go again, based on a back-off algorithm created by the protocol. In this way, the computers will be kept from creating subsequent collisions.

CSMA/CA

While using wireless communication between computers and devices, use a Carrier Sense Multiple Access with Collision Avoidance instead of Collision Detection.

The main purpose of this protocol is to guarantee that the data to be transmitted can be transmitted and received successfully between the two devices. It does this by first, listening, and then using additional frames to negotiate the network access.

Encapsulation/De-encapsulation

As data is passed from the host device to destination device by following the OSI model, before transmission of the data, each layer adds a header, or sometimes trailer, containing protocol information specific to that layer. These headers are called Protocol Data Units (PDUs), and the process of adding these headers, is called Encapsulation.

When the receiving device receives the data off the wire, reading and interpreting the header information, it is referred to as De-encapsulation.

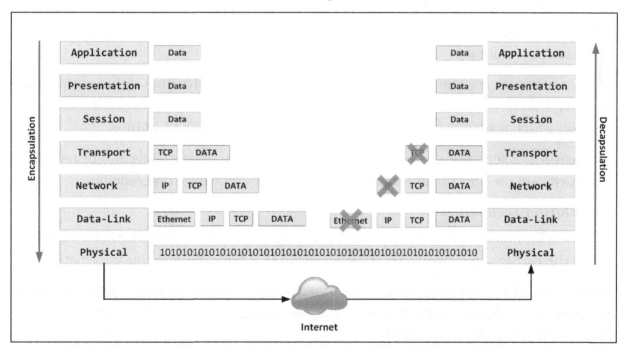

Figure 1-06: Encapsulation/De-encapsulation

During encapsulation on the sending host:

- Data from the user application is handed off to the Transport layer
- The Transport layer adds a header containing protocol-specific information, and then hands over the segment to the Network layer
- The Network layer adds a header containing source and destination logical addressing, and then hands over the packet to the Data-Link layer
- The Data-Link layer adds a header, containing source, destination physical addressing and other hardware-specific information
- The Data-Link frame is then handed over to the Physical layer to be transmitted on the network medium as bits

During de-encapsulation on the receiving host, the reverse process occurs:

- The frame is received from the physical medium
- The Data-Link layer processes its header, strips it off, and then hands it off to the Network layer
- The Network layer processes its header, strips it off, and then hands it off to the Transport layer
- The Transport layer processes its header, strips it off, and then hands the data to the user application

Unicast/Broadcast/Multicast

The Layer 2 and Layer 3 (if applicable) addresses will always be of the same type: unicast, broadcast, or multicast.

Unicast messages are sent from one source to exactly one destination. A broadcast is sent to every system in the broadcast domain. A common example of a broadcast is an ARP request, which is used to find a MAC address given that device's IP address.

Multicasts are sent from routers to networks that have at least one interested client. Multicasts are used for things like streaming, gaming, and video conferencing.

Modulation Techniques

In networks, modulation is the process of varying one or more properties of a waveform, called the carrier signal, with a transmitted signal that typically contains information.

Modulation of a waveform transforms a baseband message signal into a passband signal. In recent networks, modulation takes a digital or analog signal and puts it in another signal that can be physically transmitted.

The purpose of digital modulation is to transfer a digital bit stream over an analog bandpass channel. The purpose of analog modulation is to transfer an analog baseband (or lowpass) signal over an analog bandpass channel at a different frequency.

The digital baseband modulation methods found in our Ethernet networks, and also known as line coding, are used to transfer a digital bit stream over a baseband channel. Baseband means that the signal being modulated has used the complete available bandwidth.

Multiplexing

Multiplexing is the process, in which multiple Data Streams, coming from different Sources are combined and Transmitted over a Single Data Channel.

In networking, the two basic forms of Multiplexing are Time Division Multiplexing (TDM) and Frequency Division Multiplexing (FDM).

In Time Division Multiplexing, Transmission Time on a Single Channel is divided into non-overlapped Time Slots. Data Streams from different Sources, are divided into Parts with the same size and interleaved successively into the Time Slots.

In Frequency Division Multiplexing, Data Streams are carried simultaneously on the same Transmission medium by allocating to each of them, a different Frequency Band within the Bandwidth of the Single Channel.

De-Multiplexing

De-Multiplexing is the reverse process of multiplexing that performs at the receiving end. The multiplexed signal is separated by a device called De-Multiplexer (DEMUX).

Maximum Transmission Unit (MTU)

MTU is considered as a legacy metric that is used to signify the largest packet that could be sent across the entire route. EIGRP uses MTU but it is not used in the calculation of the best route. EIGRP uses bandwidth and delays to make decisions.

Segmentation and Interface Properties

Layer 2 switches enable many creative setups for classifying, separating, and dealing with network traffic. VLANs break up broadcast domains, and STP avoids switching loops from occurring. MAC address tables are used to cache address pairs. These concepts, as well as others are discussed in the following sections.

Virtual Local Area Network (VLAN)

Switches and routers have physical interfaces, commonly known as a physical port; these ports can be configured in a variety of ways, depending upon the topology, design, type of encapsulation, duplex, and speed of the link. On switches, the additional configuration is VLAN port assignment.

- **Native VLAN:**
  When enabling IEEE 802.1Q tunneling on an edge switch, you must use IEEE 802.1Q trunk ports for sending packets into the service-provider network.

However, packets pass through the core of the service-provider network and can be carried through IEEE 802.1Q trunks, ISL trunks, or non-trunking links. When IEEE 802.1Q trunks are used in these core switches, the native VLANs of the IEEE 802.1Q trunks must not match any native VLAN of the non-trunking (tunneling) port on the same switch because traffic on the native VLAN would not be tagged on the IEEE 802.1Q sending trunk port

- **VTP:** VTP is a Layer 2 messaging protocol that maintains VLAN configuration consistency by managing the databases of VLANs within a VTP domain. A VTP domain is made up of one or more network devices that share the same VTP domain name and that are interconnected with trunks. VTP can make configuration changes centrally on one or more network devices and have those changes automatically configured to all the other network devices in the network

VLAN Interface Configuration

A VLAN is a subnet created using a switch instead of a router. For this reason, VLANs have many advantages over subnets created by routers. One of the main advantages of VLANs is that the logical network design does not have to follow the physical network topology. It gives administrators much more flexibility in network design and in the subsequent changes of that design. All the administrator has to do is configure the interface with the right VLAN and connect the appropriate cables.

Trunking 802.1Q

VLAN Trunking (802.1Q) allows physical network interfaces in a computing environment to be shared. As data centers become more complex and the number of interconnected services increase, it is expensive to provide dedicated cabling and network switch ports to allow all the required connections. VLAN trunking allows multiple virtual network connections to be maintained on a small number of physical adapters.

Tagging and Untagging Ports

Tagging means that the port will send out a packet with a header that has a tag number that matches its VLAN tag number. Trunk Tagging protocol 802.1Q, ISL and DTP are the types of Tag VLAN.

Untagged VLAN means that the frame cannot be tagged while traveling from one switch to another switch e.g., VLAN1, Native VLAN or Management VLAN. The frame does not mention which VLAN it belongs to. Untagged VLAN is a port-based VLAN.

Port Mirroring

Port mirroring, also known as Switch Port Analyzer (SPAN) and Remote Switch Port Analyzer (RSPAN), allows you to sniff traffic on a network when using a switch.

Local SPAN supports a SPAN session entirely within one switch; all source ports or source VLANs and destination ports are on the same switch. Local SPAN copies traffic from one or more source ports in any VLAN or from one or more VLANs to a destination port for analysis.

Remote SPAN supports source ports, source VLANs, and destination ports on different switches. The traffic for each RSPAN session is carried over a user-specified RSPAN VLAN that is dedicated for that RSPAN session in all participating switches.

Switching Loops / Spanning Tree

Users can generate redundant connections in a network because they can connect switches together in any fashion. Certain redundant connections would cause switching loops, without proper control in place.

Spanning Tree (802.1d)/Rapid Spanning Tree (802.1w)

Spanning tree is used to ensure that only one active path exists between two nodes at one time on the network. If a network has more than one active path, you can block all the redundant paths by enabling spanning tree. STP prevents network switching loops. STP has two main types; the original spanning tree 802.1d and the improved rapid spanning tree 802.1w. The leading advantage of 802.1w is much faster convergence on link failure. It is accomplished by the protocol automatically, determining the designated ports that will be used as well as the backups and alternates that might be used in case of a link failure.

Flooding

When a switch does not know what to do with traffic, or the switches, or it does not have a specific destination address, then it forwards the data to all the connected ports except the host address. This process is called flooding.

Forwarding/Blocking

When switches learn the destination of the data, it forwards it. Alternatively, if users do not allow the traffic from unknown ports, then it is blocked.

Filtering

If switches want to allow traffic from only the specific port, then you must configure the switches according to it. This process is called filtering traffic.

Power over Ethernet (PoE) / PoE+ (802.3af, 802.3at)

Power over Ethernet PoE (802.3af) and PoE+ (802.3at), technologies describe a system for transmitting electrical power along with data to remote devices over twisted-pair cable in an Ethernet network. Many switches, IP telephones, embedded computers, wireless access points, cameras can use this technology for convenient installation. The main difference between PoE and PoE+ is an increase in the wattage, PoE (802.af) provides 15.4W; whereas PoE+ (802.at) provides 25.5W from the same source.

Demilitarized Zone (DMZ)

Generally, three zones are related with firewalls: Internal, External, and Demilitarized (DMZ). The internal zone is the zone inside of all firewalls, and it is considered to be the protected area where most critical servers, such as domain controllers that control sensitive information, are placed. The external zone is the area outside the firewall that represents the network against inside protection such as the internet. The DMZ is placed where the network has more than one firewall. It is a zone that is between two firewalls. It is created using a device that has at least three network connections, sometimes referred to as a three-pronged firewall. In DMZ, the servers that are used by hosts are placed on both the internal network and the external network that may include web, VPN, and FTP servers.

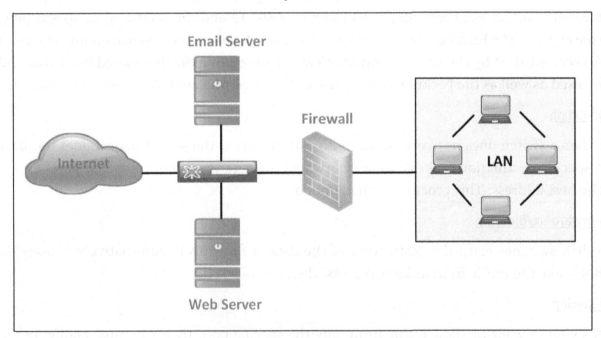

Figure 1-07: DMZ using One Firewall

MAC Address Table

The MAC address is a 48-bit binary address that is represented as a hexadecimal format. The below figure illustrates the structure of a MAC address in which the first 2 bits on the left represent whether the address is broadcast, and whether it is local or remote. The next 22 bits are assigned to vendors that manufacture network devices, such as routers and NICs. This is the Organizational Unique Identifier (OUI). The next 24 bits should be uniquely assigned to the OUI.

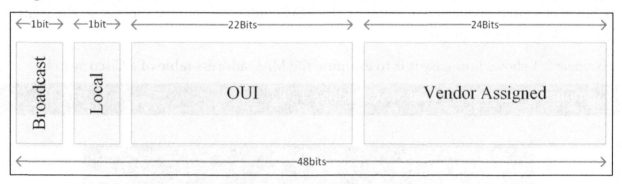

Figure 1-08: The Structure of a MAC Address

MAC Learning and Aging

To learn the MAC address of devices is the fundamental responsibility of switches. The switch transparently observes incoming frames. It records the source MAC address of these frames in its MAC address table. It also records the specific port for the source MAC address. Based on this information, it can make intelligent frame forwarding (switching) decisions. Notice that a network machine could be turned off or moved at any point. As a result, the switch must also age MAC addresses and remove them from the table after they have not been seen for some duration.

Frame Switching

Along with building a MAC address table (learning MAC address to port mappings), the switch also forwards (switches) frames intelligently from port to port. Think about this as the opposite of how a Layer 1 Hub works. Device hub takes in a frame and always forwards this frame out all other ports. In a hub-based network, every port is part of the same collision domain. The switch is too smart for that. If its MAC address table is fully populated for all ports, then it "filters" the frame from being forward out ports unnecessarily. It forwards the frame to the correct port based on the destination MAC address.

Frame Flooding

What happens when a frame has a destination address that is not in the MAC address table? The frame is flooded out all ports (other than the port on which the frame was received). This also happens when the destination MAC address in the frame is the broadcast address.

Obviously, the MAC address table is a critical component in the modern switch and act as a brain of switch operation. It contains the MAC address to port mappings so the switch can work its network magic.

Example 2-1 shows how easy it is to examine the MAC address table of a Cisco switch.

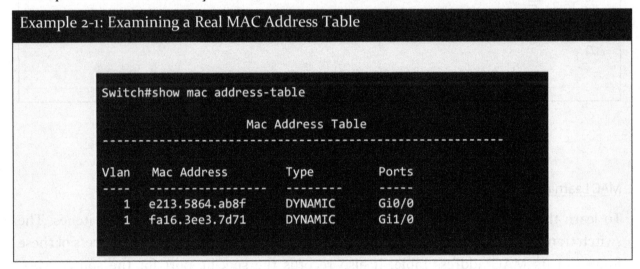

Figure 1-09: MAC Address Table

Address Resolution Protocol (ARP) Table

An Autonomous System (AS) is a group of networks under a single administrative. When Border Gateway Protocol (BGP) was in progress and standardization stage, a 16-bit binary number was used as the Autonomous System Number (ASN) to identify the Autonomous Systems. 16-bit Autonomous System Number (ASN) is also known as 2-Octet Autonomous System Number (ASN). The 16-bit binary number is used represented as (2^{16}) numbers, which is equal to 65536 in decimals. The Autonomous System Number (ASN) value 0 is reserved, and the largest ASN value (65,535), is also reserved. The values from 1 to 64,511 are available for use in Internet routing, and the values 64,512 to 65,534 are selected for private use.

BGP was also known as Border Gateway Routing Protocol, a dynamic routing protocol, which is mostly used in Global Internet. Typically, the connection between the ISPs is BGP.

Because of its complex path selection method, it allows more flexibility to configure best path selection. IBGP and EBGP are interior and exterior BGPs, which are used within an autonomous system and with different autonomous systems respectively. BGP uses TCP port number 179 to send its routing information. The main difference of BGP is that it does not need neighbors to be connected to the same subnet. ASN stands for Autonomous System Number or a unique number that makes the Autonomous System Number different from others. IANA or ICANN also provide ASN.

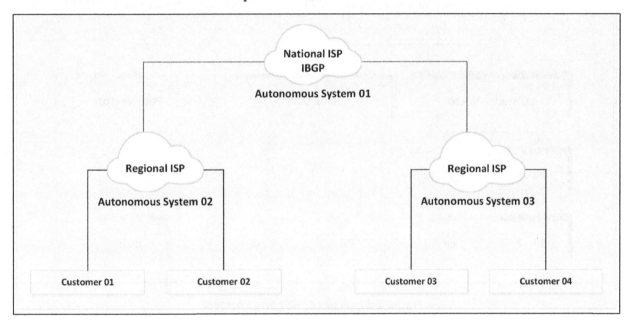

Figure 1-10: Autonomous System

BGP is a very robust and scalable routing protocol, as evidenced by the fact that BGP is the routing protocol employed on the internet. Internet BGP routing tables gas more than 600,000 routes. To achieve scalability at this level, BGP uses many route parameters, called attributes, to define routing policies and maintain a stable routing environment.

Routing

Routes in routing tables come from two sources: either they are manually entered or the router detects them dynamically.

IPv4 and IPv6 Routing Protocols

There are basically three types of routing protocols, which are as follows:

1. Distance Vector Routing Protocol
2. Link State Routing Protocol
3. Path Vector Routing Protocol

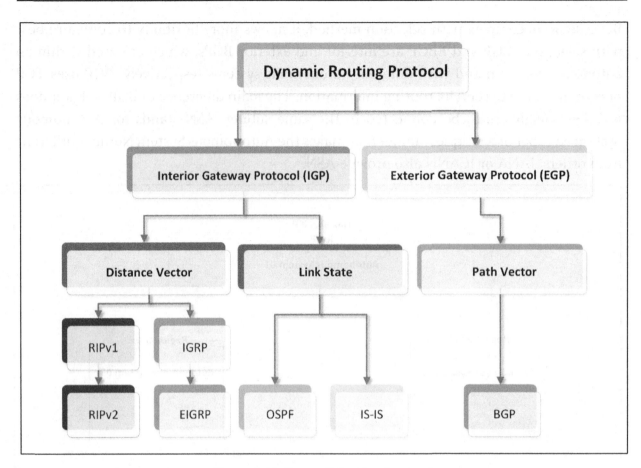

Figure 1-11: Types of Routing Protocol

Distant-Vector Routing Protocol

Distance Vector is one of the two Interior Gateway Routing Protocols. It uses Bellman-Ford, Ford-Fulkerson, or DUAL FSM (Cisco only) algorithm for the calculation of its paths. In Distance Vector, the router informs about topology changes periodically. There are two main parameters in Distance Vector routing protocol:

- Distance (Cost to the destination)
- Direction (Next Hop and the exit interface)

RIP and EIGRP are the two known Distance Vector Protocols. The others are DSDV and Babel. RIP uses hop count, EIGRP uses delay and Bandwidth as a cost to reach the destination. It also uses RIP UDP as a transport protocol with port number 520. It uses Poison reverse and Split Horizon to prevent routing loops. EIGRP, DSDV, and Babel are the loop-free routing protocols of Distance Vector. EIGRP runs over IP using Protocol no 88 (it does not use TCP or UDP).

Routing Information Protocol (RIP)

Routing Information Protocol (RIP) is a standardized Distance Vector protocol, designed for use on smaller networks. RIP was the first true Distance Vector routing protocol. It has two versions; RIPv1 and RIPv2. RIPv1 is a class-full protocol and does not support Variable Length Subnet Masks (VLSMs). RIPv2 is a classless protocol and includes the subnet mask with its routing table updates. RIPv2 supports VLSMs, and is still based on hop count metric, because of this limitation, RIPv2 cannot be used effectively in today's network.

Enhanced Interior Gateway Routing Protocol (EIGRP)

Enhanced Interior Gateway Routing Protocol (EIGRP) is a Cisco proprietary protocol. EIGRP uses more sophisticated metric than RIPv1 RIPv2. This metric depends upon the bandwidth of a connection and delay. The only drawback of EIGRP is that it operates only on Cisco routers and Cisco layer 3 switches.

Link-State Routing Protocol

Link State Routing protocol including OSPF (Open System Shortest Path First) and IS-IS (Intermediate System to Intermediate System) are the second main types of Interior Gateway Routing Protocol. In link state routing protocol, each node prepares a table or map of connectivity, about which node is connected to the other. Each node independently calculates the best logical path to every destination. This collection of best path forms the Routing Table. Link State Routing uses Dijkstra Algorithm for calculating its shortest path. OSPF does not use TCP/UDP as a transport protocol. It is encapsulated on IP with protocol no 89; whereas IS-IS is OSI Layer 2 Protocol.

A comparison of Distance Vector and Link State Routing protocols are given below:

Distance Vector		Link State
Distance vector means that routes are advertised by providing two characteristics:		In link-state protocols, also called Shortest-Path-First (SPF) protocols, the routers each create three separate tables. One of these tables keep track of directly attached neighbors, one determines the topology of the entire internetwork, and one is used as the routing table
Distance: ⟶	Identifies how far it is to the destination network and is based on a metric	A router configured with a link-state routing protocol can create a complete view or topology of the network by

	such as the hop count, cost, bandwidth, delay, and more	gathering information from all of the other routers
Vector: ⟶	Specifies the direction of the next-hop router or exit interface to reach the destination	Link-state routing tables are not exchanged periodically. Instead, triggered updates, containing only specific link-state information, are sent
A router using a Distance Vector routing protocol does not know the entire path to a destination network		Periodic keep lives that are small and efficient, in the form of hello messages, are exchanged between directly connected neighbors to establish and maintain neighborly relationships
Distance vector protocols use routers as signposts along the path to the final destination		
The only information a router knows about a remote network is the distance or metric to reach that network and which path or interface to use to get there		
Distance Vector routing protocols do not have an actual map of the network topology		
RIP is a Distance Vector routing protocol and periodically sends out the entire routing table to directly connected neighbors		

Table 1-03: Difference between Distance Vector & Link State

Basis for Comparison	Distance Vector				Link-State	
	RIPv1	RIPv2	IGRP	EIGRP	OSPF	IS-IS
Speed Of Convergence	Slow	Slow	Slow	Fast	Fast	Fast
Scalability	Small	Small	Small	Large	Large	Large
VLSM	No	Yes	No	Yes	Yes	Yes
Resource Usage	Low	Low	Low	Medium	High	High
Implementation and Maintenance	Simple	Simple	Simple	Complex	Complex	Complex

Table 1-04: Link-State and Distance-Vector Routing Protocol Comparison

Note

While EIGRP is an advanced routing protocol that combines many of the features of both link-state and distance-vector routing protocols, EIGRP's DUAL algorithm contains many features, which make it more of a Distance Vector routing protocol than a link-state routing protocol.

Open Shortest Path First (OSPF)

Open Shortest Path First (OSPF) is the most common link state protocol in use today. OSPF operates on algorithm Shortest Path First (SPF) developed by Dijkstra. The main advantage of EIGRP is that it updates the routing table immediately if any changes occur in the network. OSPF can easily be used on small, medium and large networks.

Intermediate System to Intermediate System (IS-IS)

Another important routing protocol is Intermediate System to Intermediate System (IS-IS). IS-IS is designed for large networks like Internet Service Providers. It selects the routing path by packet switched network and also follows Dijkstra's algorithm.

The below-mentioned table describes the difference between Distance Vector, Link state, and Hybrid routing protocol.

Interior Gateway Protocol vs. Exterior Gateway Protocol

Basis for Comparison	Interior Gateway Protocols	Exterior Gateway Protocols

Routing	Routing inside an autonomous system	Routing across an autonomous system
Configuration	Fast convergence and easy configuration	Slow convergence and complex configuration
Routing Decisions	Administrator influence is low on routing decisions	Administrator influence is high on routing decisions
Examples	RIP, IGRP, OSPF, and IS-IS	BGP

Table 1-05: IGP Vs. EGP

Hybrid Routing Protocol

BGP is listed as a hybrid routing protocol, because it can be used both within the backbone routers and between the backbone routers and other AS routers.

Border Gateway Protocol (BGP)

Path Vector Routing Protocols are those dynamic routing protocols, which operate over path information. This path information is dynamically updated throughout the autonomous system. It is different from the Distance Vector routing and Link State routing. Each entry in the routing table contains the destination network, the next router, and the path to reach the destination.

Routing Types

This section describes the various routing concepts and protocols.

Loopback Interface

A logical interface is a virtual interface. It is not a physical interface like fast Ethernet interface or Gigabit Ethernet interface. A loopback interface is a software interface, which can be used to imitate a physical interface. The router does not have any default loopback interfaces, but they can easily be created. Loopback interfaces are created by assigning IP addresses to the router. Loopback interface has many advantages; it is used for redirecting traffic. A loopback interface's IP Address determines an OSPF Router ID.

Routing Loops

Routing loops are issues that must be avoided in networks. Routing loops makes the routing path more difficult, so the properly configured static routes and dynamic routes avoid routing loops by assuring that only the most efficient paths are used.

Routing Tables

Routing table is a set of rules used to determine the path of the data packet traveling over an Internet Protocol network. The routing table consists of specific routing destinations,

next hop, interface, metric, and routes. Routing tables can be maintained manually or automatically. Routing tables for static network devices do not change until the network administrator changes them manually. In dynamic routing, devices update its routing table automatically by using routing protocols to exchange information about the neighborhood network topology.

<u>Static Routing</u>

Static routing is a type of network routing technique. It is the manual configuration and selection of a network route, usually managed by the network administrator.

Advantages	Disadvantages
Simple to configure, Low Processor overhead(It don't spend CPU cycles to calculate best path)	High maintenance configuration
Secure Operation	Topology Change cannot detect
Predictability	Manual update of routes after changes
Secure as only defined routes can be accessed	Misconfiguration can lead to routing loops

Table 1-06: Static Routing Advantages and Disadvantages

Configuration syntax of static route on Cisco Router:

```
Config)# Ip route Destination-Network-ID Subnet Mask Next-Hop/Exit interface
Or
ip route [destination_network] [mask] [next-hop_address or
  exitinterface] [administrative_distance] [permanent]
```

This list describes each command in the string:

IP Route: The command used to create the static route.

Destination network: The network you are placing in the routing table.

Mask: The subnet mask being used on the network.

Next-hop address: This is the IP address of the next-hop router that will receive packets and forward them to the remote network,

Exit-Interface: Used in place of the next-hop address if you want, and shows up as a directly connected route.

Administrative Distance: By default, static routes have an administrative distance of 1 or 0 if you use an exit interface instead of a next-hop address.

Permanent: If the interface is shut down or the router cannot communicate to the next-hop router, the route will automatically be discarded from the routing table by default.

Next-Hop Static Route: Only Next-Hop address is specified for the packet destined to exit the network.

Directly Connected Static Routes: By introducing the exit interface in a directly connected static route, the router assumes that the destination is directly connected to the exit interface and the packet destination is used as next-hop.

Fully Specified Static Routes: A fully specified static route, when the exit interface is a multi-access interface and you need to identify the next-hop address. The next-hop address must be directly attached to the specified out interface. In a fully specified Static route, exit interface and Nest hop IP address both are defined.

Floating Static Routes: A floating static route is what the router uses to back up a dynamic route. You need to configure a floating static route with higher Administrative Distance than the other route that it backs up. In this instance, the router prefers a dynamic route to a floating static route. Floating static route can be used as a replacement if the dynamic route is lost.

<u>Lab: Static Routing</u>

Case Study: A company requires the installation of two new routers to deploy a small static network. Being a network administrator, you have to configure static routing on these routers. Requirements are as follows:

Router 1 Ethernet interface 0/0: 10.10.1.1/24

Router 1 Ethernet interface 0/1: 10.10.2.1/24

Router 2 Ethernet interface 0/1: 10.10.2.2/24

Router 1 Ethernet interface 0/0: 10.10.3.1/24

PC1 IP Address: 10.10.1.2/24

PC2 IP Address: 10.10.3.2/24

Topology Diagram:

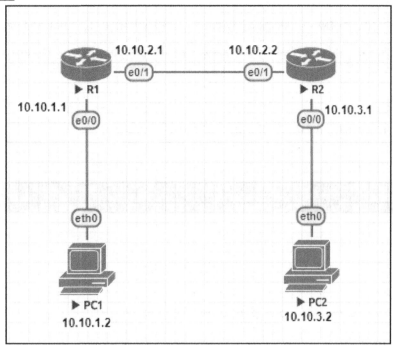

Figure 1-12: Topology Diagram

Configuration:

Router 1
Router>en

Router#config t

Enter configuration commands, one per line. End with CNTL/Z.

Router(config)#int e0/0

Router(config-if)#ip address 10.10.1.1 255.255.255.0

Router(config-if)#no shutdown

Router(config-if)#exit

*May 10 00:47:21.146: %LINK-3-UPDOWN: Interface Ethernet0/0, changed state to up

*May 10 00:47:22.150: %LINEPROTO-5-UPDOWN: Line protocol on Interface Ethernet0/0, changed state to up

Router(config)#int e0/1

Router(config-if)#ip address 10.10.2.1 255.255.255.0

```
Router(config-if)#no shutdown

Router(config-if)#exit

*May 10 01:05:34.662: %LINK-3-UPDOWN: Interface Ethernet0/1, changed state to up

*May 10 01:05:35.662: %LINEPROTO-5-UPDOWN: Line protocol on Interface Ethernet0/1,
changed state to up


Router(config)# ip route 10.10.3.0 255.255.255.0 10.10.2.2
```

Router 2

```
Router>

Router>en

Router#config t

Enter configuration commands, one per line.  End with CNTL/Z.

Router(config)#int e0/0

Router(config-if)#ip address 10.10.3.1 255.255.255.0

Router(config-if)#no shutdown

Router(config-if)#exit

*May 10 00:56:00.888: %LINK-3-UPDOWN: Interface Ethernet0/0, changed state to up

*May 10 00:56:01.892: %LINEPROTO-5-UPDOWN: Line protocol on Interface Ethernet0/0,
changed state to up


Router(config)#int e0/1

Router(config-if)#ip address 10.10.2.2 255.255.255.0

Router(config-if)#no shutdown

Router(config-if)#exit

*May 10 01:07:49.996: %LINK-3-UPDOWN: Interface Ethernet0/1, changed state to up

*May 10 01:07:50.996: %LINEPROTO-5-UPDOWN: Line protocol on Interface Ethernet0/1,
changed state to up


Router(config)# ip route 10.10.1.0 255.255.255.0 10.10.2.1
```

Virtual PC

Go to PC1 and enter the following command:

VPC> **IP 10.10.1.2/24 10.10.1.1**

Similarly, go to PC2 and enter the following command:

VPC> **IP 10.10.3.2/24 10.10.3.1**

In case you are using Windows PC, go to "Control Panel" > "Network and Internet" > "Internet and Sharing" > "Change Adapter Settings" > "Adapter" > "Properties". Select "IPv4" > "Properties" > "Manual IP Addressing" then enter your IP address, subnet and default gateway.

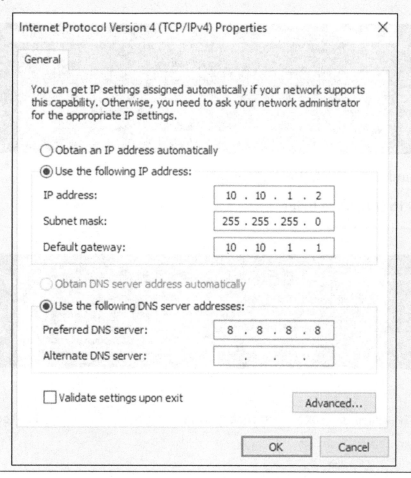

Verification

Go to PC1 and ping PC2 (10.10.3.2).

VPC> **ping 10.10.3.2**

```
PC1                                                    —  □  ✕

VPCS> ping 10.10.3.2

84 bytes from 10.10.3.2 icmp_seq=1 ttl=62 time=1.911 ms
84 bytes from 10.10.3.2 icmp_seq=2 ttl=62 time=0.850 ms
84 bytes from 10.10.3.2 icmp_seq=3 ttl=62 time=0.943 ms
84 bytes from 10.10.3.2 icmp_seq=4 ttl=62 time=0.811 ms
84 bytes from 10.10.3.2 icmp_seq=5 ttl=62 time=0.942 ms
```

Go to PC2 and ping PC1 (10.10.1.2).

VPC> **ping 10.10.1.2**

```
PC2                                                    —  □  ✕

VPCS> ping 10.10.1.2

84 bytes from 10.10.1.2 icmp_seq=1 ttl=62 time=0.944 ms
84 bytes from 10.10.1.2 icmp_seq=2 ttl=62 time=0.400 ms
84 bytes from 10.10.1.2 icmp_seq=3 ttl=62 time=0.805 ms
84 bytes from 10.10.1.2 icmp_seq=4 ttl=62 time=6.384 ms
84 bytes from 10.10.1.2 icmp_seq=5 ttl=62 time=0.802 ms
```

Go to Router and enter the following command:

Router# **show ip interface brief**

```
R1                                                     —  □  ✕

Router#show ip interface brief
Interface          IP-Address      OK? Method Status                 Protocol
Ethernet0/0        10.10.1.1       YES manual up                     up
Ethernet0/1        10.10.2.1       YES manual up                     up
Ethernet0/2        unassigned      YES unset  administratively down  down
Ethernet0/3        unassigned      YES unset  administratively down  down
Router#
```

Interface	IP-Address	OK?	Method Status	Protocol
Ethernet0/0	10.10.1.1	YES	manual up	up
Ethernet0/1	10.10.2.1	YES	manual up	up
Ethernet0/2	unassigned	YES	unset administratively down	down

```
Ethernet0/3   unassigned   YES   unset administratively down      down
```

//As shown in the output, we configured Ethernet 0/0 and 0/1 interfaces. Both interfaces are holding the configured IP address, method is manual, status is up, and protocol is up.

Router# **show ip route**

```
R1                                                    —    □    ×

Router#show ip route
Codes: L - local, C - connected, S - static, R - RIP, M - mobile, B - BGP
       D - EIGRP, EX - EIGRP external, O - OSPF, IA - OSPF inter area
       N1 - OSPF NSSA external type 1, N2 - OSPF NSSA external type 2
       E1 - OSPF external type 1, E2 - OSPF external type 2
       i - IS-IS, su - IS-IS summary, L1 - IS-IS level-1, L2 - IS-IS level-2
       ia - IS-IS inter area, * - candidate default, U - per-user static route
       o - ODR, P - periodic downloaded static route, H - NHRP, l - LISP
       a - application route
       + - replicated route, % - next hop override

Gateway of last resort is not set

      10.0.0.0/8 is variably subnetted, 5 subnets, 2 masks
C        10.10.1.0/24 is directly connected, Ethernet0/0
L        10.10.1.1/32 is directly connected, Ethernet0/0
C        10.10.2.0/24 is directly connected, Ethernet0/1
L        10.10.2.1/32 is directly connected, Ethernet0/1
S        10.10.3.0/24 [1/0] via 10.10.2.2
Router#
```

From the above output, as shown "**S   10.10.3.0/24 [1/0] via 10.10.2.2**" shows that network 10.10.3.0/24 is connected via 10.10.2.2. Here "**S**" denotes Static route.

Dynamic Routing

Dynamic Routing, also known as Adaptive Routing is a technique to automatically learn the routing table and select the best route towards the destination. Unlike static route, which are administrative overhead and not a best practice for large networks, dynamic routes ensures to measure the path cost by calculating path metrics. The dynamic routing protocol is responsible for learning, maintenance and updating the routing table.

Specification	Dynamic Routing	Static Routing
Configuration Complexity	Independent of the network size	Increases in network size
Required Administrator Knowledge	Advanced knowledge required	No extra knowledge required

Topology	Automatically adapts to topology changes	Administrative intervention required
Scaling	Suitable for simple and complex topologies	Suitable for simple topologies
Security	Less secure	More secure
Predictability	Route depends on the current topology	The route to the destination is always the same

Table 1-07: Dynamic Routing Vs. Static Routing

Default Routing

A default route is a route that is adopted when there is no other routing path available for an IP destination address. The default route usually has a next-hop address of another routing device present in a network, which performs the same process. The process repeats until a packet is delivered to the destination.

IPv6 Concept

IP addressing is used to close together the network of computers and routers and connect it to other networks and the internet. This section contains details of IPv6, IPv4, private addresses, public addresses, NAT, PAT, and so on. Additionally, it discusses the services to resolve MAC addresses to IP addresses and to use IP addresses in more creative ways such as multicast addressing. There is also a need to understand the different types of communication that the network will use, such as; unicast and broadcast, and the almost automatic domains of communication that will result from network schema.

Internet Protocol v6 (IPv6) are in hexadecimal format. This address format has been shortened using the address compression rules for IPv6. Each hexadecimal character in the address is read as a 4 bits' binary number by the network device. The below table illustrates the relationship of each decimal, binary, and hexadecimal character.

IPv6 address in this case is as the following hexadecimal number:

fe80::218:deff:fe08:6e14

The device will use a 128-bit number that looks like the following:

1111 1110 1000 0000 : 0000 0000 0000 0000 : 0000 0000 0000 0000 : 0000 0000 0000 0000 : 0000 0010 0001 1000 : 1101 1110 1111 1111 : 1111 1110 0000 1000 : 0110 1110 0001 0100

This huge addressing can be represented as:

$2^{128} = 3.4028367 \times 10^{38}$

The addressing method of IPv6 used on interfaces of routers and network interface cards is the same as IPv4 addressing, while some new methods have been introduced. These are discussed below.

Auto-configuration

In auto-configuration method, clients can obtain a unique IPv6 address by using their own Media Access Control (MAC) address and adding FF: FE into the middle of the address. It usually assures that the client has a unique address, as its MAC address is unique within that network segment.

Types of IPv6 Address

IPv6 also has different types of addresses. The following are the three main types:

- **Anycast:** Very different from an IPv4 broadcast—one-to-the-nearest interface, where many interfaces can share the same address. These addresses are taken from the unicast address space but can represent multiple devices, like multiple default gateways. For example, using an Anycast address as a default gateway address on your routers, user devices only have to know one address, and you do not need to configure a protocol like HSRP or VRRP

- **Multicast:** Address of a set of interfaces. One-to-many delivery to all interfaces in the set

- **Unicast:** Address of a single interface. One-to-one delivery to a single interface

The five types of unicast addresses are listed in the below table. Interestingly enough, multiple addresses of any type can be assigned to a device's interface: unicast, multicast, and Anycast.

Address	Value	Description
Global	2000::/3	These are assigned by the IANA and used on the public networks. They are equivalent to IPv4 global (sometimes called as public) address. ISPs summarize these to provide scalability in the internet
Reserved	(range)	Reserved addresses are used for specific types of Anycast as well as for future use. Currently, about 1/256 of the IPv6 address space is reserved

Private	FE80::/10	Like IPv4, IPv6 originally supported private addressing, which is used by devices that do not need to access a public network. The first two digits are FE, and the third digit can range from 8 to F
Loopback	::1	Like the 127.0.0.1 address in IPv4, 0:0:0:0:0:0:0:1, or ::1, is used for local testing function; unlike IPV4, which dedicates a complete class A block of addresses for local testing. Only one is used in IPv6
Unspecified	::	0.0.0.0 In IPv4 means "unknown" address. In IPv6, this is represented by 0:0:0:0:0:0:0:0, 0 ::, and is typically used in the source address field of the packet when an interface does not have an address and is trying to acquire one dynamically

Table 1-08: IPv6 Unicast Address Types

IPv6 Header

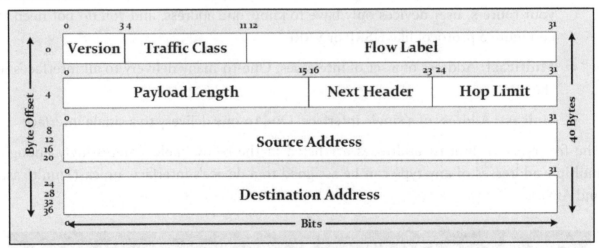

Figure 1-13: IPv6 Header Details

Version: Version of IP Protocol. 4 and 6 are valid. This diagram represents version 6 structure only.

Traffic Class: 8-bits traffic field.

Flow Label: 20-bits flow label.

Payload length: 16-bits unsigned integer length of the IPv6 payload, i.e, the rest of the packet following this IPv6 header in octets. Any extension header is considered part of the payload.

Source Address: 128-bits address of the originator of the packet.

Next Header: 8-bits selector. Identifies the type of header immediately following the IPv6 header. Uses the same values as the IPv4 protocol field.

Destination Address: 128-bits address of the intended recipient of the packet (possibly not the ultimate recipient if a routing header is present).

Hop Limit: 8-bits unsigned integer decremented by 1 by each node that forwards the packet. The packet is discarded if hop limit is decremented to zero.

IPV6 Addressing

- IPv6 addresses are 128-bits in length

- IPsec is built into the IPv6 protocol and allows device roaming without losing connectivity

- IPv6 addresses use eight sets of four hexadecimal addresses (16 bits in each set), separated by a colon (:), like this: xxxx:xxxx:xxxx:xxxx:xxxx:xxxx:xxxx:xxxx

- If you have successive fields of zeroes in an IPv6 address, you can represent them using two colons (::), but this can be used only once in an address

- An Anycast address represents the nearest interface to a device, where many devices can share an Anycast address. Multicast addresses begin with FF

- Global unicast addresses begin with 2000::/3. Private addresses range from FE8 through FFF. A loopback address is ::1

- The subnet ID is the first 64 bits, and the interface ID is the last 64 bits. EUI-64 allows dynamic creation of the interface ID portion by using the MAC address on the interface

Link Local

Similarly to IPv4, IPv6 comes with global address and link local address. Simply put, any address that starts with FE:80 has been set aside for unicast link local addressing on a private network. These addresses may be manually assigned or may be assigned using a DHCP server.

IPv6 Tunneling

One of the nicest features about IPv6 is the conversion option that does not need to convert the entire network at one time but converts some part of the network and then comes back to the previous. If you connect two dissimilar networks to each other using a router in the middle, that has both IPv6 and IPv4 addresses on it, it is referred to as 6to4 tunneling or 4to6 tunneling, depending on which direction you are traveling. If you are using Network Address Translation (NAT), then you may also use Teredo tunneling with a Miredo client. This type of tunneling is designed to allow full IPv6 connectivity to computer systems that

have no direct connection but instead are coming through NAT or even Port Address Translation (PAT).

Dual Stack

The term dual stack network refers to the network nodes capable to process IPv4 as well as IPv6 traffic simultaneously, so offering flexibility within the network. Following are the characteristics of Dual Stack network:

- Native Dual Stack does not require any tunneling
- IPv4 and IPv6 are independent of each other
- Supports gradual migration of endpoints, network and applications

Router Advertisement

RA stands for Router Advertisement message having the value of 134 in ICMP header type field. These packets are sent periodically on each interface on IPv6 device. For Stateless Auto-configuration feature to work properly, the prefix of the advertised RA message must be of 64 bits.

Router Advertisement message includes:

- IPv6 prefix
- Lifetime for each prefix
- Sets of flags
- Device default information
- Hop limit, MTU and other additional information for the hosts

Neighbor Discovery

ND stands for Neighbor Discovery or the process to discover the address of link layer of neighbors connected on a same network by using ICMP and Solicited Node Multicast Address, Verifying the neighbor is reachable and the route. There is also a static cache, which allows manual configuration of IPv6 addresses, subnet, gateway, and MAC address per interface of each device.

Mind Map of Routing and Switching

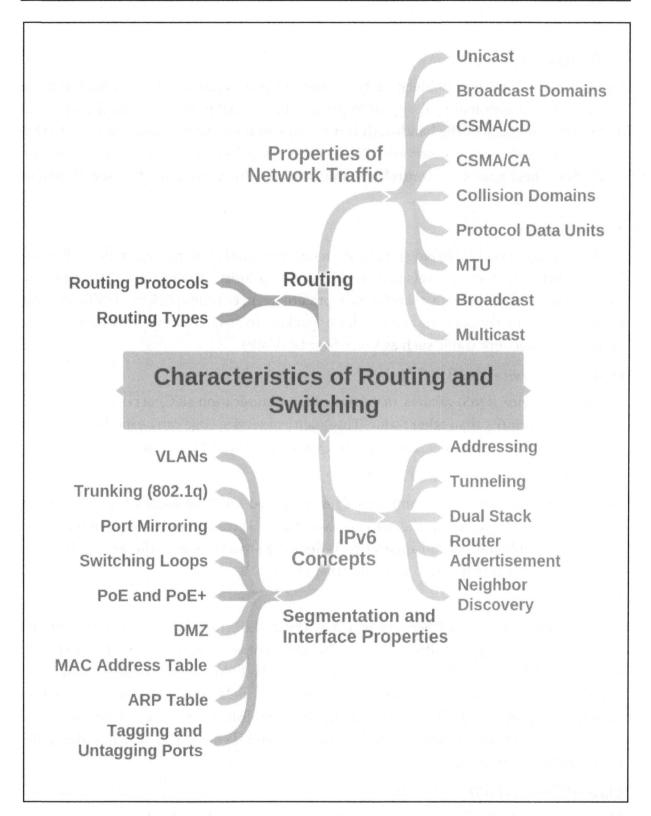

Figure 1-14: Mind Map of Characteristics of Routing and Switching

Performance Concept

Router has the capability to block packets based on port number or IP address, but these are easy mechanisms mainly designed to protect an internal network. What if users need to control how much of the bandwidth is used for certain devices or applications? In that case, users need quality of service (QoS) policies to prioritize traffic based on certain guidelines. These guidelines control how much bandwidth a protocol, PC, user, VLAN, or IP address may use.

Traffic Shaping

Traffic shaping or packet shaping is basically a network bandwidth management technique. In a network, not all the packets need high QoS and priority. Applications that need high QoS performance and priority should have preference over other packets. Traffic shaping helps to delay the flow of certain low priority packets to ensure the network performance for high QoS network traffic such as Voice over IP (VoIP).

Quality-of-Service (QoS)

Quality-of-Service (QoS) assures that Unified Communication (UC) services are treated with a higher priority than other traffic. The quality of service edge can be modeled at Layer 2 or Layer 3 of the OSI model. Two types of QoS are deployed on a network.

Differentiated Services Code Point (DSCP)

Differentiated Services Code Point (DSCP) is a method for differentiating and managing network traffic. It operates at the network layer (layer 3) using 6-bit code point within an 8-bit field. Each frame from an application is dedicated to a class of traffic, and each router on the network is configured to recognize that class.

Diffserv

Diffserver or Differentiated Services is a network architecture, which offers end-to-end Quality of Service (QoS). DiffServ uses a 6-bit Differentiated Services Code Point (DSCP) in the 8-bit Differentiated Services field (DS field) in the IP header for packet classification purposes. DiffServ uses a 6-bit DSCP in the 8-bit DS field in the IP header for packet classification purposes. In December 1998, the IETF published RFC 2474 - Definition of the Differentiated Services field (DS field) is in the IPv4 and IPv6 headers, which replaced the IPv4 TOS field with the DS field.

Class of Service (CoS)

Class of Service (COS) is an old method of classifying network traffic. It operates at Data-Link layer (layer 2) using a 3-bit designator, so there are only eight designations for traffic

(0–7). Routers and switches can be configured to recognize the classification of packets and react. Thus, applications that need more from the network will get a higher priority.

Network Address and Port Address Translation

Network Address Translation (NAT)

Network Address Translation (NAT) is a technology used for the mapping of IP addresses. It allows private IP networks that use unlisted IP addresses to connect to the public network.

NAT usually operates on router and firewall to connect at least two networks and translates the private addresses inside the network, into authorized addresses, before packets are delivered to another network.

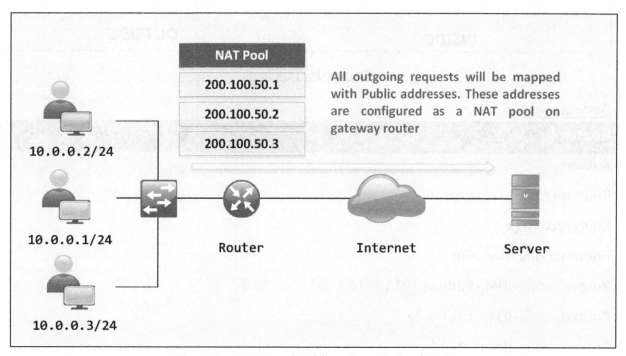

Figure 1-15: Network Address Translation (NAT)

NAT has three forms that are as follows:

1. Static NAT
2. Dynamic NAT
3. PAT

Static NAT

Static Network Address Translation allows the translation of IP addresses when the source IP address is altered but the destination IP address remains the same. Static NAT permits a host on the inside of the NAT to begin connection to a host on the outside of the NAT. Static NAT facilitates many hosts on the inside, to get any host on the outside of the NAT.

Lab: Static Network Address Translation

Case Study: In this Case, Static (One to One mapping) is performed in the shown network topology. The Source IP address 192.168.10.10 is translated into 192.168.30.2 IP address.

Topology:

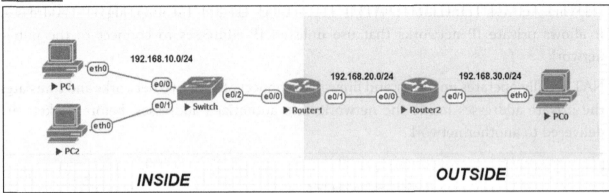

Figure 1-16: Topology

Configuration:

Router 1
Router>
Router>en
Router#config t
Router(config)#int e0/0
Router(config-if)#ip address 192.168.10.1 255.255.255.0
Router(config-if)#ip nat inside
Router(config-if)#no shutdown
Router(config-if)#ex
Router(config)#int e0/1
Router(config-if)#ip address 192.168.20.1 255.255.255.0
Router(config-if)#ip nat outside
Router(config-if)#no shutdown
Router(config-if)#ex
Router(config)#ip route 0.0.0.0 0.0.0.0 192.168.20.2

Router(config)#ip nat inside source static 192.168.10.10 100.100.100.100

Router 2

```
Router>en

Router#config t

Enter configuration commands, one per line.  End with CNTL/Z.

Router(config)#int eth 0/0

Router(config-if)#ip add 192.168.20.2  255.255.255.0

Router(config-if)#no sh

Router(config-if)#ex

*May 14 22:56:28.437: %LINK-3-UPDOWN: Interface Ethernet0/0, changed state to up

*May 14 22:56:29.441: %LINEPROTO-5-UPDOWN: Line protocol on Interface Ethernet0/0,
changed state to up


Router(config)#int eth 0/1

Router(config-if)#ip add 192.168.30.1 255.255.255.0

Router(config-if)#no sh

Router(config-if)#ex

*May 14 22:56:37.670: %LINK-3-UPDOWN: Interface Ethernet0/1, changed state to up

*May 14 22:56:38.670: %LINEPROTO-5-UPDOWN: Line protocol on Interface Ethernet0/1,
changed state to up


Router(config)#ip route 0.0.0.0 0.0.0.0 192.168.20.1
```

VPC

Go to PC0 and enter the following command:

VPC> **IP 192.168.30.2/24 192.168.30.1**

```
PC0                                                                    —  □  ✕

Welcome to Virtual PC Simulator, version 1.0 (0.8c)
Dedicated to Daling.
Build time: Dec 31 2016 01:22:17
Copyright (c) 2007-2015, Paul Meng (mirnshi@gmail.com)
All rights reserved.

VPCS is free software, distributed under the terms of the "BSD" licence.
Source code and license can be found at vpcs.sf.net.
For more information, please visit wiki.freecode.com.cn.
Modified version supporting unetlab by unetlab team

Press '?' to get help.

VPCS> ip 192.168.30.2/24 192.168.30.1
Checking for duplicate address...
PC1 : 192.168.30.2 255.255.255.0 gateway 192.168.30.1

VPCS> []
```

Go to PC1 and enter the following command:

VPC> **IP 192.168.10.10/24 192.168.10.1**

Generate some traffic to verify the connectivity.

VPC> **Ping 192.168.30.2**

```
PC1                                                    —    □    ×

Build time: Dec 31 2016 01:22:17
Copyright (c) 2007-2015, Paul Meng (mirnshi@gmail.com)
All rights reserved.

VPCS is free software, distributed under the terms of the "BSD" licence.
Source code and license can be found at vpcs.sf.net.
For more information, please visit wiki.freecode.com.cn.
Modified version supporting unetlab by unetlab team

Press '?' to get help.

VPCS> ip 192.168.10.10/24 192.168.10.1
Checking for duplicate address...
PC1 : 192.168.10.10 255.255.255.0 gateway 192.168.10.1

VPCS> ping 192.168.30.2

84 bytes from 192.168.30.2 icmp_seq=1 ttl=62 time=0.730 ms
84 bytes from 192.168.30.2 icmp_seq=2 ttl=62 time=1.339 ms
84 bytes from 192.168.30.2 icmp_seq=3 ttl=62 time=1.394 ms
84 bytes from 192.168.30.2 icmp_seq=4 ttl=62 time=1.507 ms
84 bytes from 192.168.30.2 icmp_seq=5 ttl=62 time=1.673 ms

VPCS>
```

Ping successful.

Go to PC2 and enter the following command:

VPC> **IP 192.168.10.20/24 192.168.10.1**

```
PC2                                                    —    □    ×

Welcome to Virtual PC Simulator, version 1.0 (0.8c)
Dedicated to Daling.
Build time: Dec 31 2016 01:22:17
Copyright (c) 2007-2015, Paul Meng (mirnshi@gmail.com)
All rights reserved.

VPCS is free software, distributed under the terms of the "BSD" licence.
Source code and license can be found at vpcs.sf.net.
For more information, please visit wiki.freecode.com.cn.
Modified version supporting unetlab by unetlab team

Press '?' to get help.

VPCS> ip 192.168.10.20/24 192.168.10.1
Checking for duplicate address...
PC1 : 192.168.10.20 255.255.255.0 gateway 192.168.10.1

VPCS>
```

Verification:

Ping from PC1 to PC0.

VPC> **ping 192.168.30.2**

```
PC1                                                          —   □   ×
84 bytes from 192.168.30.2 icmp_seq=5 ttl=62 time=1.452 ms

VPCS>
VPCS> ping 192.168.30.2

84 bytes from 192.168.30.2 icmp_seq=1 ttl=62 time=2.330 ms
84 bytes from 192.168.30.2 icmp_seq=2 ttl=62 time=1.384 ms
84 bytes from 192.168.30.2 icmp_seq=3 ttl=62 time=1.529 ms
84 bytes from 192.168.30.2 icmp_seq=4 ttl=62 time=1.476 ms
84 bytes from 192.168.30.2 icmp_seq=5 ttl=62 time=1.357 ms

VPCS>
```

Generate some traffic for network address translation.

Go to router 1 and enter the following command:

Router# **show ip nat statistics**

```
Router1                                                      —   □   ×
Router#
Router#show ip nat st
Router#show ip nat statistics
Total active translations: 6 (1 static, 5 dynamic; 5 extended)
Peak translations: 6, occurred 00:00:22 ago
Outside interfaces:
  Ethernet0/1
Inside interfaces:
  Ethernet0/0
Hits: 10  Misses: 0
CEF Translated packets: 10, CEF Punted packets: 0
Expired translations: 0
Dynamic mappings:

Total doors: 0
Appl doors: 0
Normal doors: 0
Queued Packets: 0
Router#
```

Translation of statistics shown in the results.

Now enter the following command:

Router# **show ip nat translation**

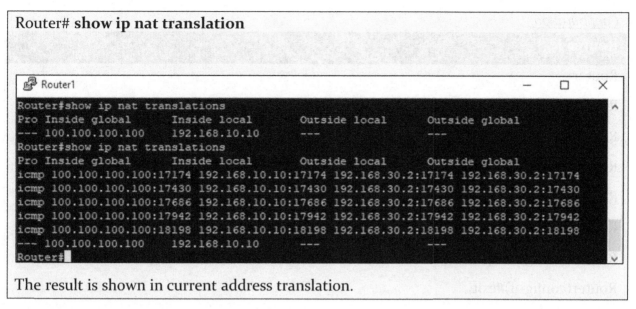

The result is shown in current address translation.

Dynamic Network Address Translation

Dynamic Network Address Translation allows the translation of IP addresses when the destination IP address is altered but the source IP address remains the same. Dynamic NAT permits a host on the outside of the NAT to begin a connection with a host on the inside of the NAT. Dynamic NAT facilitates any host on the inside to get many hosts on the outside of the NAT.

Lab: Dynamic Network Address Translation

Case Study: In this case, we are troubleshooting the process of Dynamic Network Address Translation in which the internal network 192.168.10.0/24 is dynamically translated into the pool of network 200.200.200.1 to 200.200.200.200.

Topology:

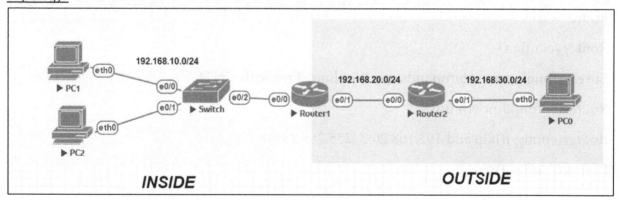

Figure 1-17: Topology

Configuration:

Router 1
Router>
Router>en
Router#config t
Router(config)#int e0/0
Router(config-if)#ip nat inside
Router(config-if)#int e0/1
Router(config-if)#ip nat outside
Router(config-if)#exit
Router(config)#access-list 10 permit 192.168.10.0 0.0.0.255
Router(config)#ip nat pool CompTIA 200.200.200.1 200.200.200.200 netmask 255.255.255.0
Router(config)#ip nat inside source list 10 pool CompTIA
Router(config)#ip route 0.0.0.0 0.0.0.0 192.168.20.2
Router#debug ip nat
IP NAT debugging is on.

Router 2
Router>en
Router#config t
Enter configuration commands, one per line. End with CNTL/Z.
Router(config)#int eth 0/0
Router(config-if)#ip add 192.168.20.2 255.255.255.0
Router(config-if)#no sh
Router(config-if)#ex
*May 14 22:56:28.437: %LINK-3-UPDOWN: Interface Ethernet0/0, changed state to up

```
*May 14 22:56:29.441: %LINEPROTO-5-UPDOWN: Line protocol on Interface Ethernet0/0,
changed state to up
```

Router(config)#int eth 0/1

Router(config-if)#ip add 192.168.30.1 255.255.255.0

Router(config-if)#no sh

Router(config-if)#ex

```
*May 14 22:56:37.670: %LINK-3-UPDOWN: Interface Ethernet0/1, changed state to up
```

```
*May 14 22:56:38.670: %LINEPROTO-5-UPDOWN: Line protocol on Interface Ethernet0/1,
changed state to up
```

Router(config)#ip route 0.0.0.0 0.0.0.0 192.168.20.1

VPC

Go to PC0 and enter the following command:

VPC> **IP 192.168.30.2/24 192.168.30.1**

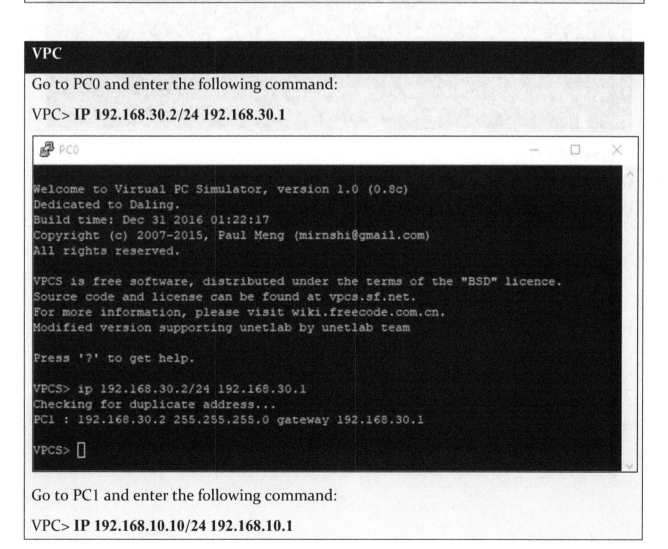

Go to PC1 and enter the following command:

VPC> **IP 192.168.10.10/24 192.168.10.1**

Generate some traffic to verify the connectivity.

VPC> **Ping 192.168.30.2**

```
PC1                                                    —  □  ×

Build time: Dec 31 2016 01:22:17
Copyright (c) 2007-2015, Paul Meng (mirnshi@gmail.com)
All rights reserved.

VPCS is free software, distributed under the terms of the "BSD" licence.
Source code and license can be found at vpcs.sf.net.
For more information, please visit wiki.freecode.com.cn.
Modified version supporting unetlab by unetlab team

Press '?' to get help.

VPCS> ip 192.168.10.10/24 192.168.10.1
Checking for duplicate address...
PC1 : 192.168.10.10 255.255.255.0 gateway 192.168.10.1

VPCS> ping 192.168.30.2

84 bytes from 192.168.30.2 icmp_seq=1 ttl=62 time=0.730 ms
84 bytes from 192.168.30.2 icmp_seq=2 ttl=62 time=1.339 ms
84 bytes from 192.168.30.2 icmp_seq=3 ttl=62 time=1.394 ms
84 bytes from 192.168.30.2 icmp_seq=4 ttl=62 time=1.507 ms
84 bytes from 192.168.30.2 icmp_seq=5 ttl=62 time=1.673 ms

VPCS>
```

Ping successful.

Go to PC2 and enter the following command:

VPC> **IP 192.168.10.20/24 192.168.10.1**

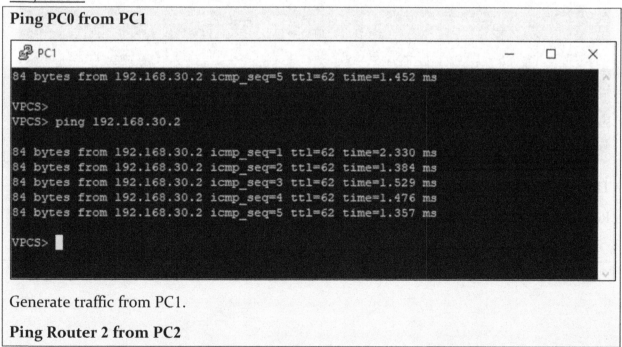

Verification:

Ping PC0 from PC1

Generate traffic from PC1.

Ping Router 2 from PC2

```
PC2                                                          —    □    ✕

VPCS> ping 192.168.20.2

84 bytes from 192.168.20.2 icmp_seq=1 ttl=254 time=1.188 ms
84 bytes from 192.168.20.2 icmp_seq=2 ttl=254 time=1.436 ms
84 bytes from 192.168.20.2 icmp_seq=3 ttl=254 time=1.330 ms
84 bytes from 192.168.20.2 icmp_seq=4 ttl=254 time=1.310 ms
84 bytes from 192.168.20.2 icmp_seq=5 ttl=254 time=1.492 ms

VPCS> █
```

Generate traffic from PC2.

Router# **show ip nat translation**

Router(config)# **do show ip nat translation**

```
Router1                                                     —    □    ✕

Router(config)#do show ip nat translations
Pro Inside global      Inside local      Outside local      Outside global
icmp 200.200.200.1:29470 192.168.10.10:29470 192.168.30.2:29470 192.168.30.2:29470
icmp 200.200.200.1:29726 192.168.10.10:29726 192.168.30.2:29726 192.168.30.2:29726
icmp 200.200.200.1:29982 192.168.10.10:29982 192.168.30.2:29982 192.168.30.2:29982
icmp 200.200.200.1:30238 192.168.10.10:30238 192.168.30.2:30238 192.168.30.2:30238
icmp 200.200.200.1:30494 192.168.10.10:30494 192.168.30.2:30494 192.168.30.2:30494
--- 200.200.200.1        192.168.10.10        ---                ---
icmp 200.200.200.2:33566 192.168.10.20:33566 192.168.20.2:33566 192.168.20.2:33566
icmp 200.200.200.2:33822 192.168.10.20:33822 192.168.20.2:33822 192.168.20.2:33822
icmp 200.200.200.2:34078 192.168.10.20:34078 192.168.20.2:34078 192.168.20.2:34078
icmp 200.200.200.2:34334 192.168.10.20:34334 192.168.20.2:34334 192.168.20.2:34334
icmp 200.200.200.2:34590 192.168.10.20:34590 192.168.20.2:34590 192.168.20.2:34590
Pro Inside global      Inside local      Outside local      Outside global
--- 200.200.200.2        192.168.10.20        ---                ---
Router(config)#█
```

The result shows dynamic network address translations.

Router(config)# **do show ip nat statistics**

```
Router1                                                               —    □    ×
Router(config)#do show ip nat statistics
Total active translations: 7 (0 static, 7 dynamic; 5 extended)
Peak translations: 17, occurred 00:04:18 ago
Outside interfaces:
  Ethernet0/1
Inside interfaces:
  Ethernet0/0
Hits: 50  Misses: 0
CEF Translated packets: 50, CEF Punted packets: 0
Expired translations: 20
Dynamic mappings:
-- Inside Source
[Id: 1] access-list 10 pool CompTIA refcount 7
 pool CompTIA: netmask 255.255.255.0
        start 200.200.200.1 end 200.200.200.200
        type generic, total addresses 200, allocated 2 (1%), misses 0

Total doors: 0
Appl doors: 0
Normal doors: 0
Queued Packets: 0
Router(config)#
```

Debugging.

```
Router1                                                               —    □    ×
Router(config)#
*May 14 23:36:58.467: NAT*: s=192.168.10.10->200.200.200.1, d=192.168.30.2 [7578]
*May 14 23:36:58.467: NAT*: s=192.168.30.2, d=200.200.200.1->192.168.10.10 [7578]
*May 14 23:36:59.469: NAT*: s=192.168.10.10->200.200.200.1, d=192.168.30.2 [7579]
*May 14 23:36:59.469: NAT*: s=192.168.30.2, d=200.200.200.1->192.168.10.10 [7579]
Router(config)#
*May 14 23:37:00.470: NAT*: s=192.168.10.10->200.200.200.1, d=192.168.30.2 [7580]
*May 14 23:37:00.471: NAT*: s=192.168.30.2, d=200.200.200.1->192.168.10.10 [7580]
*May 14 23:37:01.473: NAT*: s=192.168.10.10->200.200.200.1, d=192.168.30.2 [7581]
*May 14 23:37:01.473: NAT*: s=192.168.30.2, d=200.200.200.1->192.168.10.10 [7581]
Router(config)#
*May 14 23:37:02.475: NAT*: s=192.168.10.10->200.200.200.1, d=192.168.30.2 [7582]
*May 14 23:37:02.476: NAT*: s=192.168.30.2, d=200.200.200.1->192.168.10.10 [7582]
Router(config)#
*May 14 23:37:27.928: NAT*: s=192.168.10.20->200.200.200.2, d=192.168.20.2 [7607]
*May 14 23:37:27.928: NAT*: s=192.168.20.2, d=200.200.200.2->192.168.10.20 [7607]
*May 14 23:37:28.930: NAT*: s=192.168.10.20->200.200.200.2, d=192.168.20.2 [7608]
*May 14 23:37:28.931: NAT*: s=192.168.20.2, d=200.200.200.2->192.168.10.20 [7608]
Router(config)#
*May 14 23:37:29.933: NAT*: s=192.168.10.20->200.200.200.2, d=192.168.20.2 [7609]
*May 14 23:37:29.933: NAT*: s=192.168.20.2, d=200.200.200.2->192.168.10.20 [7609]
*May 14 23:37:30.935: NAT*: s=192.168.10.20->200.200.200.2, d=192.168.20.2 [7610]
*May 14 23:37:30.935: NAT*: s=192.168.20.2, d=200.200.200.2->192.168.10.20 [7610]
Router(config)#
```

Port Address Translation (PAT)

Port Address Translation (PAT) is an advanced form of NAT that allows multiple computers on inside network, to be mapped over the single public address, by assigning a separate port number to ongoing transmissions.

<u>Lab: Port Address Translation</u>

Case Study: In this case, we are troubleshooting the process of Port Address Translation in which a number of IP address of an internal network, i.e., 192.168.10.0/24 will be translated by PAT (Port Address Translation) into 192.168.30.0/24 network along with port numbers.

Topology:

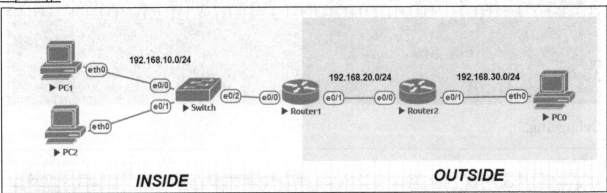

Figure 1-18: Topology Diagram

Configuration:

Router1
Router>
Router>en
Router#config t
Enter configuration commands, one per line. End with CNTL/Z.
Router(config)#hostname Router1
Router1(config)#int eth 0/0
Router1(config-if)#ip add 192.168.10.1 255.255.255.0
Router1(config-if)#no sh
Router1(config-if)#ip nat inside
*May 14 22:02:26.652: %LINK-3-UPDOWN: Interface Ethernet0/0, changed state to up
*May 14 22:02:27.657: %LINEPROTO-5-UPDOWN: Line protocol on Interface Ethernet0/0, changed state to up

```
*May 14 22:02:28.836: %LINEPROTO-5-UPDOWN: Line protocol on Interface NVI0, changed
state to up
```

Router1(config-if)#ex

Router1(config)#int eth 0/1

Router1(config-if)#ip add 192.168.20.1 255.255.255.0

Router1(config-if)#ip nat outside

Router1(config-if)#no sh

Router1(config-if)#ex

```
*May 14 22:03:11.057: %LINK-3-UPDOWN: Interface Ethernet0/1, changed state to up

*May 14 22:03:12.061: %LINEPROTO-5-UPDOWN: Line protocol on Interface Ethernet0/1,
changed state to up
```

Router1(config)#access-list 10 permit 192.168.10.0 0.0.0.255

Router1(config)#ip nat pool PAT-POOL 1.1.1.1 1.1.1.2 netmask 255.255.255.252

Router1(config)#ip nat inside source list 10 pool PAT-POOL overload

Router1(config)#ip route 0.0.0.0 0.0.0.0 192.168.20.2

Router1(config)#

Router 2

Router>

Router>en

Router#config t

Enter configuration commands, one per line. End with CNTL/Z.

Router(config)#hostname Router2

Router2(config)#int eth 0/0

Router2(config-if)#ip add 192.168.20.2 255.255.255.0

Router2(config-if)#no sh

Router2(config-if)#ex

Router2(config)#

```
*May 14 22:07:37.049: %LINK-3-UPDOWN: Interface Ethernet0/0, changed state to up

*May 14 22:07:38.053: %LINEPROTO-5-UPDOWN: Line protocol on Interface Ethernet0/0,
changed state to up
```

Router2(config)#int eth 0/1

Router2(config-if)#ip add 192.168.30.1 255.255.255.0

Router2(config-if)#no sh

```
*May 14 22:07:59.682: %LINK-3-UPDOWN: Interface Ethernet0/1, changed state to up

*May 14 22:08:00.686: %LINEPROTO-5-UPDOWN: Line protocol on Interface Ethernet0/1,
changed state to up
```

Router2(config-if)#ex

Router2(config)#ip route 0.0.0.0 0.0.0.0 192.168.20.1

VPC

Go to PC0 and enter the following command:

VPC> **IP 192.168.30.2/24 192.168.30.1**

```
PC0                                                    —  □  ✕

Welcome to Virtual PC Simulator, version 1.0 (0.8c)
Dedicated to Daling.
Build time: Dec 31 2016 01:22:17
Copyright (c) 2007-2015, Paul Meng (mirnshi@gmail.com)
All rights reserved.

VPCS is free software, distributed under the terms of the "BSD" licence.
Source code and license can be found at vpcs.sf.net.
For more information, please visit wiki.freecode.com.cn.
Modified version supporting unetlab by unetlab team

Press '?' to get help.

VPCS> ip 192.168.30.2/24 192.168.30.1
Checking for duplicate address...
PC1 : 192.168.30.2 255.255.255.0 gateway 192.168.30.1

VPCS>
```

Go to PC1 and enter the following command:

VPC> **IP 192.168.10.10/24 192.168.10.1**

Generate some traffic to verify the connectivity.

VPC> **Ping 192.168.30.2**

```
PC1                                                          —    □    ×

Build time: Dec 31 2016 01:22:17
Copyright (c) 2007-2015, Paul Meng (mirnshi@gmail.com)
All rights reserved.

VPCS is free software, distributed under the terms of the "BSD" licence.
Source code and license can be found at vpcs.sf.net.
For more information, please visit wiki.freecode.com.cn.
Modified version supporting unetlab by unetlab team

Press '?' to get help.

VPCS> ip 192.168.10.10/24 192.168.10.1
Checking for duplicate address...
PC1 : 192.168.10.10 255.255.255.0 gateway 192.168.10.1

VPCS> ping 192.168.30.2

84 bytes from 192.168.30.2 icmp_seq=1 ttl=62 time=0.730 ms
84 bytes from 192.168.30.2 icmp_seq=2 ttl=62 time=1.339 ms
84 bytes from 192.168.30.2 icmp_seq=3 ttl=62 time=1.394 ms
84 bytes from 192.168.30.2 icmp_seq=4 ttl=62 time=1.507 ms
84 bytes from 192.168.30.2 icmp_seq=5 ttl=62 time=1.673 ms

VPCS>
```

Ping successful.

Go to PC2 and enter the following command:

VPC> **IP 192.168.10.20/24 192.168.10.1**

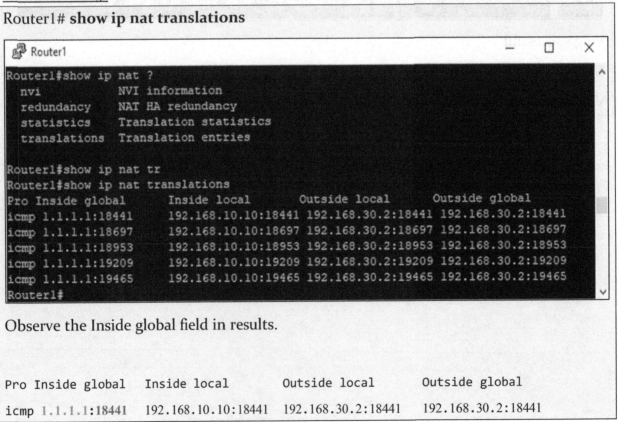

icmp 1.1.1.1:18697	192.168.10.10:18697	192.168.30.2:18697	192.168.30.2:18697
icmp 1.1.1.1:18953	192.168.10.10:18953	192.168.30.2:18953	192.168.30.2:18953
icmp 1.1.1.1:19209	192.168.10.10:19209	192.168.30.2:19209	192.168.30.2:19209
icmp 1.1.1.1:19465	192.168.10.10:19465	192.168.30.2:19465	192.168.30.2:19465

Router# **show ip nat statistics**

```
Router1#show ip nat statistics
Total active translations: 5 (0 static, 5 dynamic; 5 extended)
Peak translations: 5, occurred 00:00:51 ago
Outside interfaces:
  Ethernet0/1
Inside interfaces:
  Ethernet0/0
Hits: 10  Misses: 0
CEF Translated packets: 10, CEF Punted packets: 0
Expired translations: 0
Dynamic mappings:
-- Inside Source
[Id: 1] access-list 10 pool PAT-POOL refcount 5
 pool PAT-POOL: netmask 255.255.255.252
        start 1.1.1.1 end 1.1.1.2
        type generic, total addresses 2, allocated 1 (50%), misses 0

Total doors: 0
Appl doors: 0
Normal doors: 0
Queued Packets: 0
Router1#
```

Port Forwarding

Port forwarding is a technique that can serve a remote computer to a computer that is connected to a private IP network. This service enables the dedication of port numbers. Port forwarding usually operates on routers that allow the user to enter a port number and IP address. Therefore, all the incoming traffic automatically is forwarded to the matched port number and continues its services. The services allow the user to access data, tunneling, bypass a filter and much more.

Access Control List

An ACL is a collection of statements applied to an interface that can permit or deny traffic. They are not always for filtering traffic for security. Many types of access lists filter traffic to and from a network. These may include web/content filtering, port filtering, IP filtering,

and others. This section will discuss the main differences between web/content, port, and IP filtering access lists.

Distributed Switching

Distributed Switching is an architecture of distributed processor-controlled switching units. There is often a hierarchy of switching elements, with a centralized host switch and with remote switches located close to concentrations of users. Distributed switching is often used in telephone networks, though it is often called host-remote switching. VMware vSphere Distributed Switch (VDS) provides a centralized interface from which you can configure, monitor and administer virtual machine access switching for the entire data center.

Packet Switched Vs Circuit Switched Network

Circuit Switching	Packet Switching
The physical path between source and destination	No physical path followed
Reserves the complete bandwidth in advance	Does not reserve
Wastage of Bandwidth	No wastage of bandwidth
Does not store and forward transmission	Stores and forwards transmission
Capacity is wasted if data is burst	Efficient use of capacity
Constant delay, no reordering, no packet drops	Packets delayed, reordered, or dropped
The route is established for the entire conversation	The route is established for each packet

Table 1-09: Circuit Switching Vs. Packet Switching

Software-defined Network

The idea of programmable networks has newly regained substantial momentum due to the emergence of the Software Defined Networking (SDN) paradigm. Outdated network architectures are ill-suited to meet the requirements of today's enterprises, carriers, and end users. SDN is often referred to as a key enabler that promises dramatically simplified network management and enables innovation through network programmability.

Software Defined Networking (SDN) is an emerging network framework where network control is decoupled from forwarding and is directly programmable. Previously, the network control was firmly bound in individual network devices. This has dramatically changed into accessible computing devices, enabling the underlying infrastructure to be

abstracted for applications and network services, which can treat the network as a logical or virtual entity.

SDN Architecture

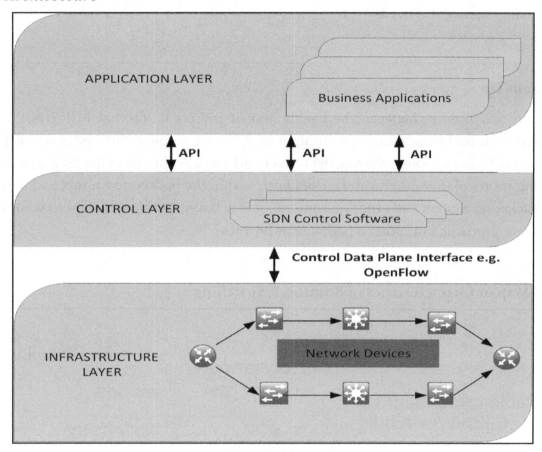

Figure 1-19: Software Defined Network Architecture

Figure 1-19 represents a logical view of the SDN framework. Network brainpower is logically integrated into software-based SDN controllers, which maintain a global view of the network. SDNs also significantly simplify the network devices themselves, as they no longer need to understand and process thousands of protocol standards but only accept instructions from the SDN controllers.

OpenFlow is the first standard communication interface defined between the controlling and forwarding layers of an SDN framework. This allows directing access and manipulation of the forwarding plane of physical, as well as virtual network devices.

SDN architecture provides a set of Application Programming Interfaces (APIs) that simplifies the implementation of common network services like routing, multicast, security, access control, bandwidth management, traffic engineering, QoS, energy

efficiency, and various forms of policy management. Therefore, enterprises, network operators, and carriers gain exceptional programmability, automation, and network control, enabling them to build highly scalable, flexible networks that cheerfully familiarize with changing business needs.

💡 Exam Tip

BGP on the interior, between the backbone exit routers is internal BGP (iBGP). BGP between the backbone router and routers in different autonomous systems is exterior BGP (eBGP). Even though the CompTIA Network+ exam objectives list BGP as a hybrid routing protocol (because it can be used both within the backbone routers and between the backbone routers and other AS routers), it is actually neither a distance vector nor a link state protocol, but rather a path vector protocol.

Mind Map of Characteristics of Routing & Switching

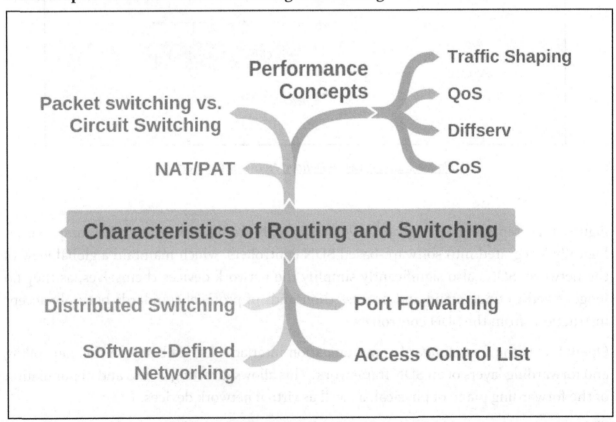

Figure 1- 20: Mind Map of Characteristics of Routing and Switching

Configuring the Appropriate IP Addressing Components

IP addresses are assigned several ways. There are number of ways that IP addresses are used and there are many different things that IP addresses represent. However, there is one thing that is certain; an IP address is nothing without a subnet mask.

Public Vs Private Network

A public IP address is an IP address that can be accessed over the internet. This address is the globally unique IP address assigned to a computing device. A public IP address can be found at "What is my IP Address" page. A private IP address, on the other hand, is used to assign computers to private network without letting them directly lead to the internet. In a scenario, where users have multiple computers within home, they may want to use private IP addresses to address each computer within home. The router gets the public IP address, and each of the devices connected to the router gets a private IP address from router by DHCP protocol.

Internet Assigned Numbers Authority (IANA) is the organization responsible for assigning IP address ranges to organizations and Internet Service Providers (ISPs). To allow organizations to assign private IP addresses freely, the Network Information Center (InterNIC) has reserved certain address blocks for private use.

The following IP blocks are reserved for private IP addresses.

Class	Starting IP Address	Ending IP Address	No. of Hosts
A	10.0.0.0	10.255.255.255	16,777,216
B	172.16.0.0	172.31.255.255	1,048,576
C	192.168.0.0	192.168.255.255	65,536

Table 1-10: Private IP Address

Loopback and Reserved Addresses

Loopback

Loopback interfaces are logical interfaces, which means they are virtual, software-only interfaces, not actual, physical router interfaces. A big reason we use loopback interfaces with OSPF configurations is that they ensure that an interface is always active and available for OSPF processes.

Loopback interfaces also come in very handy for diagnostic purposes as well as for OSPF configuration. Understand that if users do not configure a loopback interface on a router, the highest active IP address on a router will become that router's RID during boot-up.

```
Router(config)#interf loopback 0

Router(config-if)#ip address 172.31.1.2 255.255.255.0

Router(config-if)#no sh
```

Reserved Addresses

Reserved address space is the group of reserved Internet Protocol (IP) addresses. This reserved category is only for internal networks or intranets. The Internet Engineering Task Force (IETF) and Internet Address and Naming Authority (IANA) reserve these addresses for experimentation, special purposes and internal use.

Following table shows IPv4 reserved addresses:

Address Block	Number of addresses	Scope
0.0.0.0/8	16777216	Only valid as source address
10.0.0.0/8	16777216	Private network
100.64.0.0/10	4194304	Private network
127.0.0.0/8	16777216	Host
169.254.0.0/16	65536	Subnet
172.16.0.0/12	1048576	Private network
192.0.0.0/24	256	Private network
192.0.2.0/24	256	Documentation
192.88.99.0/24	256	Internet
192.168.0.0/16	65536	Private network
198.18.0.0/15	131072	Private network
198.51.100.0/24	256	Documentation
203.0.113.0/24	256	Documentation
224.0.0.0/4	268435456	Internet
240.0.0.0/4	268435456	Internet
255.255.255.255/32	1	Subnet

Table 1-11: IPv4 Reserved Addresses

Following table shows IPv6 reserved addresses:

Address block (CIDR)	Number of addresses	Usage	Purpose
::/0	2^{128}	Routing	Default route
::/128	1	Software	Unspecified address
::1/128	1	Host	Loopback address to the local host
::ffff:0:0/96	2^{32}	Software	IPv4 mapped addresses
::ffff:0:0:0/96	2^{32}	Software	IPv4 translated addresses
64:ff9b::/96	2^{32}	Global Internet	IPv4/IPv6 translation
100::/64	2^{64}	Routing	Discard prefix
2001::/32	2^{96}	Global Internet	Teredo tunneling
2001:20::/28	2^{100}	Software	ORCHIDv2
2001:db8::/32	2^{96}	Documentation	Addresses used in documentation and example source code
2002::/16	2^{112}	Global Internet	The 6to4 addressing scheme (now deprecated)
fc00::/7	2^{121}	Private network	Unique local address
fe80::/10	2^{118}	Link	Link-local address
ff00::/8	2^{120}	Global Internet	Multicast address

Figure 1-12: IPv6 Reserved Addresses

Default Gateway

Default Gateway is the gateway used by the network device to send packets unless the specific gateway is defined. It allows the network devices to communicate with other networks.

Virtual IP

Virtual IP is a similar concept to VRRP; it consists of a virtual IP address assigned to any physical router present in the network. Therefore, the traffic coming to the virtual IP

addresses may be sent to any router behind it. It provides load-balance to increase traffic throughput and to increase stability.

Subnet Mask

Subnet Mask is a 32 bits long address used to distinguish between network address and host address in IP address. Subnet mask is always used with IP address. Subnet mask has only one purpose, to identify which part of an IP address is network address and which part is host address.

For example, how will we figure out network partition and host partition from IP address 192.168.1.4? Here, we need subnet mask to get details about network address and host address.

In decimal notation subnet mask 255 represent network address and value 0 [Zero] represent host address.

In binary notation subnet mask ON bit [1] represent network address while OFF bit [0] represent host address.

In decimal notation
IP address   192.168.1.4
Subnet mask   255.255.255.0

Network address is 192.168.1.0 and host address is 192.168.1.4.

In binary notation
IP address 11000000.10101000.00000001.00000100
Subnet mask 11111111.11111111.11111111.00000000

Network address is 11000000.10101000.00000001 and host address is 00001010

Subnetting

Subnetting allows a large network block to be logically subdivided into multiple smaller networks, or subnets. The use of multiple smaller networks allows the use of varying physical networks, such as Ethernet or Token Ring, which could not otherwise be combined. Additionally, the smaller subnets can improve the speed of traffic and permit easier management.

Subnet masks provide the logical segmentation required by routers to be able to address logical subnets. A default gateway IP address on a router interface, allows clients to access

networks outside their local subnets. The number of bits used in a subnet mask determines the number of subnets available.

An IPv4 address is a 32-bits binary address represented in dotted decimal format. The following is an example of an IPv4 address:

192.168.1.1

IPv4 comes with a subnet mask that distinguishes which portion belongs to host portion and which belongs to network portion. IPv4 is in the dotted decimal format, but the network devices show the IPv4 addresses as binary numbers.

In fact, 192.168.1.1 ends up looking like the following:

11000000	10101000	00000001	00000001

It happens as the dotted decimal form uses the first 8 bits of binary, repeatedly, four times. The bits of the address are then valued based on the following template of values:

128 64 32 16 8 4 2 1	128 64 32 16 8 4 2 1	128 64 32 16 8 4 2 1	128 64 32 16 8 4 2 1

The address would then line up with the template as follows:

Everywhere there is not a 1, is a 0.

Advantages of Subnetting

- Subnetting breaks large network in smaller networks as smaller networks are easier to manage
- Subnetting reduces network traffic by removing collision and broadcast traffic, overall improving performance
- Subnetting allows users to apply network security polices at the interconnection between subnets
- Subnetting allows users to save money by reducing requirement for IP range

Classful Subnetting

IPv4 develops a class-based system of IP addresses that have five classes of addresses. The first three bits in the addresses identify the type of class. Remember that all class A addresses begin with 000, all Class B addresses begin with 100, all Class C addresses begin with 110, and all Class D addresses begin with 111, since Class D addresses are used for multicasting. There is also a class E, which begins at 240 in the first octet and is used only for experimental purposes.

Class	First Octet Range	Subnet Mask	No. of Networks	No. of Hosts/Network
A	0.0.0.0 – 126.0.0.0	255.0.0.0	126	16,777,214
B	128.0.0.0 – 191.0.0.0	255.255.0.0	16,384	65,534
C	192.0.0.0 – 223.0.0.0	255.255.255.0	2,097,152	254
D	224.0.0.0 – 239.0.0.0	NA	NA	NA
E	240.0.0.0 – 255.0.0.0	NA	NA	NA

Table 1-13: IP Addressing

Classless Subnetting

Classless Inter-Domain Routing (CIDR) is a method of IP addressing proposed by IETF in 1993 to replace Classful network design to overcome the exhaustion of IPv4 addresses. The difference in Classful and Classless networking is of network prefix. In Classful network, Class A, B and C addresses contains 8, 16, and 24 network bits respectively. Whereas, Classless addresses contains CIDR notation or subnet mask to define network and host bits regardless of bit-boundaries. CIDR encompasses several concepts. It is based on the Variable-Length Subnet Masking (VLSM) technique, which allows the specification of arbitrary-length prefixes.

Variable Length Subnet Masking (VLSM)

Variable-Length Subnet Masking (VLSM) is a technique that allows the network administrator to divide the IP address space into different subnets as per required sizes without wasting large number of addresses.

Exercise:

Consider a network 192.168.1.0/24. The requirement is to divide the network into five subnetworks where the following number host addresses are required.

- Network A requires 14 hosts
- Network B requires 28 hosts
- Network C requires 2 hosts
- Network D requires 7 hosts
- Network E requires 28 hosts

Subnetting

Decimal	192	168	1	0
Binary	11000000	10101000	00000001	00000000

Subnet Mask	255	255	255	0

We are considering the last octet to create four subnetworks.

Decimal	192	168	1	0
Binary	11000000	10101000	00000001	00000000
Subnet Mask	255	255	255	0

Rearrange the requirement; it will be easy to divide:

- Network B requires 28 hosts
- Network E requires 28 hosts
- Network A requires 14 hosts
- Network D requires 7 hosts
- Network C requires 2 hosts

Now, calculate the number of hosts using the following formula:

Total Number of Hosts = 2^N

Total Usable Number of Hosts = $2^N - 2$

Calculating Hosts for Network B:

Total Usable Number of Hosts = $2^N - 2$

Total Usable Number of Hosts = $2^5 - 2 = 30$

The requirement of 28 hosts can be fulfilled with this condition.

Calculating Hosts for Network E:

Total Usable Number of Hosts = $2^N - 2$

Total Usable Number of Hosts = $2^5 - 2 = 30$

The requirement of 28 hosts can be fulfilled with this condition.

Calculating Hosts for Network A:

Total Usable Number of Hosts = $2^N - 2$

Total Usable Number of Hosts = $2^4 - 2 = 14$

The requirement of 14 hosts can be fulfilled with this condition.

Calculating Hosts for Network D:

Total Usable Number of Hosts = $2^N - 2$

Total Usable Number of Hosts = $2^4 - 2 = 14$

The requirement of seven hosts can be fulfilled with this condition.

Calculating Hosts for Network C:

Total Usable Number of Hosts = $2^N - 2$

Total Usable Number of Hosts = $2^2 - 2 = 2$

The requirement of two hosts can be fulfilled with this condition.

	1st Octet	2nd Octet	3rd Octet	4th Octet							
Bits	8-bits	8-bits	8-bits	8-bits							
IP	192	168	1	0							
				128	64	32	16	8	4	2	1
Net B	11000000	10101000	00000001	0	0	0	0	0	0	0	0
	11000000	10101000	00000001	0	0	0	1	1	1	1	1
Net E	11000000	10101000	00000001	0	0	1	0	0	0	0	0
	11000000	10101000	00000001	0	0	1	1	1	1	1	1
Net A	11000000	10101000	00000001	0	1	0	0	0	0	0	0
	11000000	10101000	00000001	0	1	0	0	1	1	1	1
Net D	11000000	10101000	00000001	0	1	0	1	0	0	0	0
	11000000	10101000	00000001	0	1	0	1	1	1	1	1
Net C	11000000	10101000	00000001	0	1	1	1	0	0	0	0
	11000000	10101000	00000001	0	1	1	1	0	0	1	1

Network Bits	Host Bits

Network B: 192.168.1.0/27

Network E: 192.168.1.32/27

Network A: 192.168.1.64/28

Network D: 192.168.1.80/28

Network C: 192.168.1.96/30

CIDR Notation

CIDR notation is the representation of IP address along with its associated prefix. The notation is represented as IP address with a slash (/) and decimal number. The number is the count of leading 1-bits in the subnet mask.

For example:

- 192.168.100.14/24 represents the IPv4 address 192.168.100.14 and its associated routing prefix 192.168.100.0, or equivalently, its subnet mask 255.255.255.0, which has 24 leading 1-bits
- The IPv4 block 192.168.100.0/22 represents the 1024 IPv4 addresses from 192.168.100.0 to 192.168.103.255
- The IPv6 block 2001:db8::/48 represents the block of IPv6 addresses from 2001:db8:0:0:0:0:0:0 to 2001:db8:0:ffff:ffff:ffff:ffff:ffff
- ::1/128 represents the IPv6 loopback address. Its prefix length is 128, which is the number of bits in the address

Address Assignment

There are two methods to give a host an IP address, subnet mask, and default gateway: either by typing in all the data (called static addressing) or by having a server program operating on a system that automatically passes out all the IP data to systems as they boot up on or connect to a network (called dynamic addressing).

Dynamic Host Configuration Protocol (DHCP)

Dynamic Host Configuration Protocol (DHCP) provides administrators with a methodology to dynamically assign IP addresses rather than manually.

DHCP can provide the following parameters:

- IP Addresses
- Subnet Masks
- Default Gateways
- DNS Server and much more

There are four processes to complete the DHCP operation:

1. **DHCPDiscover:** When a DHCP client boots up, it broadcasts a DHCP discover message, looking for a DHCP server

2. **DHCPOffer:** If a DHCP server exists on the local site, it will reply with a DHCP offer, containing the offered IP address, subnet mask, etc.

3. **DHCPRequest:** Marks that it will accept the offered protocol information

4. **DHCPAck:** At last, the server acknowledges the client's approval of offered protocol information

Lab: DHCP Configuration

Case Study: In a small network, configure Dynamic Host Configuration Protocol (DHCP) to obtain IP address automatically by creating a DHCP pool on Router.

Topology:

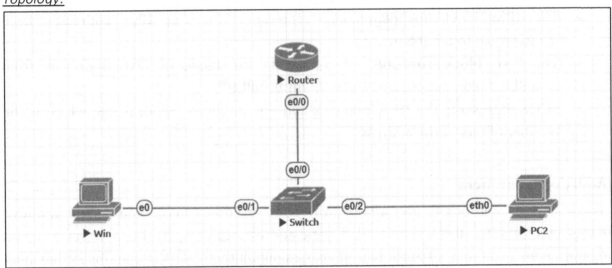

Figure 1-21: DHCP Configuration Topology Diagram

Configuration:

Router 1
Router>
Router>en
Router#config t
Enter configuration commands, one per line. End with CNTL/Z.
Router(config)#host R1
R1(config)#int e0/0
R1(config-if)#ip address 192.168.10.1 255.255.255.0

```
// Assigning IP address to Ethernet interface of Router

R1(config-if)#no shutdown

R1(config-if)#

*May  9 01:10:57.996: %LINK-3-UPDOWN: Interface Ethernet0/0, changed state to up

*May  9 01:10:59.000: %LINEPROTO-5-UPDOWN: Line protocol on Interface Ethernet0/0,
changed state to up

R1(config-if)#exit


R1(config)#ip dhcp pool IP10

R1(dhcp-config)#network 192.168.10.0 255.255.255.0

R1(dhcp-config)#default 192.168.10.1

R1(dhcp-config)#exit

// Configuring DHCP pool


R1(config)#ip dhcp exc 192.168.10.1 192.168.10.10

// Configuring DHCP excluded addresses

R1(config)#exit

R1#

*May  9 01:20:11.810: %SYS-5-CONFIG_I: Configured from console by console


R1#show ip dhcp pool
```

```
Router                                                        —    □    ×

*May 14 20:59:07.322: %LINK-3-UPDOWN: Interface Ethernet0/0, changed state to up
*May 14 20:59:08.330: %LINEPROTO-5-UPDOWN: Line protocol on Interface Ethernet0/
0, changed state to up
R1#show ip dhcp ?
  binding    DHCP address bindings
  conflict   DHCP address conflicts
  database   DHCP database agents
  import     Show Imported Parameters
  pool       DHCP pools information
  relay      Miscellaneous DHCP relay information
  server     Miscellaneous DHCP server information

R1#show ip dhcp pool

Pool IP10 :
 Utilization mark (high/low)     : 100 / 0
 Subnet size (first/next)        : 0 / 0
 Total addresses                 : 254
 Leased addresses                : 0
 Pending event                   : none
 1 subnet is currently in the pool :
 Current index        IP address range              Leased addresses
 192.168.10.1         192.168.10.1   - 192.168.10.254   0
R1#
```

As shown in the output, no DHCP address is leased yet.

Windows PC (PC1) Configuration:

Go to Windows PC and Login with password "**ipspecialist**".

Logging in to Windows 7.

Go to "**Control Panel**".

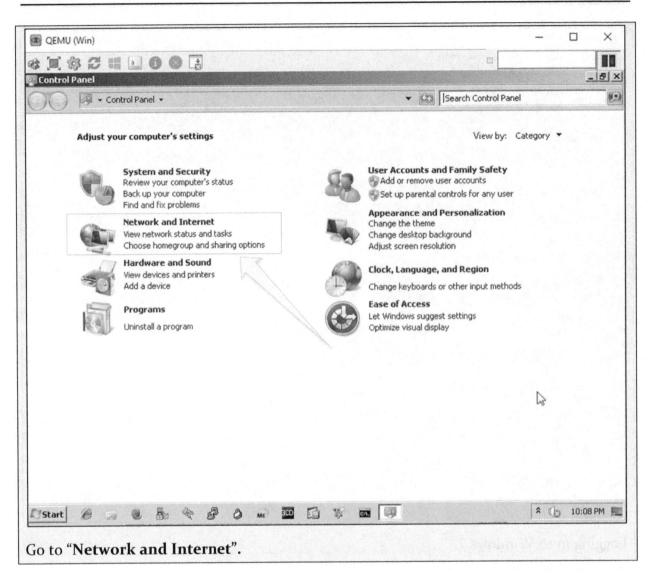

Go to "**Network and Internet**".

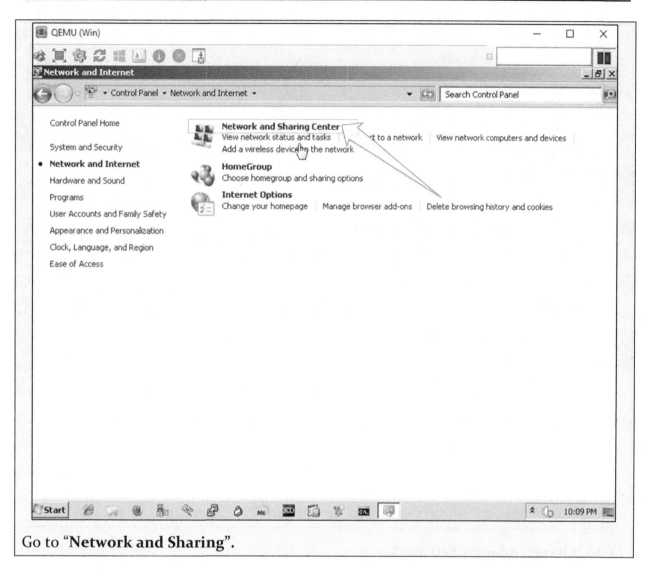

Go to "**Network and Sharing**".

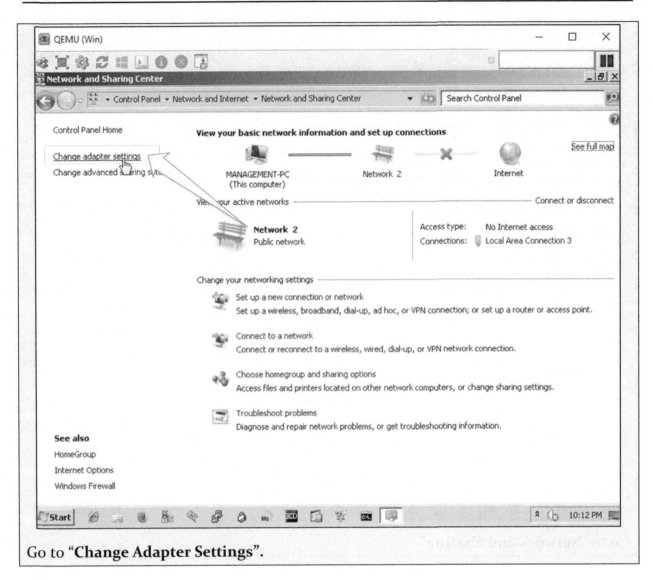

Go to "**Change Adapter Settings**".

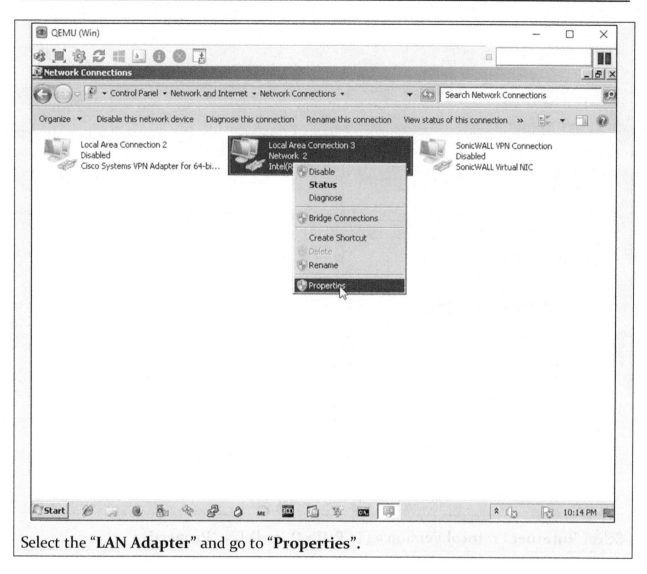

Select the "**LAN Adapter**" and go to "**Properties**".

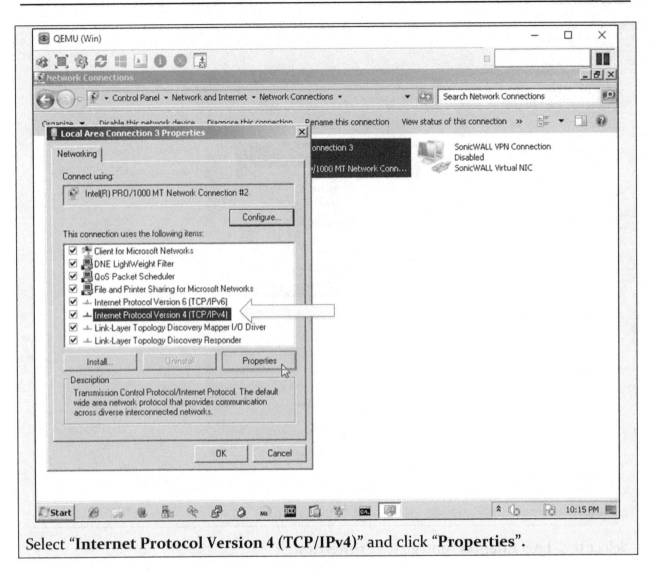

Select "**Internet Protocol Version 4 (TCP/IPv4)**" and click "**Properties**".

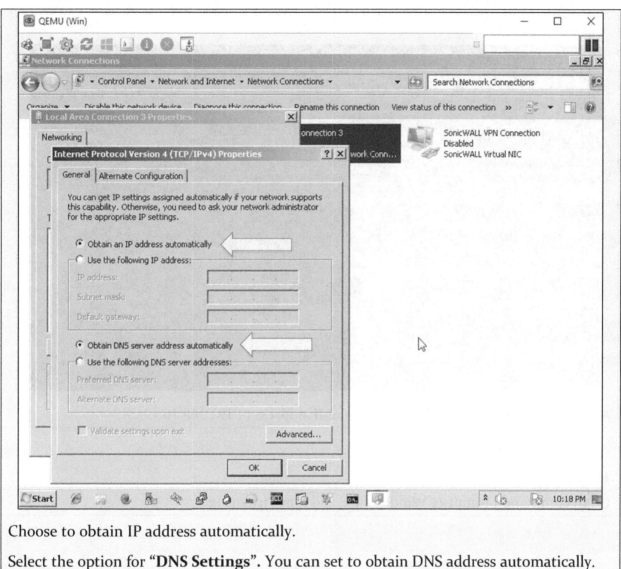

Choose to obtain IP address automatically.

Select the option for **"DNS Settings"**. You can set to obtain DNS address automatically.

Virtual PC (PC2) Configuration:

Go to VPC and type **"IP DHCP"** to configure VPC to obtain IP address via DHCP.

```
PC2                                                          —    □    ×

Welcome to Virtual PC Simulator, version 1.0 (0.8c)
Dedicated to Daling.
Build time: Dec 31 2016 01:22:17
Copyright (c) 2007-2015, Paul Meng (mirnshi@gmail.com)
All rights reserved.

VPCS is free software, distributed under the terms of the "BSD" licence.
Source code and license can be found at vpcs.sf.net.
For more information, please visit wiki.freecode.com.cn.
Modified version supporting unetlab by unetlab team

Press '?' to get help.

VPCS> ip dhcp
DDORA IP 192.168.10.12/24 GW 192.168.10.1

VPCS>
```

As shown in the output, VPC obtained the IP address of 192.168.10.12/24.

Verification:

Go to command prompt of Windows PC and type "**ipconfig**".

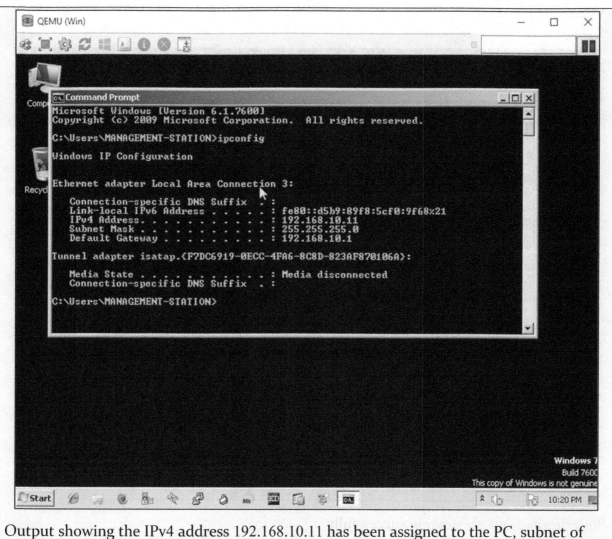

Output showing the IPv4 address 192.168.10.11 has been assigned to the PC, subnet of 255.255.255.0 and default gateway 192.168.10.1.

Ping 192.168.10.1 (gateway) and 192.168.10.12 (PC2).

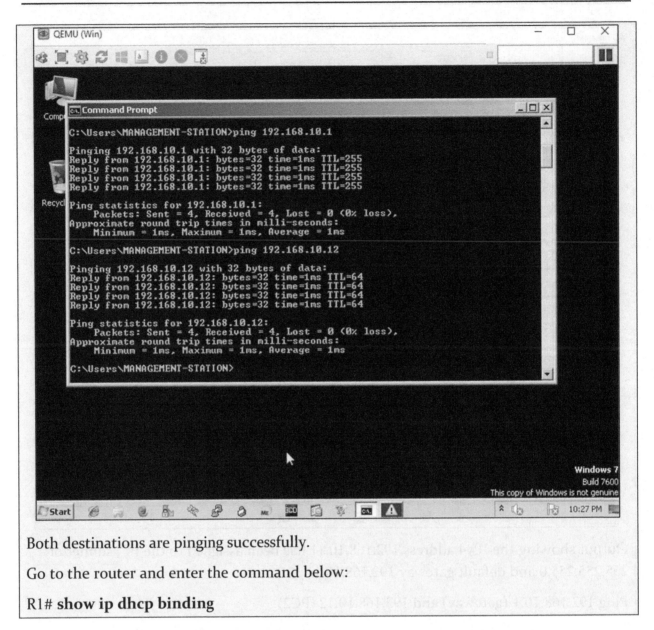

Both destinations are pinging successfully.

Go to the router and enter the command below:

R1# **show ip dhcp binding**

```
Router                                                    —    □    ×

 terminal   Write to terminal
 <cr>

R1#wr me
Building configuration...
[OK]
R1#show ip dhcp ?
  binding    DHCP address bindings
  conflict   DHCP address conflicts
  database   DHCP database agents
  import     Show Imported Parameters
  pool       DHCP pools information
  relay      Miscellaneous DHCP relay information
  server     Miscellaneous DHCP server information

R1#show ip dhcp binding
Bindings from all pools not associated with VRF:
IP address           Client-ID/              Lease expiration         Type
                     Hardware address/
                     User name
192.168.10.11        0150.0000.0300.00       May 15 2018 11:20 PM     Automatic
192.168.10.12        0100.5079.6668.04       May 15 2018 11:24 PM     Automatic
R1#
R1#
```

The result shows DHCP bindings.

R1#show ip dhcp pool

```
Router                                                    —    □    ×

R1#show ip dhcp pool

Pool IP10 :
 Utilization mark (high/low)    : 100 / 0
 Subnet size (first/next)       : 0 / 0
 Total addresses                : 254
 Leased addresses               : 2
 Pending event                  : none
 1 subnet is currently in the pool :
 Current index       IP address range                    Leased addresses
 192.168.10.13       192.168.10.1    - 192.168.10.254     2
R1#
```

DHCP pool information.

R1#show ip dhcp server statistics

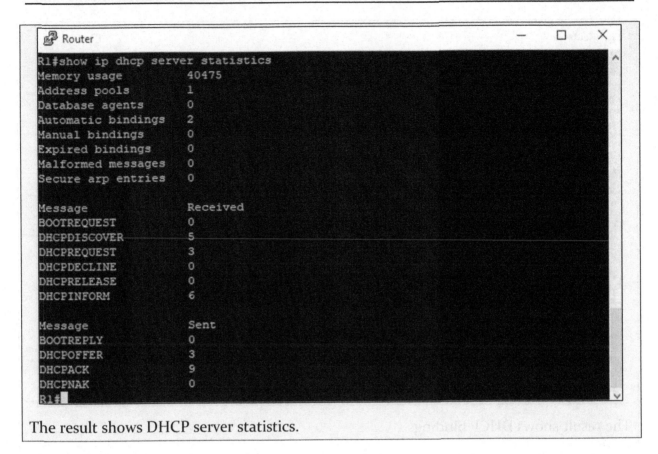

The result shows DHCP server statistics.

DHCPv6

As discussed earlier, Dynamic Host Configuration Protocol (DHCP) server is used to configure IP addresses, DNS servers automatically, and so on for clients joining a network.

In IPv6, there are two types of IPv6 auto configuration addresses. The first one is the automatically configured IP address by the DHCPv6, called State-full Auto configuration. Another way of auto configuration in IPv6 is Stateless Auto configuration SLAAC. Stateless Auto configuration uses Neighbor Discovery Protocol and EUI-64 to work with. EUI-64 is very important in SLAAC as IPv6 address needs to be globally unique. As we discussed earlier about EUI-64, 64 bit is received by EUI-64, remaining 64 bits are received by NDP through Router Advertisement. As discussed above, RA message includes Network Prefix resulting the 128 bits of IPv6 address.

DHCPv6 works as similar to DHCPv4, with the exception that DHCP uses Anycast communication instead of broadcast communication. Anycast communication is a more efficient type of signaling that is unique to IPv6. In Anycast, a packet is sent to the addresses of the Anycast members. By using Anycast, a router can become a DHCP server for a client or direct it to a DHCP server.

DHCPv6 uses two different ports:

- UDP port 546 for clients
- UDP port 547 for servers

```
Command Prompt                                                    _ |□| X|

C:\Users\MANAGEMENT-STATION>ipconfig

Windows IP Configuration

Ethernet adapter Local Area Connection 3:

    Connection-specific DNS Suffix  . :
    IPv6 Address. . . . . . . . . . . : aabb::a1dd:aae:7330:3227
    Temporary IPv6 Address. . . . . . : aabb::58b7:a743:de5e:ed6b
    Link-local IPv6 Address . . . . . : fe80::a1dd:aae:7330:3227%16
    Autoconfiguration IPv4 Address. . : 169.254.50.39
    Subnet Mask . . . . . . . . . . . : 255.255.0.0
    Default Gateway . . . . . . . . . : fe80::a8bb:ccff:fe00:2100%16

Tunnel adapter isatap.{82E8C9B2-A443-4F12-8820-86527DD00AF8}:

    Media State . . . . . . . . . . . : Media disconnected
    Connection-specific DNS Suffix  . :

C:\Users\MANAGEMENT-STATION>
C:\Users\MANAGEMENT-STATION>
C:\Users\MANAGEMENT-STATION>
C:\Users\MANAGEMENT-STATION>
```

Figure 1-22: IP Configuration

Static IP Addressing

There are two possible ways to configure IP addressing on a host device. Network Administrator can either manually approach each and every network device or assign an IP address to each device. This technique is called Static IP Addressing. Static IP addressing can be easy to deploy on a small-scale network, but it is very difficult to deploy on a large-scale network having hundreds or thousands of networking devices. Another limitation of static IP addressing is that an administrator has to remove the IP address from the network device when it is not used to assign any other device.

Another approach is Dynamic IP addressing. Dynamic IP addressing is an automated procedure of assigning IP addresses and other network related parameters such as DNS information to the client. Using Dynamic Host Configuration Protocol (DHCP), the network administrator can configure a DHCP server and assign a pool of addresses. DHCP automatically listens for DHCP request packets and binds the IP addresses from the pool with a lease. When the lease expires, the address is sent back to the pool.

Static Vs. Dynamic IP Addressing

DHCP devices such as servers, network printers, plotters, and router interfaces are statistically configured and cannot be changed. The client computers get their IP addresses from a DHCP server when required.

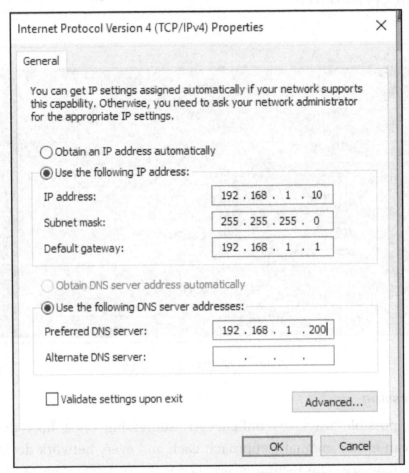

Figure 1-23: Static Configuration on Windows 10

APIPA

All client computers are configured by default to obtain their IP address from a DHCP server. When a DHCP server is not available, clients can configure by default to use an address in the range of 169.254.0.1 to 169.254.255.254. These addresses are called Automatic Private Internet Protocol Addressing (APIPA) addresses. The advantage of using APIPA is that the clients in the same network segment that could not obtain a true IP address from a DHCP server can still communicate with each other. The disadvantage is that the clients can communicate with each other, but not with the true network.

```
Command Prompt                                              _ □ ×

Packet Tracer PC Command Line 1.0
C:\>
Packet Tracer PC Command Line 1.0
C:\>ipconfig

FastEthernet0 Connection:(default port)

   Link-local IPv6 Address.........: FE80::210:11FF:FEDC:572B
   Autoconfiguration IP Address....: 169.254.87.43
   Subnet Mask.....................: 255.255.0.0
   Default Gateway.................: 0.0.0.0

C:\>
C:\>|
```

Figure 1-24: APIPA

EUI64

Extended Unique Identifier 64 (EUI-64) addresses that are in use in many organizations provide an address space that far exceeds that of our current MAC-48 addresses. In the coming years, EUI-64 addresses will be used more often, essentially replacing MAC-48 addresses, when companies begin the transition to IPv6.

IP Reservation

DHCP reservation is a process of assigning a permanent IP address. These reserved IP addresses are configured on the DHCP server for internal servers, printers, routers, workstations, etc. This IP address uses the DHCP scope that is reserved for leased use to a particular DHCP client.

> **Exam Tip**
>
> Make sure you can quickly tell the difference between a private IP address and a public IP address and memorize the IP class ranges for the CompTIA Network+ exam.

Mind Map of IP Addressing Components

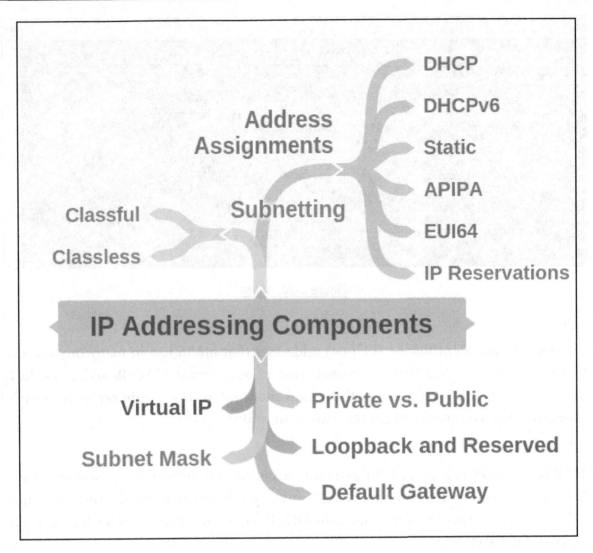

Figure 1-25: Mind Map of IP Addressing Components

Compare and Contrast the Characteristics of Network Topologies, Types and Technologies

Network topologies are classified into two basic types with respect to transmission medium:

1. Wired Topology
2. Wireless Topology

Wired Topologies

Several topologies are in use on networks today. Some of the more common topologies are the bus, ring, star, mesh. The following sections provide an overview of each.

Logical Vs Physical Topologies

Network topology can be classified into two different types:

1. Physical Topology
2. Logical Topology

Physical topology demonstrates how the network devices are physically connected with each other along with cabling and devices connection. Logical topology differs from physical topology in the way that it only demonstrates the logical diagram of the network.

> **Note**
>
> A physical topology diagram identifies the physical location of intermediary devices, configured ports, and cable installation.
>
> A logical topology diagram identifies devices, ports, and the IP addressing scheme.

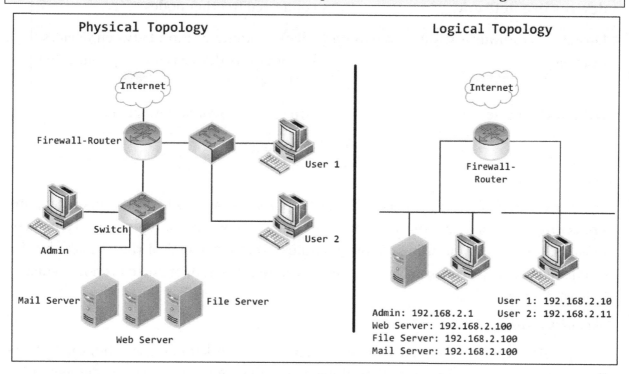

Figure 1-26: Logical Vs Physical Topologies

Star Topology

A star topology is the most common topology in use today. A star topology consists of a group of computers connected to a central point such as hub or switches. The flow of information must pass through the central device. Each device present in star topology has an individual connection with the central device. Therefore, if one connection fails, it does not affect the network, but if a central device fails, all the connections will be affected.

Ring Topology

A ring topology is a network topology that connects network devices in a circular path. Each network device is connected to two other devices. In the most ring network, data packets travel only in one direction to avoid a collision, but some networks allow data packets to travel in both directions.

Mesh Topology

Any network that has multiple paths, or redundant connections, in network topology, is referred to as, Mesh Topology. There are two types of Mesh topology, i.e., Full Mesh and Partial Mesh.

Full Mesh	Partial Mesh
Every device is connected to all devices in a network	Devices are grouped into nodes that are connected to other nodes
Direct communication between devices	Allows communication between devices, but not every device is directly connected to the other
Difficult to scale	Typically used for larger networks

Table 1-14: Full Mesh Vs. Partial Mesh

Bus Topology

To connect all the PCs on the network, a bus topology uses a trunk or backbone. Systems connect to this backbone using T connectors or taps (known as a vampire tap). To prevent signal reflection, a physical bus topology requires that every end of the physical bus be terminated, with one end also being grounded. Note that a hub or switch is not needed in this installation.

Hybrid Topology

The hybrid network topology is a combination of two network topologies. They can be Star-Ring, Star-Bus topologies, etc. Hybrid network topology has many advantages, like; flexibility, reliability, and maximum fault tolerance.

Point-to-Point Vs. Multipoint

Point-to-point and point-to-multipoint are the two types of line patterns. The main difference between point-to-point and the multipoint connection is that in a point-to-point connection, the link connects only two devices, i.e., a sender and a receiver. On the other hand, in a multipoint connection, the link is between many devices, i.e., a sender and multiple receivers.

BASIS FOR COMPARISION	POINT-TO-POINT	MULTIPOINT
Link	The dedicated link between two devices	The link is shared between two or more devices
Channel Capacity	Entire channel capacity is shared between two devices	Channel capacity is shared among the connected devices
Sender and Receiver	The single transmitter and a single receiver	The single transmitter and multiple receivers
Example	Frame relay, T-carrier, X.25, etc.	Frame relay, token ring, Ethernet, ATM, etc.

Table 1-15: Point-to-Point Vs. Multipoint

Client-Server Vs. Peer-to-Peer

There are two common network models for use in networking. Client-Server and Peer-to-Peer network, The Client-Server network model concentrates on information sharing whereas; the Peer-to-Peer network model concentrates on connectivity to the remote computers.

BASIS FOR COMPARISON	CLIENT-SERVER	PEER-TO-PEER
Basic	Specific server and specific clients are connected to the server	No specific server, no specific client, each node acts as client and server
Service	Client requests for service and server responds with the service	Each node can request for services and can also provide the services
Concentration	Sharing the information	Connectivity
Expense	Expensive to implement	Less expensive
Stability	More stable and scalable	Stability affected if the number of peers increases

Table 1-16: Client-Server Vs. Peer-to-Peer

Wireless Topologies

The topology is an arrangement of a network including nodes and connections lines. The network topology may be physical or logical. There are three basic types of wireless network topologies.

Mesh

This is one of the complex wireless topologies as it involves one or more than one WAPs. The user can connect to the network through a specific WA, depending on the placement in premises. This type of topology is called Basic Service Set (BSS).

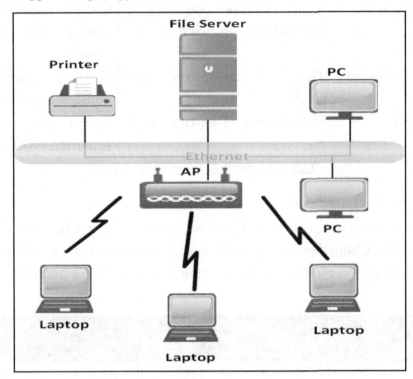

Figure 1-27: Mesh Topology

Note

Wireless Mesh is generated through the connection of wireless access points installed at each network user's locale. Data signals in a wireless mesh depend on all nodes to propagate signals. Wireless mesh networks can be identified by the interconnecting signals between each node.

Ad Hoc

A wireless device connecting to another wireless device with no need for a WAP is referred to as an ad hoc topology. It is also sometimes called an Independent Basic Service Set (IBSS) because it is independent of the WAP.

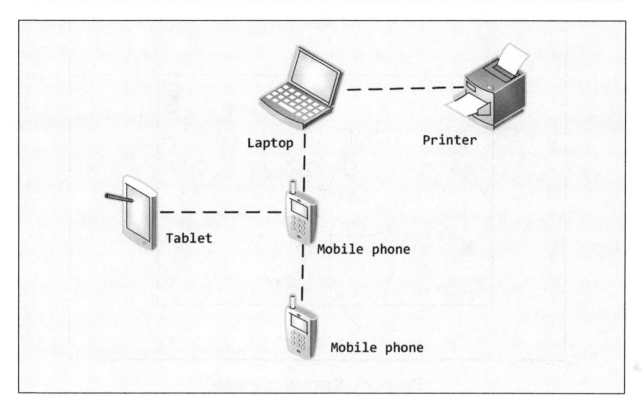

Figure 1-28: An Ad Hoc Topology

Infrastructure

In infrastructure topology, devices that are connected to one WAP can be automatically switched to another WAP. It is useful if the device is used in many parts of your premises and needs to maintain connectivity throughout the entire area once connected. This type of topology is also called Extended Service Set (ESS).

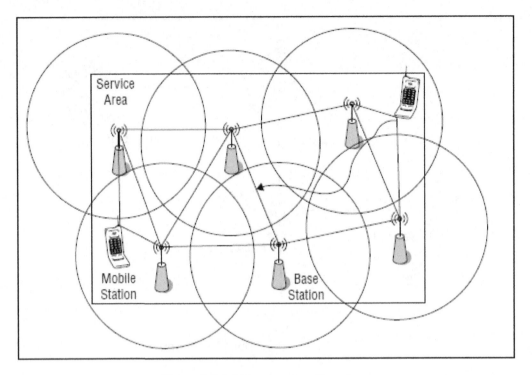

Figure 1-29: Infrastructure Topology

Network Types

Networks are categorized by geographic size and coverage. Local Area Networks (LANs) and Wide-Area Networks (WANs) are the two most common network categories. Choosing between the two is often a matter of understanding the requirements.

LAN

A Local Area Network (LAN) is an information network that is limited to a single geographic location and typically covers a relatively small area, such as an office building or school. The function of the LAN is to interconnect workstation PCs for sharing files and resources. The LAN typically is high speed and cheaper to set up than a WAN, due to its localized nature.

WLAN

Wireless Local Area Network (WLAN) is an extended form of LAN with wireless technology. It is not difficult to connect to the wired networks wirelessly. Wireless LANs are designed to operate in license-free bands, making their operation and maintenance costs more effective than cellular and PCS networks. The use of the license-free band increases the risk of network security and spectral interference. The key advantages of wireless networks are; mobility, flexibility, ease of installation and maintenance, and reduced cost.

MAN

Metropolitan Area Network (MAN) is confined to a certain geographic location, such as a university campus or city. No formal instructions dictate the differences between a MAN and a WAN; technically, a MAN is a WAN. The term MAN is used less often than WAN. If any distinction exists, it is that a MAN is smaller than a WAN. A MAN is usually bigger than a LAN. MANs utilize an Internet Service provider (ISP) or telecommunications (telco) provider.

WAN

A Wide Area Network (WAN) is a network that spans more than one geographic location, often connecting separate LANs. WANs are slower than LANs and often need additional and expensive hardware, such as routers, dedicated leased lines, and complicated implementation procedures

Comparison between LAN, MAN and WAN

A computer network allows networking devices to connect and communicate with different computers. LAN, MAN, and WAN are the three types of networks designed to operate over the coverage area.

BASIS OF COMPARISON	LAN	MAN	WAN
Acronym	Local Area Network	Metropolitan Area Network	Wide Area Network
Purpose	Connects a group of computers in a small geographical area	Covers a relatively large region such as cities, towns	Connects a larger area such as countries
Deployment and Maintenance	Easy	Difficult	Difficult
Speed	High	Moderate	Low
Fault Tolerance	More	Less	Less
Congestion	Less	More	More
Application	School, Hospital	Small Towns, City	Country, Continent

Table 1-17: LAN Vs. MAN Vs. WAN

CAN

Campus Area Network (CAN) is also termed as Campus Network, Corporate Area Network. It is a network of interconnected campuses. Each campus has users with different roles.

Consider a university CAN where administrative buildings, academic buildings, university library and finance building are connected with each other. Each building is connecting different type of users. Administrative building contains admin users, Finance building connects the users which need the access to finance information whereas library connects students, which are only allowed to access internet. Much like a university campus network, a corporate campus network serves to connect buildings. Examples of such are the networks at Googleplex and Microsoft's campus. Campus networks are normally interconnected with high speed Ethernet links operating over optical fiber such as gigabit Ethernet and 10 Gigabit Ethernet.

SAN

A Storage Area Network (SAN) consists of networked/shared storage devices. Consumers can use multiple devices to increase performance, with clustered storage. SANs are subsets of LANs and offer block-level information storage that appears within the OS of the connected devices as locally attached devices.

PAN

Personal Area Network (PAN) is a small personal network of devices at individual workspace. PAN is carried over a low-powered, short-distance wireless network technology such as IrDA, Wireless USB, Bluetooth or ZigBee.

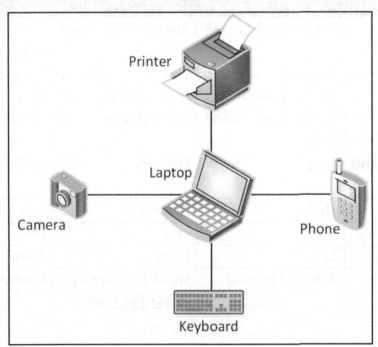

Figure 1-30: PAN Network

Internet-of-Things (IoT) Technologies

In today's IT world, embedded devices such as thermostats, water softeners, and other appliances are one of the fastest growing areas. This interconnection of computing devices embedded in everyday objects via the Internet is known as the Internet of Things (IoT). The goal is to allow data to be sent and received. To do this, technologies are required that facilitate such interaction. These technologies are discussed in the following section:

Z-Wave

Z-Wave is another popular wireless communication protocol. It is used for home automation like connecting home appliances such as lighting control, security systems, thermostats, windows, and locks. Z-Wave network follows mesh topology via low-energy radio waves. It operates in 800-900 MHz radio frequency and covers around 100 meters.

Ant+

Adaptive Network Topology is a wireless sensor network designed by ANT Wireless (Garmin Canada). ANT technology defines a wireless communication that operates at 2.4 GHz ISM band. ANT technology nodes acts as master-slave concurrently. ANT is incorporated in fitness sensors, which allow monitoring devices to communicate with each other.

Bluetooth

Bluetooth is designed for short-range connectivity, for mobile personal devices. Operational frequency of Bluetooth is 2.45 GHz and coverage area is less than 10 meters.

Exam Tip

Up until the most recent version, the numbers have always included a point and a decimal: 1.0, 1.2, and so on. With the latest version, there is no point or decimal. After much discussion, it was decided it was less confusing to go with a whole number: Bluetooth 5.

NFC

Near Field Communications (NFC), is a special standard designed for smartphones that qualifies them to dynamically form a mini PAN by keeping them only a few centimeters away from each other. This network can then be used to exchange data for things such as a door key, a ticket for a train, a payment for services rendered, a photo, a telephone number and contact information, etc.

IR

Infrared (IR) is the PAN technology used over short distances. The infrared (IR) initially offered a 115.2-kbit/s data rate over a range of up to 1 m. A 4-Mbit/s version was soon developed and has been widely integrated into laptops and PDAs for printer connections and short-range PANs. A 16-Mbit/s version is also available. The problem with IR is not only its very short range, but also, its need for a Line-of-Sight (LOS) connection.

RFID

Radio Frequency Identification (RFID) uses electromagnetic fields to automatically identify and track tags attached to objects. The e-tags contains the information for unique identification. These tags can be either active or passive. Passive tags do not need any power source whereas active tags have low power source. RFID is one method of automatic identification and data capture (AIDC). RFID systems can be classified by the type of tag and reader.

1. Passive Reader Active Tag (PRAT) System
2. Active Reader Passive Tag (ARPT) System
3. Active Reader Active Tag (ARAT) System

802.11

802.11 is the wireless standards specified by IEEE used for wireless LAN technology. It operates over-the-air interface between a wireless client and a base station or between two wireless clients. The IEEE specification was accepted in 1997. The original 802.11 standard used a Frequency-Hopping Spread Spectrum (FHSS) radio signal. There have been many versions since the beginning.

Hotspot

A hotspot is any location where internet access is available, usually using Wi-Fi through a Wireless Local Area Network (WLAN). WLAN uses a router connected to an internet service provider.

Exam Tip

Loose or missing terminators from a bus network disrupt data transmissions. The Network+ objectives require you to be familiar with wireless topologies such as mesh, ad hoc, and infrastructure.

Mind Map of Network Topologies Types & Technologies

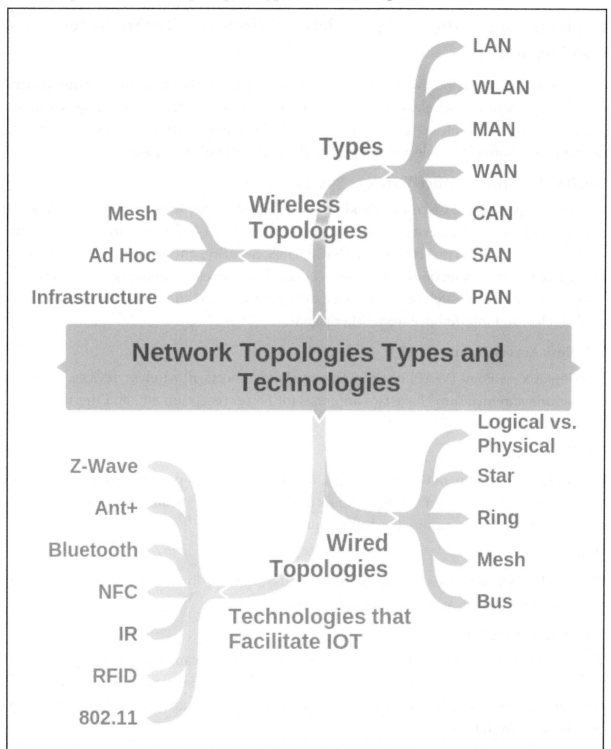

Figure 1-31: Mind Map of Network Topologies Types & Technologies

Implementing the Appropriate Wireless Technologies and Configurations

This section will describe the implementation of wireless LAN infrastructure and discuss the challenges of the wireless network. Some of the challenges of installing a wireless network area are Wireless Access Point (WAP) placement, antenna types, interference, frequencies, channels, wireless standards, SSID, and compatibility issues.

Small Office, Home Office Wireless Router

Vendor companies like Cisco and Belkin provide a router that is usually installed in small offices and homes. The devices come with an intelligent wizard built into the router and configure the appropriate settings for DHCP, DNS, Security, and so on. To make it easier, the cables and connections are color-coded. The wireless network is affected by environmental factors such as the distance between the client and the wireless router, type of obstacles, and interference from other signals.

Wireless Access Points (WAP)

Wireless Access Point (WAP) is a component that connects all wireless devices. WAP has at least one antenna; some have two antennas for better reception and an Ethernet port to connect them to a wired network.

Device Density

To increase the density of wireless devices, use multiple access points to overlap with each other. The amount of overlapping depends upon the range of installation; usually 10 to 20 percent overlapping is required at a minimum.

Roaming

The overlapping in wireless access points provides roaming for the users, so they connect to them while moving around buildings or campuses.

Wireless Controllers

The wireless controller collects all the data from the control plane and sends out streaming orders to individual APs. Depending on the type of controller, and how the network is configured, the controller may also process all data plane traffic as well, which has its benefits and limitations.

- **VLAN Pooling**
  VLAN pooling is a feature that enables the user to group multiple wireless controller VLANs to form a VLAN pool. Configure a VLAN pool to load-balance sessions evenly

across multiple VLANs. Individual VLANs are then assigned dynamically from the pool when a wireless client accesses the network. It uses a round robin algorithm

- **LWAPP**

  Lightweight Access Point Protocol (LWAPP) is a protocol proposed by a division of Cisco called Airespace. LWAPP is used by the wireless access controller that organizes the hand-off signals among many WAPs

Wireless Bridge

A wireless bridge is a network device that connects Ethernet network to a wireless network and also connects one wireless network to another wireless network. The wireless bridge does not provide a wireless access point for end users; it only connects the different wireless and wired networks throughout an organization's premises.

SSID Broadcast

When a wireless device like mobile phones and laptops want to connect WAPs, it will scan for Service Set Identifiers (SSIDs) in its instant area, which is a network name. In wireless LAN, if it wants the devices to find the SSID that are broadcasting, so it will make sure that WAP is enabled for broadcast. For security purpose, SSID broadcasting can be disabled.

Mobile Devices

Mobile Devices such as cell phones, laptops, tablets, gaming devices and media devices that want to connect to wireless LAN infrastructure, must have enabled Wireless features and be capable of uploading and downloading data.

802.11 Standards

802.11 is the wireless standards specified by IEEE used for wireless LAN technology. It operates over-the-air interface between a wireless client and a base station or between two wireless clients. The IEEE specification was accepted in 1997. The original 802.11 standard used a Frequency-Hopping Spread Spectrum (FHSS) radio signal. There have been many versions since the beginning. The following are the major 802.11 standards in use today:

802.11a

802.11a uses Orthogonal Frequency Division Multiplexing (OFDM) to increase bandwidth. This standard uses the 5 GHz radio band and can transmit data at up to 54 Mbps. It is not commonly used today.

802.11b

802.11b uses Direct Sequence Spread Spectrum (DSSS) modulation technique that operates in the 2.4 GHz wireless band. This standard can transmit data at up to 11 Mbps with

fallback rates of 5.5 Mbps, 2 Mbps, and 1 Mbps. It has been updated by the newer and faster standards.

802.11g

802.11g uses dual modulation techniques; DSSS and OFDM, and operates at 2.4 GHz wireless band. This standard enhances the 802.11b standard and can transmit data at speeds up to 54 Mbps. It is backward compatible with 802.11b, since both can use DSSS and the 2.4 GHz band.

802.11n

802.11n also uses DSSS and OFDM at the 2.4 GHz and the 5 GHz bands. This standard enhances the 802.11g standard and can transmit data at speeds up to 600 Mbps, although most devices support speeds only up to about 300 Mbps. This standard is backward compatible with 802.11g and 802.11b and 802.11a.

802.11ac

802.11ac uses the 5 GHz band and Multiple Input Multiple Output (MIMO) technologies. This standard enhances the 802.11n standard and can transmit data at speeds up to 1-Gbps, although most devices in use today, support speeds only up to about 500 Mbps. Devices that support 802.11n standard also support 802.11ac.

Cellular Standards

Anyone with a smartphone these days appreciates the convenience of using wireless cellular technology on the road. Who does not love firing up an Android phone or iPhone and cruising the internet from anywhere? As cellphone technology converges with internet access technologies, competent techs need to understand what is happening behind the scenes.

The voice and data people use on their smartphone moves via a cellular wireless network with towers that now cover the world. All of these technologies are nothing more than signaling standards that use the same cellular infrastructure in different manner to improve speed, latency, configuration, and dependability over the years.

Global System for Mobile (GSM)

The Global System for Mobile (GSM) is the first group of wireless technology that has been widely utilized in mobile devices. It uses time division multiple access techniques to share the same channels among the users, at different time spaces. GSM operates by SIM cards that enable access to the cellular networks and hold some information. GSM operates at 900 MHz in Asia and Europe, and 1900 MHz in the USA. GSM provides features like phone

call encryption, data networking, caller ID, call forwarding, call waiting, SMS, and conferencing.

Time Division Multiple Access (TDMA)

Time Division Multiple Access (TDMA) is channel access method used in digital cellular telephone such as Global System for Mobile Communications (GSM), IS-136, Personal Digital Cellular (PDC) and iDEN, and in the Digital Enhanced Cordless Telecommunications (DECT) standard for portable phones. It allows multiple users to share a frequency channel by dividing the signals into different time slots.

Code Division Multiple Access (CDMA)

Code Division Multiple Access is the technology developed just after the GSM, it uses spread spectrum codes to communicate with the users, in which different codes have been assigned to users, to time and frequency allocations. CDMA provides better voice quality, efficient use of spectrum, and facilitates more users at the same time.

Frequencies

The wireless network operates on 2.4 GHz frequency band and 5 GHz band frequency. Sometimes these two frequency bands combine to form a band that provides greater bandwidth for the user.

> **Note**
>
> Hertz (Hz) is the standard of measurement for radio frequency. Hertz is used to measure the frequency of vibrations and waves, such as sound waves and electromagnetic waves. One hertz is equal to one cycle per second. RF is measured in Kilohertz (KHz), 1000 cycles per second; Megahertz (MHz), one million cycles per second; or Gigahertz (GHz), one billion cycles per second.

Speed and Distance Requirements

Goodput is an application level throughput that measures the number of useful bits per unit of time sent by the network, from source to destination, excluding protocol overhead such as retransmissions. The main goal of wireless communication is to configure all settings to maximize goodput. Some wireless software and firmware can manage and monitor goodput.

Wireless networks have many standards that have developed over time, such as 802.11a, 802.11b, 802.11g, and 802.11n. Standards and connection types continue to develop, to make wireless networks even faster and more powerful. Some standards are backward compatible with others while some are not. Some devices cannot be configured to be

compatible with 802.11a standard because it uses 5 GHz frequency whereas 802.11 b and g use only 2.4 GHz frequency band.

Standard	802.11a	802.11b	802.11g	802.11n	802.11ac	802.11ad
Maximum Throughput	54 Mbps	11 Mbps	54 Mbps	Up to 600 Mbps	3.2 Gbps	Up to 7 Gbps
Maximum Range	~ 150 feet	~ 300 feet	~ 300 feet	~ 300 feet	~ 100 feet	~ 15 feet
Frequency	5 GHz	2.4 GHz	2.4 GHz	2.4/5 GHz	5 GHz	60 GHz
Backward Compatibility			802.11b	802.11a/b/g	802.11a/b/g/n	802.11a/b/g/n

Table 1-18: Wireless Network Standards

Signal strength is an important factor to consider while installing a wireless network. The signal strength varies according to many factors. They are; distance between the client and WAPs, walls and other barriers, protocol used, and interference with another signal.

Channel Bandwidth

Various frequency bands (2.4GHz, 3.6 GHz, 4.9 GHz, 5 GHz, and 5.9 GHz) have their range of channels. Usually, wireless routers will use the 2.4GHz band with a total of 14 channels, but in reality, it may use 13 channels around the world. All Wireless versions through 802.11n (a, b, g, n) work between the channel frequencies of 2400 and 2500 MHz. This 100 MHz in between them are split into 14 channels, 20 MHz each. Therefore, each 2.4GHz channel overlaps with two to four other channels as shown in the following diagram. Overlapping makes wireless network throughput quite poor.

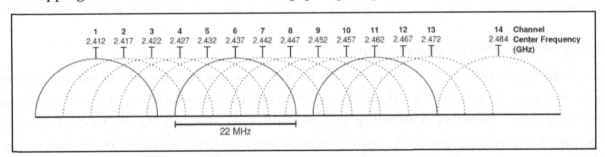

Figure 1-32: Channel Overlapping

Most popular channels for 2.4 GHz Wireless channels are 1, 6, and 11 because they do not overlap with each other.

Channel Bonding

With channel bonding, two channels can be used at the same time. As users might guess, the ability to use two channels at once increases efficiency. Bonding can help increase wireless transmission rates from the 54 Mbps provided with the 802.11g standards to a theoretical maximum of 600 Mbps with 802.11n. 802.11n uses the OFDM transmission strategy.

MIMO/MU-MIMO

Multiple-Input and Multiple-Output (MIMO) is an emerging technology that offers a substantial increase in speed and distance without additional need of transmission power. MIMO is a technique of using multiple antennas at both the transmitter and receiver to improve communication performance. MIMO is used with 802.11n and with 4G technologies.

When MIMO is used throughout a network with multiple users connecting to multiple antennas with multiple outputs, it is referred to as Multiple-User Multiple-Input and Multiple-Output (MU-MIMO).

Exam Note

Multiple Input, Multiple Output (MIMO) and Multiuser Multiple Input, Multiple Output (MU-MIMO) are advanced antenna technologies that are key in wireless standards such as 802.11n, 802.11ac, HSPA+, WiMAX, and LTE.

Unidirectional and Omni-Directional Antennas

There are many types of antennas, but the two common types of antennas are an omnidirectional antenna and unidirectional antenna. Antennas can even be placed away from the WAP but connected to it with a cable.

Omnidirectional

Omnidirectional antennas radiate its energy with equal strength in all direction. It has the advantage that any device within the signal radius can potentially access the network.

Unidirectional

Unidirectional antennas radiate its energy only in one direction. It is used to increase the strength of the signal.

Optimal antenna placement varies according to the space to fill and security concerns. Users can find the best place for antenna by site survey, also using wireless analyzer tools to find the dead spots and odd corners, and then use the right kind of antenna on each WAP to fill in space.

WAP antennas are available in many shapes and sizes. Previously, it was common to see WAPs with only one antenna. Some WAPs have two antennas, and some (802.11n and 802.11ac) have more than two antennas.

Site Survey

Before the deployment of wireless LAN, infrastructure performs a site survey that helps in frequency planning, cost estimation, coverage area and other parameters.

Heatmaps

A diagram of signal strength in a Wi-Fi network is referred to as Heat Maps. It is like a wireless monitoring tool that provides a visual map of a workstation to the network administrator that will give invaluable knowledge about the adjustment of the Access Points (APs) for better coverage.

Mind Map of Wireless Technologies

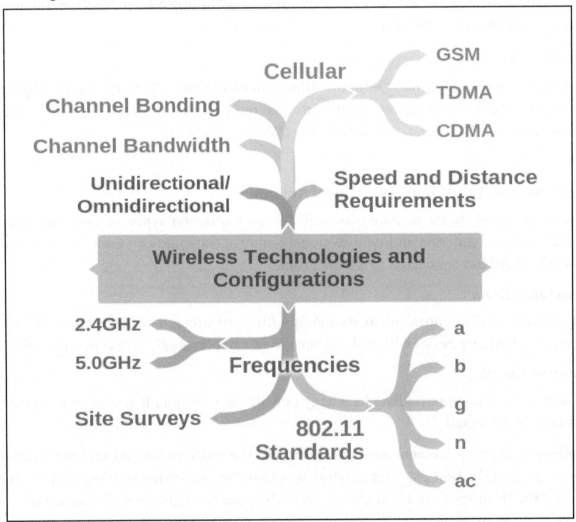

Figure 1-33: Mind Map of Wireless Technologies and Configurations

Cloud Concepts and their Purposes

Cloud Computing is a service that delivers computing resources that can be provided when needed. Major Cloud concepts include; public, private, hybrid, and community relating to Infrastructure as a Service (IaaS), Software as a Service (SaaS), and Platform as a Service (PaaS) individually.

Types of Cloud Computing Services

Cloud Computing services are categorized into the following three types:

- Infrastructure as a Service (IaaS)
- Platform as a Service (PaaS)
- Software as a Service (SaaS)

Software as a Service (SaaS)

Software as a Service (SaaS) is one of the most popular types of cloud computing services that is most widely used. Wherever users have an internet connection, SaaS model provides access to necessary applications, often without having to transfer information or regularly update software. At the enterprise level, the subscription model of several SaaS providers makes it easier for organizations to budget software expenses and to keep hundreds or thousands of PCs up to date with office software, messaging software, payroll processing software, database management software, management software, and much more. An example of SaaS is office software such as office 365, Cisco WebEx, Citrix GoToMeeting, Google Apps, messaging software, DBMS, CAD, ERP, HRM, etc.

Infrastructure as a Service (IaaS)

Infrastructure as a Services (IaaS), also known as cloud infrastructure service is a self-service model. IaaS is used for accessing, monitoring and managing purpose. For example, instead of purchasing additional hardware such as firewall, networking devices, server, etc. and spending money on deployment, management, and maintenance, IaaS model offers cloud-based infrastructure to deploy remote data centers. Most popular examples of IaaS are Amazon EC2, Cisco Metapod, Microsoft Azure, Google Compute Engine (GCE).

Platform as a Service (PaaS)

Platform as a service is another cloud computing service. It allows the users to develop, run and manage applications. PaaS offers development tools, configuration management, deployment platforms, and it migrates apps to hybrid models. It helps to develop and

customize applications, manage OSs, visualization, storage and networking, etc. Examples of PaaS are Google App Engine, Microsoft Azure, Intel Mash Maker, etc.

Cloud Deployment Models

The following are the deployment models for Cloud Services.

Deployment Model	Description
Public Cloud	Public Clouds are hosted by a third party offering different types of Cloud Computing services
Private Cloud	Private Clouds are hosted personally, individually. Corporate companies usually deploy their private Clouds because of their security policies
Hybrid Cloud	Hybrid Clouds are comprised of both private and public Cloud, allowing communication between them
Community Cloud	Community Clouds are accessed by multiple parties having common goals and shared resources

Table 1-19: Cloud Deployment Model

Public Cloud

The philosophy behind the public cloud is to get the computing resources immediately. In public cloud, the client has a choice to decide from a variety of offerings from public cloud vendors such as Amazon Web Service or Microsoft's Azure.

Private Cloud

Individuals can make a platform for the private cloud using virtualization software from VMware and other companies. The cloud gives complete authority and decision-making. It takes some time to develop but the complete authority is in IaaS, PaaS, and SaaS components of the system.

Hybrid Cloud

The hybrid cloud infrastructure is a composition of two or more distinct cloud infrastructures (private, community, or public) that remain unique entities, but are bound together by standardized or proprietary technology that allows information and application portability.

> **Note**
>
> A common reason for using cloud computing is to be able to offload traffic to resources from a cloud provider if your own servers become too busy. This is known as cloud bursting, and it requires load-balancing/prioritizing technologies such as Quality of Service (QoS) protocols to make it possible.

Community Cloud

A group of organizations from the business community that share the same common content such as compliance, security, and so on, uses a community cloud. Therefore, the costs to create the cloud are divided over a few organizations to save money for each organization but still maintain more control over IaaS, PaaS, and SaaS decisions than with a public cloud.

Connectivity Methods

There are several ways to communicate and access to the cloud environment. Connecting to a virtual server that is hosted on a cloud environment, following methods can make the access:

- Virtual Private Network (VPN)
- Remote Desktop Protocol (RDP)
- Secure Shell (SSH)
- File Transfer Protocol (FTP)
- VMware Remote Console

Security Implications and Considerations

Following are some security considerations for cloud environment:

- Cloud computing is trending day by day. High availability, ease of access and multi-tenancy model helps to collect information rapidly. As the computing becomes easy and fast, it also raises the security considerations. It also makes the cloud more susceptible to attacks as on-premises environments are
- Saleforce.com phishing incident reminds the security consideration towards social engineering attacks. Saleforce.com staff reveals the personal identification of their customer, which led to a phishing attack
- IT tools designed for on-premises environments are sometimes incompatible with cloud or virtualized environment. This raises not only the compatibility issue but also the visibility and control gaps. These gaps may lead an organization to the risk of data leakage, vulnerability exploits, excessive privileges access and compliance issues
- Although cloud computing is on trend, customers are still facing trust issues. Cloud customers are failing to ensure that their data, security keys and other confidential information are secure, protected and private.

Relationship between Local and Cloud Resources

Comparison of cloud and local infrastructure shows different aspect to be considered before selecting any one option. Following table shows the relationship among cloud and local resources.

Cloud Environment	Local Environment
Low cost overhead on customer	High cost overhead on customer
No maintenance overhead on customer	Maintenance overhead on owner
Scalable (On-demand / Auto-Scaling)	Scaling requires more investment
Monthly fee	Capital expenditure
Cloud Service Provider (CSP) takes some control	Total control on infrastructure
Stored data location may change rapidly	Fixed or known storage location

Table 1-20: Local and Cloud Environment

Exam Tip

For the exam, you should keep in mind that the most deployed cloud delivery models are private, public, and hybrid.

Mind Map of Cloud Concepts

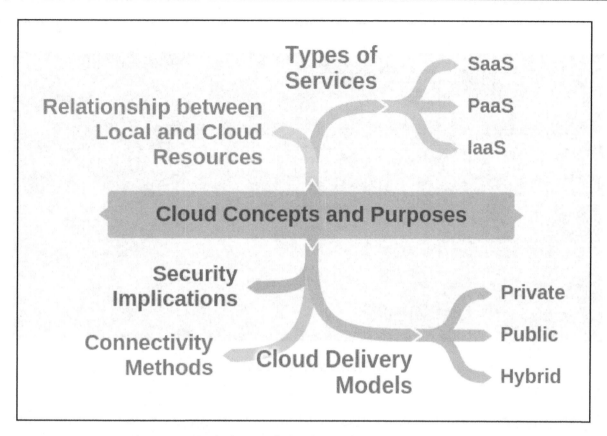

Figure 1-34: Mind Map of Cloud Concepts and their Purposes

Functions of Network Services

PCs use IP addresses to communicate with each other over a TCP/IP network; individuals prefer names to IP addresses. To solve this issue, a protocol known as Domain Name System (DNS) converts Fully Qualified Domain Names (FQDN) to IP addresses, to make it simpler for individuals to communicate with PCs.

It also covers Dynamic Host Configuration Protocol (DHCP), which enables customers to automatically get IP addresses, instead of being manually configured with a static address, Network Time Protocol (NTP), which synchronizes clocks, and IP Address Management (IPAM), which integrates DNS and DHCP, NTP, and IPAM.

Domain Name Service (DNS)

Domain Name Systems (DNS) translate between the human-readable domain names and IP addresses and are supported by all operating systems on the network. It comprises of specific servers that manage records.

```
Command Prompt                                          —    □    ✕

Microsoft Windows [Version 10.0.17763.615]
(c) 2018 Microsoft Corporation. All rights reserved.

C:\Users\tbi>ping www.google.com

Pinging www.google.com [172.217.19.4] with 32 bytes of data:
Reply from 172.217.19.4: bytes=32 time=48ms TTL=52
Reply from 172.217.19.4: bytes=32 time=46ms TTL=52
Reply from 172.217.19.4: bytes=32 time=51ms TTL=52
Reply from 172.217.19.4: bytes=32 time=41ms TTL=52

Ping statistics for 172.217.19.4:
    Packets: Sent = 4, Received = 4, Lost = 0 (0% loss),
Approximate round trip times in milli-seconds:
    Minimum = 41ms, Maximum = 51ms, Average = 46ms

C:\Users\tbi>
```

Figure 1-35: DNS Records

DNS Server

A DNS server is a special type of server that directs, holds and processes internet domain names, and their related records. DNS server involves software and configuration that allows resolving hostnames to IP addresses for an IP network. It performs its functions individually and can communicate with other DNS servers to exchange their databases and records.

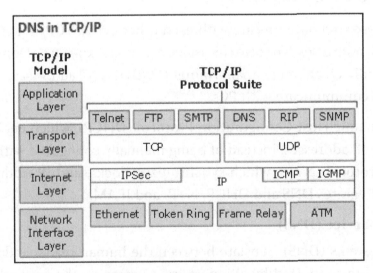

Figure 1-36: DNS in TCP/IP

DNS Records

DNS servers use different types of records, some of them are described below with their specifications:

- **Address (A) record:** Used to resolve a simple hostname to an IPV4 address
- **Mail Exchange (MX) record:** Directs the mail server about the routing of mail
- **AAAA Record:** Deals to resolve IPV6 addresses
- **CNAME Record:** Aliases on other records
- **PTR Record:** Recall a resolution for a service or host
- **NS (Name Server):** Represents DNS server
- **TXT-Records (Descriptive text)**
  - **TXT (SPF):** Used to provide authentication of mail sent and received by the same email system
  - **TXT (DKIM):** Used to provide authentication of mail sent and received by the same email system
- **SRV-Records (Location of Service):** Generalized service location record

Dynamic DNS

Dynamic DNS, commonly known as DDNS, is a service that converts domain names to IP addresses. DDNS has similar functions to DNS, but it deals with dynamic IP addresses. It can solve the problem of changing domestic IP addresses, by combining with a stable domain name without purchasing of static IP. It can update the server if any changes occur in the databases.

Internal vs External DNS

DNS server can be placed inside the private network as well as in DMZ, depending upon the requirements, Internal and External DNS servers can also be setup in a network.

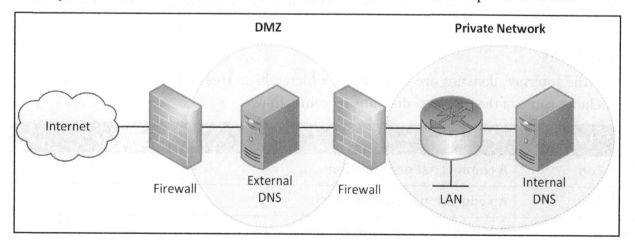

Figure 1-37: Internal vs External DNS

As shown in the above figure, when a DNS server is placed in DMZ, it contain the records of the devices that are placed in DMZ such as web servers, proxy servers, email servers, FTP servers and other devices.

Similarly, the DNS server placed in private network contains the records of internal devices. Deploying internal and external DNS server needs to import the external DNS records at the internal DNS server to access the resources in the DMZ by their IP addresses.

Third Party / Cloud Hosted DNS

Configuring DNS within the network is really a tough job. Smaller organizations and networks usually outsource the DNS service to cloud-based DNS providers or third-parties instead of hiring professional IT staff to configure and maintain the DNS function. There are number of cloud DNS providers in the market providing the reliable services. Popular cloud DNS providers are:

- Oracle Dyn Managed DNS
- CloudFlare
- Cisco Umbrella
- Amazon Route 53
- NS1
- Azure DNS
- Google Cloud DNS

There are many advantages of cloud-based DNS, including affordability, scalability, resiliency and security. Other advantages of cloud-based DNS services may include advanced traffic routing, such as AWS's Route 53 cloud DNS service, which offers round-robin, latency-based routing, geographic DNS and geo-proximity routing in addition to simple failover.

Hierarchy

On the Internet, domains are arranged in a hierarchical tree structure. The following list includes some of the top-level domains currently in use:

Domain	Use
.com	A commercial organization
.edu	An educational establishment
.gov	A branch of the U.S. government

.int	An international organization
.mil	A branch of the U.S. military
.net	A network organization
.org	A nonprofit organization

Table 1-21: Top-Level Domains

DNS tree structured hierarchy is known as DNS Namespace. In Domain Name System (DNS) inverted tree structure, top is called the Root. The DNS namespace tree has a unique root and large number of sub-trees. After the Root, the next layer is TLDs (Top Level Domains) such as edu., net., org., com., gov., etc.

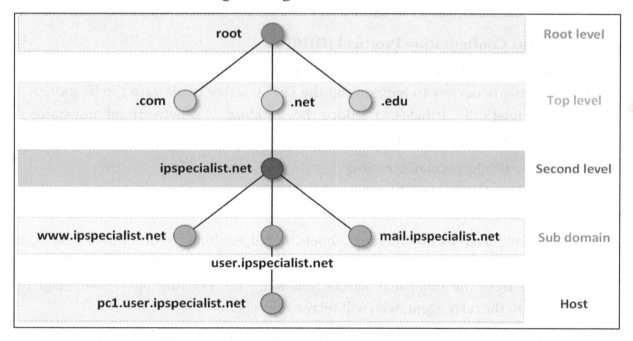

Figure 1-38: DNS Name Space Tree

Forward vs Reverse Zone

Forward DNS lookup is the address resolution of domain name to find an IP address. Reverse DNS lookup is using an Internet IP address to find a domain name.

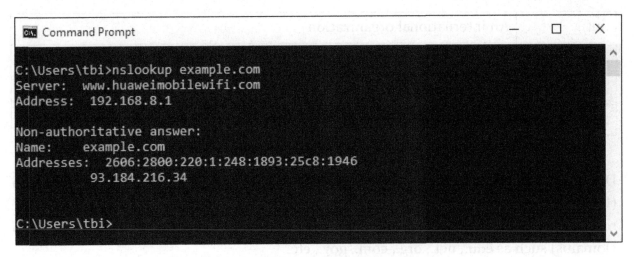

Figure 1-39: DNS Lookup

Dynamic Host Configuration Protocol (DHCP)

DHCP is a dynamic IP addressing protocol working on client-server based model, which allows the network devices to request and the DHCP server to allocate the IP address to this host automatically. It helps to reduce the workload of a network administrator to manually assign an IP address to each device. DHCP provides the following benefits:

- Reliable IP address configuration
- Reduced network administration

DHCP Relay and Server:

If the client and server are on different subnets, IP helper shifts a router into a relay agent where it will take a broadcast from one domain and forward it, as a unicast, to the client address listed from the original broadcast domain. The receiving device will send the relevant data to the relay agent, who will relay to the client.

DHCP Relay agent forwards the DHCP packets from server to client and client to server. Relay agents help the communications like forwarding request and reply between client and servers. Relay agents, when receiving a DHCP message; generate a new DHCP request to send it out from another interface with including default gateway information as well as Relay-Agent information option (Option-82). When the Relay Agent gets the reply from the server, it removes the Option 82 and forwards it back to the client.

Determining the Packet Forwarding Address

By using UDP broadcast, DHCP client sends an initial DHCP-Discover packet because it initially does not have network information to which they are connected. As we know, the router does not forward the broadcast request, by configuring the router interface that is receiving the DHCP-Discover broadcast packets to forward it to a helper address. More than one helper address can also be configured on an interface. This is what DHCP relay

agent is. In a Cisco Router, by using "IP helper-address" commands in interface configuration mode, DHCP relay agent can be configured.

Relay Agent Information Option

When a DHCP relay agent adds the information in the DHCP-Discover broadcast packet, it adds Remote ID and Circuit ID as a relay agent information (Option 82) and unicasts it to the DHCP Server. The server uses this information to assign IP addresses, security policies, Quality of Service and Access Control. When the Server sends the packet back to the relay agent, Option 82 information will be stripped from the packet and sent back to the client who initiated the request.

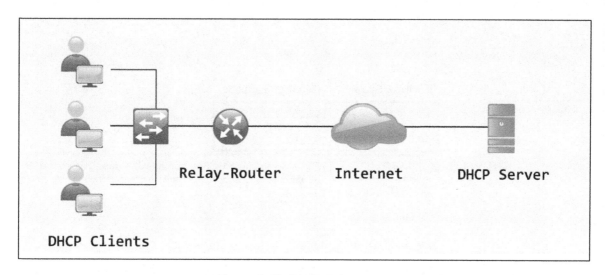

Figure 1-40: DHCP Relay Agent

DHCP Protocol Operations:

DHCP is the process of allocating the IP address dynamically so that these addresses are assigned automatically and also that they can be reused when hosts do not need them. Round Trip Time is the measurement of time from discovery of DHCP server until obtaining the leased IP address. RTT can be used to determine the performance of DHCP.

IP SLAs DHCP Relay Agent Options

IP SLA (Service Level Agreement) DHCP option uses relay agent option 82 information and is used for releasing the IP address when it is not in use, or when the DHCP operation ends.

DHCP Lease

DHCP Lease can be defined as time configured on a DHCP server to allow a host to use the assigned IP address. When this lease expires, the client has to renew the lease.

DHCP Pool

DHCP pool is a range of IP address, which are used in dynamic host address allocation process. Whenever a host requests for an IP address, an address from the pool is allocated and the lease time starts. Once a lease expires, the IP address is free. If the user requests it again, an address is reassigned.

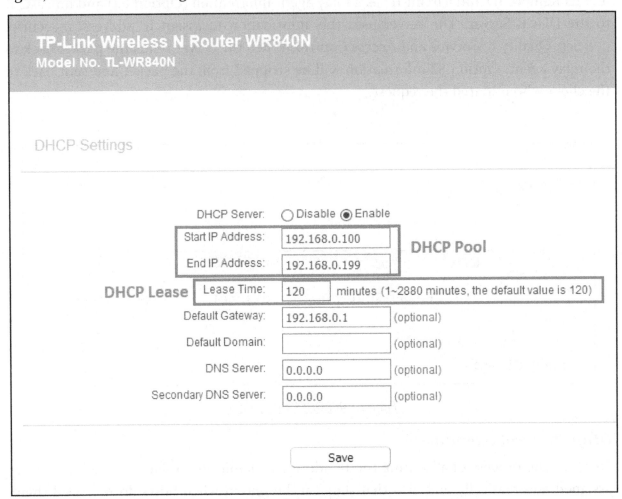

Figure 1-41: DHCP Pool

Scopes

A scope is a range of IP addresses that can be assigned to clients. The scope can be set by IP subnet, which is using the organization. However, you must be careful that scopes do not overlap with other scopes as it causes conflict.

IP Reservation / Excluded addresses

DHCP reservation is a process of assigning a permanent IP address. These reserved IP addresses are configured on the DHCP server for internal servers, printers, routers, workstations, etc. This IP address uses the DHCP scope that is reserved for leased use to a

particular DHCP client. Following command is used for Cisco routers to exclude an address from DHCP pool.

Router(config)# ip dhcp excluded-address 192.168.1.2 192.168.1.10

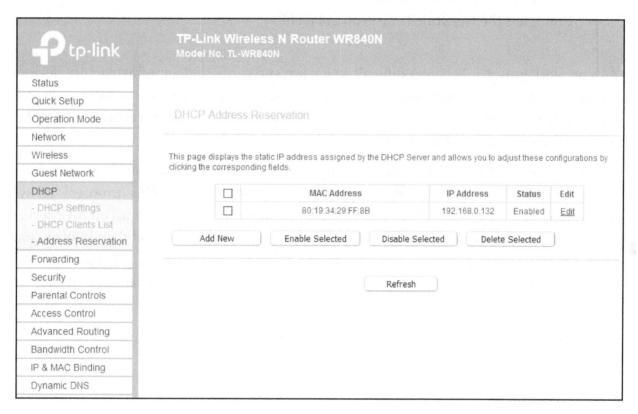

Figure 1-42: DHCP Address Reservation

Time To Live (TTL)

Time to Live (TTL) or hop limit is a lifespan of a packet in a network. The purpose of TTL is to discard the packet when the timespan has elapsed to avoid circulating indefinitely. TTL is commonly used to improve the performance and manage the caching of data. TTL is an 8-bit field. In the IPv4 header, TTL is the 9th octet of 20. In the IPv6 header, it is the 8th octet of 40. The maximum TTL value is 255, the maximum value of a single octet. A recommended initial value is 64.

Network Time Protocol (NTP)

There are many things involved in the securing of a network such as security logs along with an accurate date and timestamp. Secondly, when an attack is encountered on a network, it is important to identify when the attack occurred and the order in which a specified attack was encountered on a network. Log messages can be accurately time

stamped by the synchronization of clocks on hosts and network devices manually as well as using Network Time Protocol.

Typically, the date and time settings on the router can be set using one of two methods:

- Manually set the date and time
- Configure the Network Time Protocol (NTP)

As a network grows, it becomes difficult to ensure and verify that all infrastructure devices within a network are operating with synchronized time. Even in a smaller network environment, the manual method is not ideal. For example, if a router reboots, how will it get an accurate date and timestamp?

A better solution to prevent manual configuration of time and date in a network is to configure the Network Time Protocol (NTP) on the network. This protocol allows networking devices on the network to synchronize their time and date with an NTP server device. This is a better way that a group of NTP clients obtain time and date information from a single source has more consistent time settings. When NTP is configured in the network, it can synchronize to a NTP server, which is publicly available, or it can be synchronize to a private master clock.

Here is an example to set manually time and date on a Cisco router.

R1#clock set 11:00:00 12 may 2017

// To set time 11 hr 00 min 00 sec and date 12th May 2017

R1#show clock

// To check the Time and date running on the device

```
R1                                                          —    □    ✕

Press RETURN to get started.




R1>
R1>en
R1#clock set 11:00:00 12 may 2017
R1#
May 12 09:00:00.000: %SYS-6-CLOCKUPDATE: System clock has been updated from 11:00:46 EET Fri
May 12 2017 to 11:00:00 EET Fri May 12 2017, configured from console by console.
R1#
R1#show clock
11:00:12.369 EET Fri May 12 2017
R1#
R1#
R1#
```

NTP Authentication

NTP version 3 (NTPv3), and later versions, supports a cryptographic authentication technique between NTP peers. This authentication can be used to mitigate an attack.

Three commands are used on the NTP master and the NTP client:

- **ntp authenticate**
- **ntp authentication-key** *key-number* **md5** *key-value*
- **ntp trusted-key** *key-number*

Without NTP Authentication configuration, network time information will still be exchanged between servers and clients but the difference is these NTP clients do not authenticate the NTP server as a secure source such as what if the legitimate NTP server goes down and a fake NTP server overtake the real NTP server.

> Use the **show ntp associations detail** command to confirm that the server is an authenticated source.

```
NTP-CLient                                              —    □    ×

NTP-Client>
NTP-Client>
NTP-Client>en
NTP-Client#show ntp associations

  address          ref clock       st   when   poll reach  delay  offset  disp
*~1.0.0.2         127.127.1.1      10     6      64    17  1.000  -0.500 940.01
 * sys.peer, # selected, + candidate, - outlyer, x falseticker, ~ configured
NTP-Client#
NTP-Client#
NTP-Client#
```

Use the **show ntp status** command to confirm that the server and client are synchronized.

```
NTP-CLient                                              —    □    ×

NTP-Client>
NTP-Client>
NTP-Client>en
NTP-Client#config t
Enter configuration commands, one per line.  End with CNTL/Z.
NTP-Client(config)#ntp up
NTP-Client(config)#ntp update-calendar
NTP-Client(config)#end
NTP-Client#show
May 12 06:16:56.468: %SYS-5-CONFIG_I: Configured from console by console
NTP-Client#show ntp st
NTP-Client#show ntp status
Clock is synchronized, stratum 11, reference is 1.0.0.2
nominal freq is 250.0000 Hz, actual freq is 250.0000 Hz, precision is 2**10
ntp uptime is 16800 (1/100 of seconds), resolution is 4000
reference time is DCBFD1B8.59168820 (08:16:24.348 EET Fri May 12 2017)
clock offset is 0.5000 msec, root delay is 1.00 msec
root dispersion is 7942.70 msec, peer dispersion is 7938.47 msec
loopfilter state is 'CTRL' (Normal Controlled Loop), drift is 0.000000000 s/s
system poll interval is 64, last update was 38 sec ago.
NTP-Client#
```

IP Address Management (IPAM)

IP Address Management (IPAM) is an integrated suite of tools, which allows the network administrator for end-to-end planning, deploying, managing and monitoring the IP addresses. IPAM automatically discovers IP addresses of infrastructure servers and Domain Name System (DNS) servers on the network and enables users to manage them from a central interface.

IPAM provides highly customizable administrative and monitoring capabilities for the IP address and DNS infrastructure on an Enterprise or Cloud Service Provider (CSP) network. Users can monitor, audit, and manage servers running Dynamic Host Configuration Protocol (DHCP) and Domain Name System (DNS) by using IPAM.

 Exam Tip

Be very comfortable with the hierarchical way DNS works. The most popular DNS server used in UNIX/Linux systems is called BIND.

Mind Map of Network Services

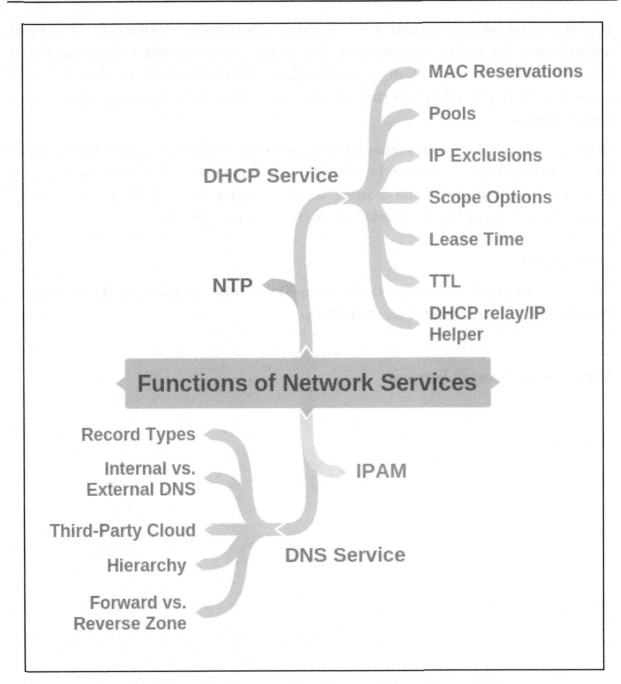

Figure 1-43: Mind Map of Functions of Network Services

Summary

Purposes and Uses of Ports and Protocols

- TCP is used for connection-oriented, guaranteed, acknowledged communication

- UDP is used for connectionless, unguaranteed, and unacknowledged
- TCP segments and UDP datagrams are encapsulated in IP packets at Layer 3
- ICMP provides informational and error reporting to devices

Devices, Applications, Protocols and Services at their Appropriate OSI Layers

- Routers are found at Layer 3 of OSI
- Frames at Layer 2 contain MAC addresses
- Layer 4 is where the sending application chooses between connection-oriented TCP and connectionless UDP

The Concepts and Characteristics of Routing and Switching

- Wi-Fi networks use carrier sense multiple access with collision avoidance (CSMA/CA) rather than CSMA/CD
- A Protocol Data Unit (PDU) represents a specific set of data at each layer of a model, like OSI
- There are three types of ways to send a frame or packet: broadcast, multicast and unicast
- Trunking is the process of transferring VLAN traffic between two or more switches

Configuring the Appropriate IP Addressing Components

- A subnet mask is needed to identify the network ID and host ID portions of the IP address
- IPv4 addresses are 32 bit numbers, written in dotted decimal notation

Compare and Contrast the Characteristics of Network Topologies, Types and Technologies

- The switch acts as the central device in a star topology
- The infrastructure topology uses a wireless access point
- The 802.11 standards define every aspect of wireless networks

Implementing the Appropriate Wireless Technologies and Configurations

- An omnidirectional antenna radiates outward from the WAP in all directions, while a unidirectional antenna focuses a radio wave into a beam of sorts
- The site survey helps determine the best location for the WAPs
- GSM introduced SIM cards

Cloud Concepts and their Purposes

- In a private cloud model, the cloud is owned by the organization and it acts as both the provider and the consumer
- The hybrid cloud delivery model is a composition of two or more distinct cloud infrastructures (public, private, and so on)

- A common reason for using cloud computing is to be able to offload traffic to resources from a cloud provider

Functions of Network Services

- DHCP relay agents take broadcasts from clients and unicast them to DHCP servers
- Routers never forward broadcasts, nor do they turn unicasts into broadcasts
- The Sender Policy Framework (SPF) and Domain Keys Identified Mail (DKIM) are implemented through the TXT record

Practice Questions

1. What are the advantages of using DHCP in a network? (Choose 2)
   A. Easier Administration
   B. Static IP Addressing
   C. Difficult Network Administration
   D. Assigning IP Addresses to Hosts

2. What role does the Address (A) record in a Domain Name Service (DNS) server have in your network?
   A. Translates IP address to human name
   B. Translates human name to IP address
   C. Aliases on other records
   D. Recalls a resolution for a service or host

3. Which type of server performs the mapping of private IP address into public IP address?
   A. IPS/IDS Server
   B. NAT Translation Server
   C. DNS Server
   D. Proxy Server

4. Which connector provides communication and controlling factor in network devices.
   A. RJ-11
   B. RJ-48C
   C. RJ-45
   D. DB-9

5. Select three Fiber Optic connectors.
   A. ST
   B. SC
   C. BNC
   D. LC

6. Which physical topology connects computers to central devices, and is the most common for LANs?
   A. Mesh

B. Star

C. Ring

D. Bus

7. Which wireless technology utilizes a short-range communication facilitating data transmission from fixed and/or mobile devices, creating wireless Personal Area Networks (PANs)?
   A. IR (Infrared)
   B. NFC (Near field Communication)
   C. Bluetooth
   D. Comsat

8. Select two right statements regarding IPv4 and IPv6 addresses.
   A. An IPv6 address is 128 bits long, represented in decimal
   B. An IPv4 address is 32 bits long, represented in decimal
   C. An IPv6 address is 32 bits long, represented in hexadecimal
   D. An IPv6 address is 128 bits long, represented in hexadecimal

9. Which routing protocol belongs to hybrid routing protocols and Cisco proprietary protocol?
   A. OSPF
   B. RIP
   C. EIGRP
   D. BGP

10. Which version of SNMP provides plaintext authentication with MD5 or SHA with no confidentiality?
    A. SNMPv2
    B. SNMPv1
    C. SNMPv2c
    D. SNMPv3

11. Which of the following is not a SNMP utility?
    A. GET
    B. Trap
    C. Run
    D. Walk

12. Which switching protocol can prevent switching loops in a network?
    A. STP
    B. VTP
    C. RSTP
    D. Tunneling Protocol

13. Which cable is used by PoE and PoE+ for transmitting power and data for remote devices?
    A. Fiber Optic Cable
    B. Twisted-pair Cable
    C. Coaxial Cable
    D. E1/T1

14. Which of the following best describes Goodput?
    A. The average size of a file to be transferred
    B. The size of a pipe between the receiver and sender
    C. The amount of time it takes to pass data from sender to receiver
    D. The amount of usable bits transferred in a given period of time

15. Which of the following are valid frequency bands for wireless networks?
    A. 2.4 MHz
    B. 5.0 GHz
    C. 2.4 GHz
    D. 5.0 MHz

16. Sublayer that serves as midway between Physical Link and Higher Layer protocols, performing flow-control and error-control is called as
    A. Media Access Control (MAC)
    B. Logical Link Control (LLC)
    C. Session Layer
    D. Transport Layer

17. Which of the following does not belongs to Data-Link Layer?
    A. Token Ring
    B. FDDI
    C. Frame Relay
    D. IP

18. Connection Oriented Protocol of Transport layer is _____.
    A. TCP
    B. UDP
    C. IP
    D. ICMP

19. The process in which multiple Data Streams coming from different sources are combined and transmitted over a Single Data Channel is called _____.
    A. Modulation
    B. Encapsulation
    C. Multiplexing
    D. Sampling

20. Which two common wireless standards use only the 2.4 GHz frequency band? (Choose 2)
    A. 802.11a
    B. 802.11n
    C. 802.11g
    D. 802.11b

21. Which layer is responsible for the reliable transfer of data, by ensuring that data arrives at its destination are error-free and in order?
    A. Session Layer
    B. Transport Layer
    C. Network Layer
    D. A and B

22. FTP, HTTP, and Telnet are all related to which layer of the OSI model?
    A. Presentation Layer
    B. Session Layer
    C. Application Layer
    D. Network Layer

23. Which layer controls the formatting and syntax of user data for the application layer?
    A. Layer 6
    B. Layer 4

C. Layer 1

D. Layer 5

24. In encapsulation, PDU stands for _____.

   A. Packet Data Unit

   B. Port Data Unit

   C. Package Datagram Unit

   D. Protocol Data Unit

25. The most common functionality of Internet Control Message Protocol (ICMP) is _____.

   A. Collision Avoidance

   B. Broadcasting

   C. Ping Utility

   D. Error Checking

26. UDP, instead of connection less protocol but it is quite demanding due to?

   A. High Payload

   B. Low Overhead

   C. Low Payload

   D. High Overhead

27. UDP header has 4 fields whereas TCP header has _____.

   A. 10

   B. 14

   C. 11

   D. 16

28. For secure communications using HTTPS, which port number is used by default?

   A. 80

   B. 110

   C. 25

   D. 443

Chapter 02: Infrastructure

Technology Brief

When infrastructure equipment is purchased and deployed, the ultimate success of the deployment depends on selecting the proper equipment, determining its proper location in the facility, and installing it correctly. Let's look at some common data center or server room equipment and a few best practices for managing these facilities.

Deploy the Appropriate Cabling Solution

All cables used in the networking industry can be categorized in two distinct groups: copper (with names like UTP, STP, and coax) and fiber-optic. All styles of cables have distinct connector types that you need to be familiar with.

Intermediate Distribution Frame

An Intermediate Distribution Frame (IDF) serves as a distribution point for cables from the Main Distribution Frame (MDF) to individual cables connected to equipment in areas distant from these frames. It is connected to the MDF and is used to provide greater flexibility regarding the distribution of the communication lines to the building. It is typically a sturdy metal rack, designed to hold the bulk of cables that are coming from all over the building.

Main Distribution Frame

The main distribution frame connects equipment to cables and subscriber carrier equipment. It also terminates cables that run to intermediate distribution frames, distributed throughout the facility. It often has protection devices for lightning or other electrical spikes. It is also used as a central testing point.

Cable Management

There are a large number of cables coming from the distribution frames. Managing these cables is important, both to protect the integrity of the cables, and to prevent overheating of the networking devices caused by masses of disruptive cabling.

Media Types

All media type cables used in the networking industry can be categorized in two distinct groups: copper (with names like UTP, STP, and coax) and fiber-optic.

Copper Cables

Copper cables are the most common type of cabling uses copper wire wrapped up in some kind of protective sheathing. Coaxial and twisted pair are the two primary types of copper cabling.

Coaxial Cables

Coaxial is another type of copper cable which conducts electricity. Tubular insulating layer surrounds inner conductor. The tubular insulating layer is surrounded by a conducting shield. Outer most shield or jacket is again of insulating material. The term coaxial arises from the inner conductor and the outer shield. It is used to carry high frequency electrical signals with low losses. Coaxial cables are popularly used for cable TV.

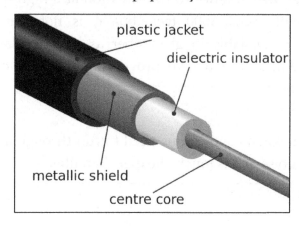

Figure 2-01: Coaxial Cable

Shielded Vs. Unshielded

Shielded Twisted Pair Cable	Unshielded Twisted Pair Cable
STP is more expensive than UTP	UTP cable is cheapest
Harder to install as it is thick and heavy	Easy to install
STP reduces EM interference by a braided shield	Affected by external EM interference
Used in computer networking	Used in ordinary telephone wires

Table 2-01: Shielded Vs. Unshielded

Fiber

Fiber-optic cables are often used in network backbones to provide high bandwidth for fast and stable communications. Two main types of fiber-optic cables are:

Single Mode Fiber

Single Mode Fiber-optic (SMF) cable is a high-speed, long coverage media. It typically consists of a single strand, or rarely two strands of glass fiber that carry the signal. SMF usually uses laser, or sometimes Light Emitting Diodes (LEDs), as a light source. A single light source transmits from end to end and provides communication by creating pulses.

SMF is used for long distance because it can transmit data at a much faster rate as 50 times greater than multimode fiber.

<u>Multimode Fiber</u>

Multimode Fiber-optic (MMF) cable provides communication by using light signals and spreading it into multi-paths as it travels from the core and reflects back through the cladding. MMF provides high bandwidth transmission at a high speed, as it travels along the medium distance of about 3000 feet, but it is not suitable for long-distance communication. MMF is available in glass fiber as well as plastic fiber. Plastic fiber installation is easier and flexible, and MMF provides immunity to electrical interference.

 Exam Tip

Coax is often preferred when connections need to run through elevator shafts because it is resistant to radio noise and is much cheaper than fiber.

Plenum vs. PVC

There is no significant fire protection for Polyvinyl Chloride (PVC) Cable. Loads of smoke and noxious fumes are produced when users burn a PVC cable. Burning cables with a plenum rating produces far less smoke and fumes, but it costs about three to five times as much as PVC cable. Plenum cables are covered with non-flammable material, often Teflon or Kynar, and when they catch fire, they do not release toxic fumes.

Connector Types

The associated network media uses a different type of connectors. Media connectors connect to the transmission media and enable the physical connection into the computing device. For the Network+ exam, users need to know the connectors associated with a specific medium. The following sections define the connectors and associated media.

Copper

Copper connectors are used to connect copper cables; copper connectors are not certainly made up of copper. There are many types of copper connectors and the most common types are discussed below:

<u>RJ-45</u>

Registered Jack (RJ)-45 connector is the most common connector for all networks. It is used to connect all physical layer devices like Network Interface Cards (NICs). RJ-45 provides communication and control factors in network devices. The RJ-45 connector can accommodate four pairs of UTP cables and mainly used in LANs for a shorter distance (100 meters).

Figure 2-02: RJ-45 Connector with Cables

RJ-11

Registered Jack (RJ)-11 connector is used to connect UTP cables and mainly used to connect telephone lines and DSL connections. RJ-11 can accommodate two pairs of wires. RJ connectors are attached to UTP cable with the help of a crimper.

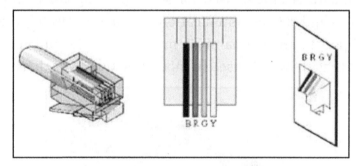

Figure 2-03: RJ-11 Connector with Cables

RJ-48C

Another type of copper connector is RJ-48C that is similar to the RJ-45 connector. RJ-48c has four pairs of shielded wires. It is used for long distance Wide Area Networks (WANs) with a T1 connection.

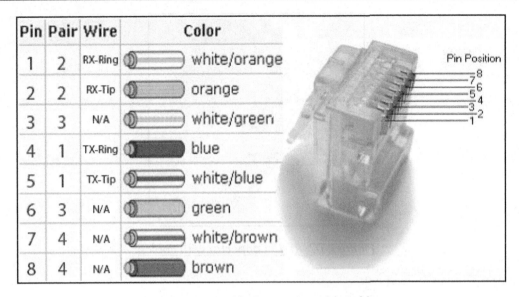

Figure 2-04: RJ-48c Connector with Cables

DB-9/RS-232

The DB-9 cable standard is mostly used for serial data signals to provide a connection between data terminal and data communication equipment. DB-9 is often used to connect a computer's serial port to an external modem. DB-9 female connector might be used in RS-232 connections that are widely used in modern networks such as USB.

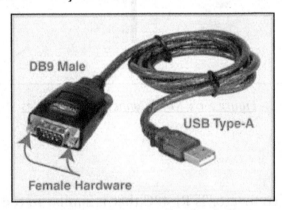

Figure 2-05: DB-9 Connector

DB-25

DB-25 connectors have been used mostly in everything, from modems to printers. In DB-25, 25 indicates the number of pins that can be used. It is configured in such a way to provide serial communication as well as parallel communication.

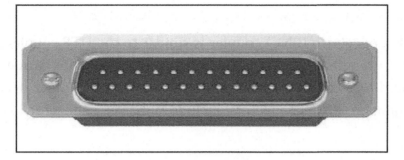

Figure 2-06: DB-25 Connector

UTP Coupler

A Universal Twisted Pair (UTP) coupler is a small plastic box that has two female RJ-45 or RJ-11 ports on any side of it. UTP coupler is usually used to extend the length of a cable by installing another cable to it.

Figure 2-07: UTP Coupler with Cables

BNC

A Bayonet Neill–Concelman (BNC) connector is used to connect coaxial cables. BNC is not very useful in today's networking. The BNC connector is pushed in and then locked onto the connection to hold it securely in place while connecting the core wire.

Figure 2-08: BNC

BNC Coupler

A Bayonet Neill–Concelman (BNC) coupler is similar to the UTP coupler. BNC coupler is used to extend the length of a coaxial cable. BNC coupler contains two female connectors on any one end. BNC connectors are used on some networks, older network cards, and older hubs. Common BNC connectors include a barrel connector, T-connector, and terminators.

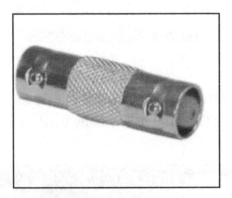

Figure 2-09: BNC Connector

F-Connector

The F-Connector is a coaxial type connector used to connect cable TV and cable modems. It is mostly attached to RG-6 or RG-59 cable. It is responsible for providing a solid connection to promote the carrying of data or television signals.

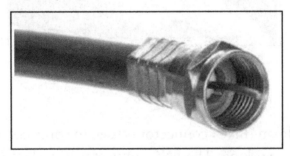

Figure 2-10: F-Connector

Fiber Connectors

There are many types of connectors used to connect fiber optic cables to the network device. The following section will describe the various fiber connectors and their general purpose:

LC

A Local Connector (LC) is a fiber-optic cable connector that is made into the body of an RJ-style jack. The LC connector is perfect for an organization's telecom room, connected with Local Area Network.

ST

Straight Tip (ST) connectors are similar to small BNC connectors but are made up of small, hard plastic. ST connectors use a half-twist bayonet type of a lock. ST connectors are most commonly used with single-mode fiber-optics that travel long distances.

SC

The Standard Connector (SC) is another type of fiber-optic cable connector. It is based on a push-pull connector mechanism, identical to common audio and video plugs. SC connectors are usually used with a multimode fiber-optic cable that provides a backbone section for Local Area Networks.

APC

The quality of fiber cable and connectors is increasing day by day, as well as improving the ability to connect to devices without signal loss due to back reflection of light. The first quality of a connector is the physical contact, which provides a physical connection with devices.

Angled Physical Contact (APC) connectors add an 8-degree angle to the curved end, lowering signal loss further. Plus, their connection does not degrade from multiple insertions, unlike earlier connection types.

UPC

Ultra Physical Contact (UPC) connectors are polished extensively for a superior finish. These reduce signal loss significantly over PC connectors.

MTRJ

Mechanical Transfer Registered Jack (MTRJ) is becoming popular because of its flexible sizes and stability. It consists of two fibers, adjacent to each other, and similar to an RJ-45 connector. It was designed to replace the SC; it is half in size of the SC and provides two fiber connections.

FC

Ferrule Connector (FC) is a thread like structure that is designed for use in the vibrational environment and is usually used with a single-mode fiber-optic cable. FC connectors are used less frequently than SC and LC connectors.

Transceivers

A transceiver plugs into networking devices, enabling conversion from one media type to another.

Gigabit Interface Converter (GBIC)

GBIC is a standard for transceivers such as Gigabit Ethernet and Fiber channel. One Gigabit port can support a wide range of physical media, from copper to long-wave single-mode optical fiber, at lengths of hundreds of kilometers. Now, GBIC is obsoleted by SFP.

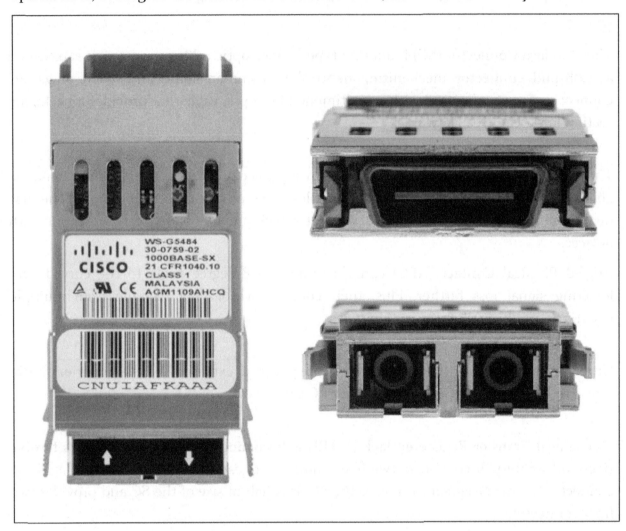

Figure 2-11: Cisco 100Base-SX GBIC WS-G5484

Small Form-factor Pluggable (SFP)

A variation of the GBIC called the small form-factor pluggable transceiver (SFP), also known as mini-GBIC, has the same functionality but in a smaller form factor. SFP is smaller than GBIC in size. For every type of GBIC and SFP transceivers, it works with different wavelengths at a designated location or distance. SFP specifications are based on IEEE802.3 and SFF-8472.

Figure 2-12: Cisco 100Base-FX SFP mini-GBIC 1310nm GLC-GE-100FX

SFP+

Both, SFP and SFP+ modules look the same and mostly, the switches can support both SFP and SFP+ modules. SFP+ is an enhanced version of the SFP. SFP+ specifications are based on SFF-8431. SFP supports up to 4.25 Gbps where as SFP+ supports upto 16 Gbps data rates.

Quad Small Form-Factor Pluggable (QSFP)

Quad in QSFP refers to four lanes. QSFP uses four lanes (each of 1x10G). The QSFP is a hot-pluggable transceiver for Ethernet, Fiber Channel and Infiniband standards.

The QSFP comes as Short Range (SR), i.e., short distance multimode up to 300 meters and Long Range (LR), i.e., ten kilometers single mode versions.

Characteristics of Fiber Transceivers

Fiber transceivers have two common characteristics: duplex and bidirectional capabilities.

Bidirectional

Bidirectional fiber optics transceivers are called BiDi transceivers. These transceivers use WDM (Wavelength Division Multiplexing) for bidirectional communication.

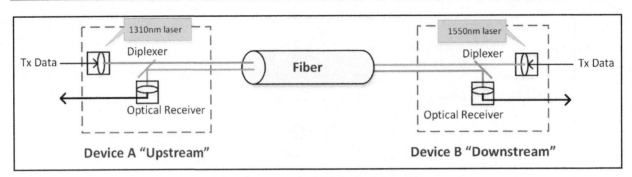

Figure 2-13: BiDi Transceiver Communication

BiDi doubles your network capacity by fully utilizing all the fiber strands. It has become more reliable because single strand solutions are less prone. BiDi also reduces the cost of cabling, labor and material.

<u>Duplex</u>

The most common forms of fiber-optic networking, where fiber is installed in pairs, with one cable to send and the other to receive, were discussed up to this point. These are still the most common fiber-based networking solution out there. All the transceivers used in these technologies have two connectors, a standard duplex format.

Termination Points

While we might see the network cables that carry information, including the connection into the NICs, it is not common to see the other side of the cable. What happens to that cable after it enters into a wall plate? Where is the location where that cable run ends? This location is called a termination point.

66 Block

The 66-block wiring distribution was the standard for telephone companies. It was used for terminating sets of telephone wires with the help of a punch down tool. It was mainly designed in multiple sizes. It was bound for analog voice communications. Therefore, it has been replaced by new hardware, like 110 blocks.

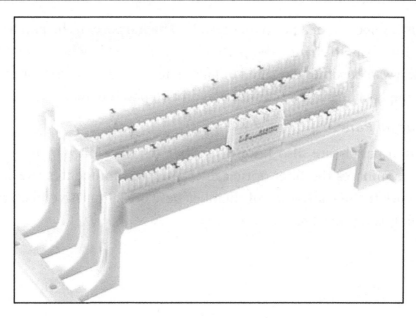

Figure 2-14: 66 Block

110 Block

110 block is a type of wiring distribution point. 110 block has replaced 66-block telephone wire installation and is used for computer networking. On either side of it, wires are punched down while the other side of it is connected with RJ-11 or RJ-45. 110 block supports variable sizes from 25 to 500 wire pairs. It delivers 1-Gbps connections when connected with CAT6 cables.

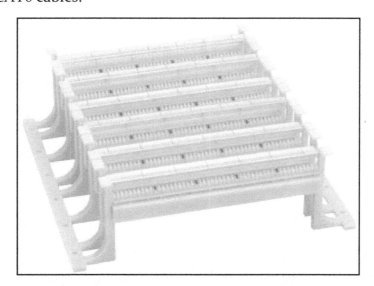

Figure 2-15: 110 Block

Patch Panels

A patch panel is generally a rack or wall-mounted structure that arranges cable connections. A patch cable generally plugs into the front side, while the back holds the

punched-down connection of a permanent cable. The purpose of the patch panel is to offer the administrator a way to change the path of a signal quickly when needed. For example, if a cable inside a wall becomes damaged or fails, a network administrator can patch around that cable by simply changing the connection on two patch panels.

Fiber Distribution Panel

Fiber optic patch panels are also known as fiber distribution panels. This distribution panels usually terminates the fiber optic cables, and accommodates the connections and patching. Network technicians control the fiber network of massive fiber cables and their connection point using this distribution panel.

Mind Map of Cabling Solution Deploymnet

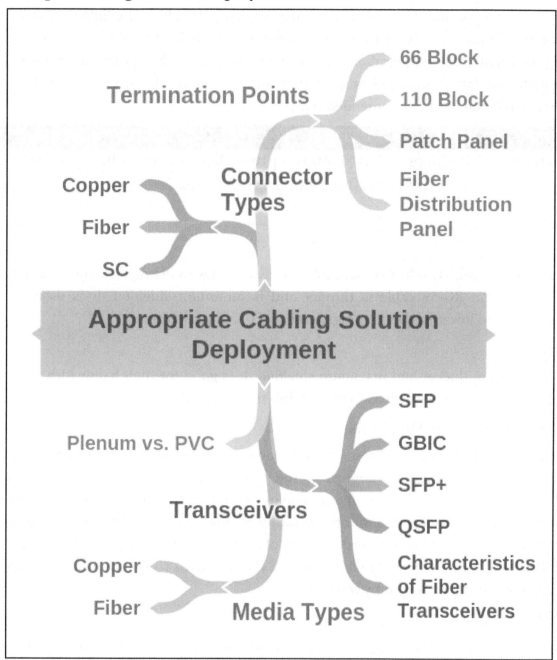

Figure 2-16: Mind Map of Cabling Solution Deployment

Copper Cable Standards

Coax cable was initially a baseband and was used as a medium for data transmission on digital computer networks. Nowadays, the only sort of coax cable users will see is broadband, which is not used to transmit information on digital networks, but rather broadband services, like TV and Internet transcieving into homes.

CAT 3, 5, 5e, 6, 6a and 7

CAT 3, 5, 5e, 6, 6a and 7 is the category of a twisted-pair cable. The following categories define the tightness of the twist applied to the wire pairs in the cable. Twisting in wires prevents them from electrical interference or crosstalk. This cable can transmit the information as faster as the twists are tighter without the interference of crosstalk. CAT5e (enhanced) is the most recommended type.

CAT3	CAT5	CAT5e	CAT6	CAT6a	CAT7
10 Mbps	100 Mbps	**1000 Mbps**	1000 Mbps	1000 Mbps	100Gbps

Table 2-02: Cable Categories and Maximum Speeds

RG-59

RG stands for Radio Guide. Coaxial cable uses RG ratings to distinguish amongst different cable types. An RG-59 cable is thinner and is minimum shielded. It is used for low bandwidth and lower frequency usage, such as CCTV installations.

RG-6

RG-6 cables are thicker and maximum shielded. It is good for high bandwidth and high-frequency requirements such as Cable TV, Internet, and Satellite signals.

Copper Termination Standards

UTP cables and connectors come with associated color codes and wiring schemes. Every wire inside a UTP cable must connect to the proper pin on the connector at each end of the cable. The wires are color-coded to help in properly matching the ends. Two industry organizations, the Telecommunications Industry Association (TIA) and the Electronic Industries Alliance (EIA) developed a variety of standard color coding schemes to facilitate installation. EIA disbanded in 2011 and moved the standards to TIA, but the term TIA/EIA or EIA/TIA are still discussed by the technicians.

EIA/TIA 568A/568B

T568A and T568B are two major wiring standards that determine the order of the wires placed in the RJ-45 connector. Using an established color-coded scheme guarantees that the wires match up properly at each end of the cable. This regularity makes troubleshooting and repair much easier.

The T568A wiring standard has the wires in the following order: white/green, green, white/orange, blue, white/blue, orange, white/brown, and finally brown. The only difference between the two standards is that the orange and green pairs of wires are interchanged regarding their pin assignment. The most common wiring standard in use today is the T568B standard.

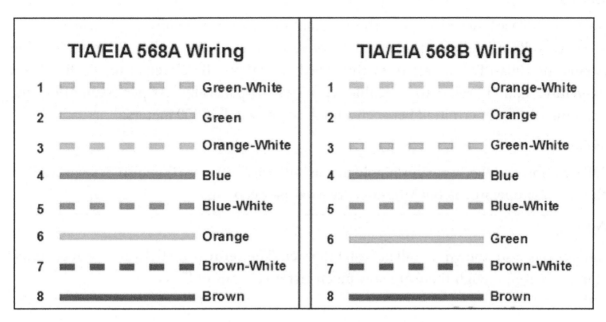

Figure 2-17: EIA/TIA 568A/568B

Straight-through Vs. Crossover Vs. Rollover Cable

Cable Types	Standard	Application
Straight-Through	Both ends T568A or both ends T568B	-Used to connect dissimilar network devices -Connects a network host to a network device e.g., Switch or Hub
Crossover	One end T568A and another end 568B	-Used to connect similar network devices -Connects two network hosts to network intermediary devices e.g., switch to switch, router to router
Rollover	Cisco Proprietary	-Connects a workstation serial port to a router console port

Table 2-03: Straight-Through Vs. Crossover Vs. Rollover

Ethernet Deployment Standards

In the early 1980's, the Institute of Electrical and Electronics Engineers (IEEE), that defines industry-wide standards in the fields of electronics and computing, adopted the DIX Ethernet standard as a general standard for networking. The IEEE working group (or committee) responsible for general networking standards known as the 802 committees, and Ethernet became IEEE 802.3 standard.

Ethernet Standardization are as follows:

10BaseT

The term 10BaseT describes an Ethernet cabling system generally used in a star bus topology. 10BaseT follows the naming convention used for earlier Ethernet cabling systems. In 10BaseT, "10" refers to the speed: 10 Mbps, "Base" refers to the Baseband modulation, and "T" refers to the cable type: Twisted-pair cable. As per assumption, the maximum distance permitted between a node and a switch is 100 meters.

100BaseT

100BaseT follows the same terminologies as 10BaseT. 100BaseT is also known as Fast Ethernet that operates at 100 Mbps over twisted-pair cabling.

> **Note**
>
> 100BaseT is also known as called Fast Ethernet. The term still sticks to the 100-Mbps standards even though there are now much faster versions of Ethernet.

1000BaseT

1000BaseT uses four-pair UTP or STP cabling to achieve gigabit performance. 1000BaseT has a maximum of 100-meter cable length on a segment just like 10BaseT and 100BaseT. 1000BaseT connections and ports look exactly like the ones on a 10BaseT or 100BaseT network. 1000BaseT is the dominant Gigabit Ethernet standard.

1000BaseTX

1000BaseTX belongs to category 5 cabling. It contains two-pair UTP wiring up to 100 meters long. It is not used today, and has been replaced by Category 6 cabling.

1000BaseSX and 1000BaseLX

1000BASE-LX and 1000BASE-SX SFP are two common forms of optical transceiver modules. 1000BASE in these terms refers to a Gigabit Ethernet connection that uses the unfiltered cable for transmission. "X" means 4B/5B block coding for Fast Ethernet or 8B/10B block coding for Gigabit Ethernet. "L" means long-range single - or multi-mode optical cable (100 m to 10 km). "S" means short-range multi-mode optical cable (less than 100 m).

10GBaseT

10GBaseT is a standard created by the IEEE 802.3an committee to provide 10Gbps connections over conventional UTP cables (Category 5e, 6, or 7 cables). 10GBaseT supports RJ-45 used for Ethernet LANs. It can support signal transmission at a full 100-meter distance, specified for LAN wiring. If users need to implement a 10Gbps link, this is the most economical way.

100BaseFX

100BaseFX (IEEE 802.3u) uses 62.5/125-micron multimode fiber cabling, and supports up to 412 meters long and point-to-point topology. It uses ST and SC connectors, which are media-interface connectors.

10Base2

10Base2 is also known as thinnet and can support up to 30 workstations on a single segment. It uses 10Mbps of baseband technology, coax up to 185 meters in length, and a physical and logical bus with Attachment Unit Interface (AUI) connectors. In 10Base2, "10" means 10Mbps, "Base" means baseband technology, and the "2" means almost 200 meters. 10Base2 Ethernet cards use BNC (Bayonet Neill-Concelman) and T-connectors to connect to a network.

10GBaseSR

It is an application of 10 Gigabit Ethernet that uses short-wavelength lasers at 850 nm over multimode fiber. It has a maximum transmission distance between 2 and 300 meters, depending on the size and quality of the fiber.

10GBaseER

It is an application of 10 Gigabit Ethernet, running over single-mode fiber, that uses extra-long-wavelength lasers at 1,550 nm. It has the longest transmission distances possible of all the 10 Gigabit technologies: anywhere from 2 meters up to 40 km, also depending on the size and quality of the fiber used.

10GBaseSW

10GBaseSW defined by IEEE as 802.3ae is a mode of 10GBaseS for Multimode Fiber (MMF) with an 850 nm laser transceiver and a bandwidth of 10Gbps. It can support up to 300 meters of cable length. This media type is designed to connect to SONET equipment.

 Exam Tip

For the exam, know the order of wires in the TIA/EIA 568A and TIA/EIA 568B standards and also know which wires are switched in a crossover cable.

Mind Map of Cabling Solution Deployment

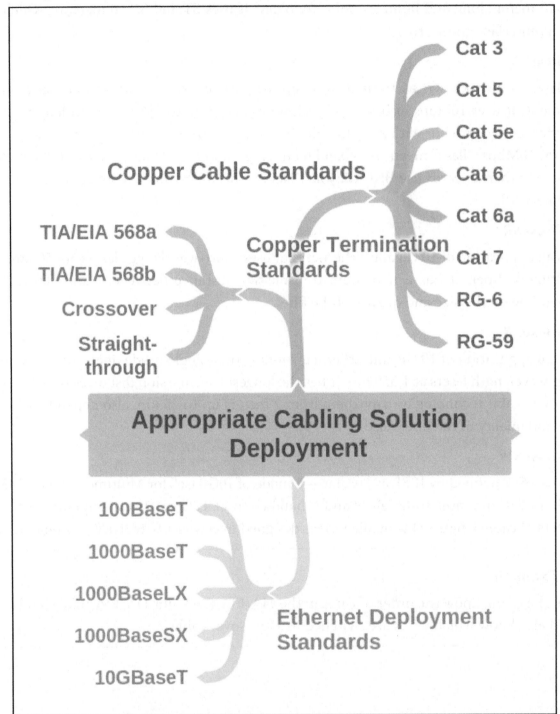

Figure 2-18: Mind Map of Cabling Solution Deployment

Determine the Appropriate Placement of Networking Devices on a Network and Install/Configure them

The integrant of a network architecture consists of numerous devices that perform a definite function or set of functions in a network. It is essential to understand the purpose of each device so that the individual would be familiar with the functionalities of the devices that are used in a network. In this section, we will cover these requirements.

Firewall

Firewalls are the physical devices and software that defend an internal network or system from unauthorized access by performing as a filter. Firewalls are an essential mechanism to fight against the malicious activities on the internet.

Functions

- Firewalls filter the flow of traffic that are either inbound or outbound traffic of a network
- It inspects each packet by certain rules and policies
- By functioning, the firewall has two types: network-based firewall and host-based firewall
- Network-based firewall is mostly implemented on hardware appliances as they protect the whole network, but they cannot fight against the traffic generating from inside the network itself
- Host-based firewall is installed on the 'host' that provides the firewall services; it will come across a network technology in future

Applications

- The firewall provides IPSec for the platform to implement virtual private networks
- Monitores security-related actions
- Protects from several sorts of IP spoofing and routing attacks
- Provides a suitable platform for various internet activity that does not require security such as NAT, internet usage audits or logs

Router

Routers are the main networking devices designed to route traffic towards the destination. Router functions at layer 3 (Internet layer of OSI Model). Routers are the devices that link up with the internet and make the World Wide Web conceivable. They also split and combine the network. Routers are more intelligent than switches.

Functions

- Routers work on Internet Protocol (IP), specifically on the logical address, also known as IP address
- Routers perform actions on the layer 3, i.e., Network Layer of the OSI model

- They route traffic from one network to the desired destination network
- As described, a router is an intelligent device that first finds out the network, or the traffic relating to their network
- After deciding, the router forwards the traffic the to the required destination

Applications

- Routers provide interfaces for different physical network connections, such as; copper cables, optic fiber, or wireless transmissions
- The Network Administrator can configure the routing table manually, as well as dynamically
- Routers learn its routing table by using static and dynamic routing protocols
- Multiple routers are used in interconnected networks
- Dynamic exchange of information about the destination is possible by the dynamic routing protocol; the administrator will have to advertise routing path manually for static networks

---

Router Interface Configuration

Router(config)#interface ethernet 0/0

Router(config-if)#ip address 10.0.0.2 255.0.0.0

Router(config-if)#no shutdown

Router(config-if)#exit

Switch

Switches are the network devices that optimize traffic flow on the network. Switches connect the network devices by providing physical interfaces in a network. Switches are smarter than hubs; they learn the Media Access Control (MAC) Address, also known as the physical address of the device.

Functions

- Switches filter the MAC addresses of all the connected devices
- Switches perform functioning on Data Link layer (layer 2) of the OSI model
- Switches learn the physical address of all the devices that are connected to them and then uses the MAC address to control traffic flow
- Switches forward the data frames only to the destination address rather than forwarding the data to all the connected ports
- Switches reduce the traffic by spontaneous segmentation of the network

Applications

- They connect the departments of one company to the other without involving in their communication
- They can transfer large files within the local area network without affecting the upper layer traffic flow of the network
- They can be used to create Virtual Local Area Networks(VLANs) to improve the flexibility of the network
- They are very efficient as they do not forward the data that have errors
- They avoid collision domains

Hub

A hub is a device that possesses many ports into which connections can be built. Hub connects all the nodes of the network in a star topology network. All the devices in the network connect directly through a single cable via Ethernet cable.

Functions

- Hub performs its function at the physical layer (Layer 1) of the OSI model
- The basic function of a hub is to transfer data from one device and send it to all the connected ports including the transmitting device
- It broadcasts the data but the further procedure is handled by the intended receiver that is addressed in the frame
- To avoid a broadcasting collision, the hub applies Carrier Sense Multiple Access with Collision Detection (CSMA/CD) techniques on the transmitter

Applications

- Active hubs regenerate a signal before forwarding it to all the nodes and need a power supply
- Small hubs that include four to five hubs with necessity cables are enough to create a small network at a low cost
- Hubs with more ports are also accessible for the networks that demand a higher capacity

Modem

Modem, is an acronym for MOdulator and DEModulator. The modulator modulates an analog carrier signal to encode digital information whereas; the demodulator demodulates the signal to decode the transmitted information.

Functions

- The main objective of a modem is to generate a signal that can be transmitted easily and decoded to regenerate the original data

- These signals are transmitted through telephone lines and demodulated by another modem at the receiver end to understand the digital data

Applications

- Permits an entirely non-digital way to provide connectivity between network areas
- Enables devices to discuss existing infrastructure, as phone-lines or coax

Access Point(Wired/Wireless)

An access point consists of a wireless switch with a router module. Furthermore, access points are both wireless and wired. An access point is a device that connects a Wireless Local Area Network (WLAN), mostly in buildings, offices or homes. An access point connects to a wired router, switch, or hub through Ethernet cable, and designs a Wi-Fi signal to the specified area.

Functions

- Is responsible for connecting the number of wired/wireless network host
- Allows the communication between the connected wired/wireless networks
- WAPs have antennas to provide signal wirelessly and an Ethernet port to connect to wired networks

Applications

- Can be used as a wireless bridge between the two wired networks
- APs with a router module possess the ability to connect wired/wireless clients to the internet
- QoS is achieved by the access points on wired networks that access the information confidentially

---

Note

Many manufacturers drop the word "wireless" from wireless access points and simply call them access points. Furthermore, many sources abbreviate both forms, so you may see the former written as WAP and the latter as AP.

Media Converters

Media converters convert one media technology, into another, according to their requirement. If the requirement is to change the media from fiber to Ethernet, or Ethernet to copper, a media converter is used for the convertion. Some common media converters are described below:

Single Mode Fiber to Ethernet

A single Mode Fiber is used among building campuses. In this situation, Single-Mode Fiber to Ethernet converters are used in each building because the light based fiber signals come into the building to be carried farther through the building, in the form of electricity.

Multimode Fiber to Ethernet

Multimode fiber is used as the backbone of the network, across the building that allows the backbone to carry more data at a much faster speed than that is fulfilled by copper cables. Multimode Fiber to Ethernet converter could be used between the backbone section and patch panels that connect with wall jacks, and finally to the computers themselves.

Fiber to Coaxial

In early times, coaxial cables were used as a backbone in some buildings, but they are not used anymore. To provide internet connections, coaxial cables are used to connect cable modems. Fiber to coaxial converters are used to provide high-bandwidth communications from a cable provider and divide it through the entire network backbone.

Single Mode Fiber to Multimode Fiber

Single mode fiber is used between buildings for long distance areas, whereas multimode fibers provide some channels for communication. In a Single Mode Fiber, the signal pulses of light convert the signal into multiple channels in multimode fiber.

Wirelss Range Extender

Wireless range extenders are the devices, which helps to eliminate the dead zones by strengthening the wireless signals. These wireless extenders are also called repeaters because of their signal extending capability. Existing wireless network is extended by rebroadcasting the signals.

Application

- Strengthening the signals in dead zones
- Strengthening the signals in the area with much interference
- Covering large geographical area

VoIP Endpoints

VoIP (Voice over IP) endpoints are usually desktop or wireless telephone systems. These endpoints are usually placed in conferencing rooms. VoIP endpoints may also include softphone applications, mobile phones and WebRTC-enabled browsers.

 Exam Tip

An Access Point can operate as a bridge connecting a standard wired network to wireless devices or as a router passing data transmissions from one access point to another.

Mind Map of Placement of Networking Devices

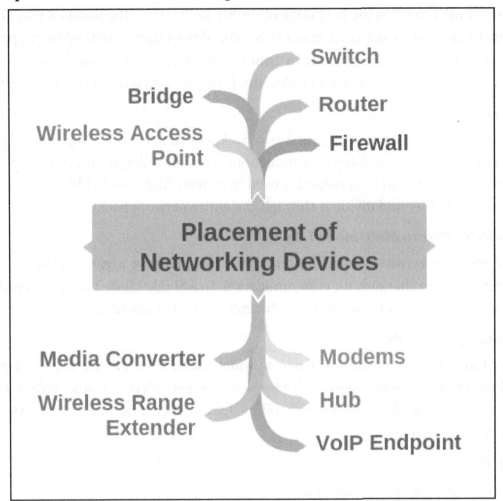

Figure 2-19: Mind Map of Placement of Networking Devices

Purposes and Use Cases of Advance Networking Devices

An internetwork should contain advanced networking devices. These special devices allow for fault tolerance, load balancing, Virtual Private Network (VPN) services, authentication, authorization, and accounting, sophisticated security, integration of voice and data, and much more.

Multilayer Switch:

Although a basic switch works entirely on Data-Link layer (layer 2) of the OSI model, a multilayer switch can perform its function on both layer 2 and layer 3. Multilayer switches are also called layer 3 switches and intelligent switches.

Functions

- A multilayer switch has an advance functioning, a switch with some router characteristics
- A multilayer switch can be connected to other multilayer switches to provide scalability to the network
- It can be logically segmented into multiple broadcast domains
- A layer 3 switch must be capable enough to make a forwarding decision
- All switches must store network flows so that forwarding can occur in hardware

Applications

- Multilayer switches are efficiently used in VLAN networks
- Multilayer switches can create VLANs and decide VLAN routes
- Multilayer switches can connect to other multilayer switches and basic switches to extend the VLANs throughout the organization

Wireless LAN Controller

Wireless LAN Controller is the important device in Wireless Secure Network Architecture. These Wireless LAN Controllers are deployed with Light Weight Access Points. These Access points offer endpoint connectivity. On the other end these access points are connected directly (next hop) or indirectly (through the network) to the Wireless LAN Controller. Wireless LAN Controllers offers HTTP or HTTPS Web User interface for configuring and monitoring WLC. Command Line Interface is also available with Wireless LAN Controllers. The main function of Wireless LAN Controllers is Monitoring and Controlling of Endpoint Clients, and Monitoring of Access Points if any rogue access point is connected.

A WLAN controller provides centralized management and monitoring of WLANs. WLAN are integrated with Authentication servers such as Identity Service Engine (ISE) to enforce the authorization and authentication on end-point devices.

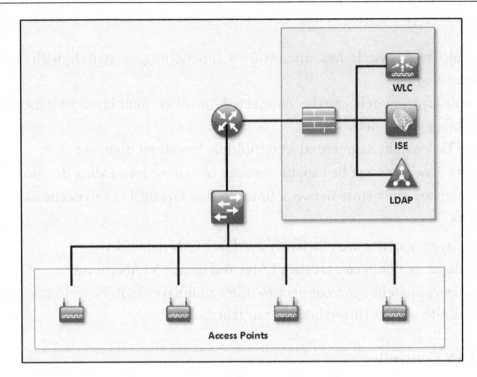

Figure 2-20: Wireless LAN Controller

Load Balancer

A Load Balancer is a device that acts as a reverse proxy and divides network or application traffic across some servers. A load balancer acts as the traffic police sitting in front of the servers and routes client requests across the servers, which execute in a way that the speed and capacity will not be compromised and also assures that no server is overloaded, which might cause degradation in performance.

Functions

A Load Balancer performs the following functions:

- It distributes the load of a network and client requests efficiently
- Assures great accessibility and stability by sending client request only to the active servers
- Provides flexibility by increasing or decreasing the servers on demand

Applications

- Load Balancer acts upon layer 4 and layer 7 of the OSI model
- Layer 4 Load Balancer manages data found in networks and transports layer protocols such as IP, TCP, FTP, and UDP
- Layer 7 Load Balancers divide request based upon data found in application layer protocols such as HTTP

- The Load Balancer can handle changeable workloads and rank up to millions of requests per seconds
- Assist routing requests to multiple applications on a single EC2 instance

> **Exam Tip**
>
> Remember that load balancing increases redundancy and therefore information availability. Also, load balancing increases performance by distributing the workload.

Host-based Intrusion Detection System

Host-based Intrusion Detection System (HIDS) is a system of sensors that are installed on various servers within the organization and maintained by some central manager. HIDS can protect only the events associated with the servers on which they are installed.

Functions

Based upon the functionalities, HIDS can be divided into five basic types:

- *Log Analyzer:* Finds out log entities that may predict a security incident
- *Signature-based Sensors:* Analyses inbound traffic and contrasts them with a set of built-in security action signatures
- *System Call Analyzer:* Inspects an application's system calls, analyses the action and contrasts it to a database of signatures
- *Application Behavior Analyzer:* Inspects an application's system call to see if it allows performing such action
- *File Integrity Reviewer:* Provides a review for changes in files

Applications

- Protects specific system activities
- Certifies success or failure of an attack
- Is appropriate for encrypted and switched domains
- Is used along with the IDS/IPS and firewalls to provide an extra layer of protection from anything that penetrates the previous layer

Intrusion Detection System /Intrusion Prevention System

An Intrusion Detection System (IDS) is much greater than a firewall. Effectively, an IDS is an intelligent proctor of network traffic. It looks after the normal traffic and points out the odd traffic as a threat but not to prevent them.

An Intrusion Prevention System (IPS) is quite similar to an IDS but can acquire more actions in response to a threat than an IDS. IPS points out the attacks from inside and outside intruders, as well as preventing them from being successful.

Functions

- It is designed to detect security violations
- Aids in reducing damage caused by hacking
- Gathers the prevent the action of a firewall with the in-depth packet analysis function of an IDS
- IDS/IPS can be configured to notify the network administrator when the threat has been detected
- IPS can address the detected threat by adjusting connections or even shut down a port

Applications

- Easy deployment as one sensor can protect hundreds of systems
- A single control point for traffic can protect thousands of systems placed below the device, not concerned about the operating system or application
- Protects against network Dos, DDoS attacks, and SYN flood, etc.
- IPSs are reconfigurable to each application that requires protection

Proxy/Reverse Proxy Server

A proxy server is a server that builds a connection on behalf of the other user-operated in another location, specifically, a website.

A reverse proxy server builds a connection back to the user on behalf of the intended server that possesses information.

VPN Concentrator

A Virtual Private Network (VPN) is a network connection that is designed to secure, although it flows through an unsecured network, usually the internet. Tunneling between two private networks over the public internet make VPN networks secure. VPN concentrators create tunneling in VPN networks that receive multiple VPN connections from the remote access site.

Functions

- VPN concentrators perform the following functions:
    1. Settlement of tunnels

    2. Managing tunneling parameters

    3. Authenticating users and assigning user addresses

    4. Encoding and decoding data

    5. Managing security keys

    6. Managing data transfer over the tunnel

- The VPN concentrators perform these functions by using standard protocols such as Point-to-Point Tunneling Protocol (PPTP) or Layer 2 Tunneling Protocol (L2TP)

Applications

- VPN concentrators provide high availability, high-performance scalability components
- VPN concentrators are capable of supporting 100 to 10,000 remote-access users simultaneously

AAA/ RADIUS Server

Remote Authenticate Dial-In User Service (RADIUS) offers a centralized system for AAA that describes Authentication, Authorization, and Accounting. RADIUS servers, also referred to as remote access servers, become the clients of another remote access server.

RADIUS server's performance is based on certificates, Kerberos, and other authentication types. RADIUS uses UDP protocol between the servers to broadcast their communication.

Exam Tip

RADIUS is a protocol that enables a single server to become responsible for all remote-access authentication, authorization, and auditing (or accounting) services; this is referred to as AAA.

UTM Application

A Unified Threat Management (UTM) system performs a function of a traditional firewall. It also provides many security solutions in one component. UTM can perform many functions such as Network Firewalling, Network Intrusion Prevention, Gateway Anti-virus, Gateway Anti-spam, VPN Content Filtering, Load Balancing, Data Leak Prevention, and On-Appliance Reporting. It is commonly installed as a single physical, rack-mountable appliance.

Next-Generation Firewall / Layer 7 Firewall

A firewall can employ a variety of techniques to ensure security. Modern firewall applications can perform a range of other functions, often through the addition of add-on modules directed at the application layer (Layer 7) of the OSI model; they are then often referred to as Unified Threat Management (UTM) devices or Next Generation Firewalls (NGFW).

Evolution of Application and Traditional Firewalls

The basic purpose of deploying firewall in a network is to control the traffic between the secure, trusted network such as Private Network or Corporate LAN and the untrusted networks such as Public Network or the internet. Common and traditional firewalls offer

Port-based or packet level filtering and Stateful inspection. These firewalls are easy to deploy and configure. These are inexpensive and offers good throughput.

Port based firewalls requires Source or Destination IP address and Port Information (TCP/UDP) in order to filter the packet from the incoming traffic and determine whether to proceed or deny the packets in case of compliance of conditions. These firewalls only inspect fist few bytes of the header of the packet to determine Application Protocol.

Evolution of internet enhances the services by offering efficient and increased performance and productivity to users which may be accessing through the public internet or connected through a secure trusted network. These enhanced services include the evolution in application by launching new generation of application that are used by various users, personally and for business. These application not only offers services but also increase the risk of security and threats in term of data loss, using Non-Standard Ports, Port Hopping, and Tunneling.

Classification of Application

Applications functioning with in the network play an important role in the productivity of an organization. These applications cannot just be classified as good & bad application according to the Risk and Advantages ratio. For example, an application that offers low risks as compared to rewards offered by the application can be classified as Good Application. Whereas, some of the application lies in between them.

Using applications including Social Media Applications within the corporate network for any purpose like promotions, sales and other reasons may increase production and benefits for the organization. While using the application, the user may not understand how the application is being used against the organization like for governing purpose. Data loss can also propagate threats into the corporate network. Completely or blindly trusting an application, even on the applications that are classified as good, is not a good approach. Blocking the entire application is also an inappropriate action.

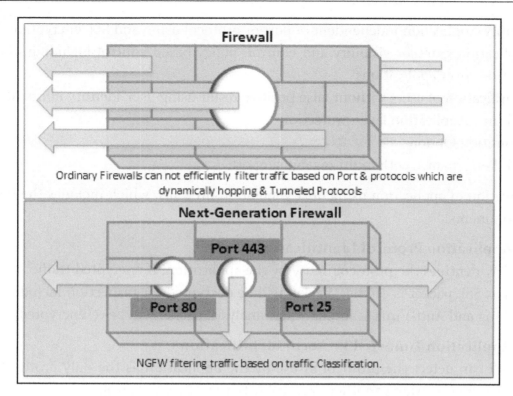

Figure 2-21: Ordinary Firewall vs NGFW

New Generation Applications are designed to offer high availability and performance. These Applications can adjust their communication dynamically to offer high availability from anywhere. The key features that these applications use are:

- **Port Hopping**

  Port and protocol using by these applications can be dynamically allocated between end users.

- **Non-Standard Ports**

  Application may use Non-Standard Ports instead of using Standard Ports such as any Application using non-standard instead of using Port 80 for HTTP.

- **Tunneling**

  Application may be tunneled within the service such as Tunneling within running HTTP.

- **Masking**

  Application may hide traffic within SSL Encryption.

Application Identification using Next-Generation Firewalls

Next Generation Firewalls offer the solution of security of the corporate network from these applications. They classify the traffic and offer visibility and control over the Application. The next generation firewalls are capable of:

- Identify Application independent of port or protocol using and SSL encryption
- Application granular visibility and control, policy based control including individual functions over applications
- Identification of users without false positive result using user-identity information
- Real time Application layer protection
- Integration Option
- High Performance with multi-gigabit support

Identification of application using next generation firewalls, which includes the following key components:

- **Application Protocol Identification**

NGFW identifies the protocol in use by the application. If encrypted traffic is detected such as SSL packet is catcher, packet will be decrypted for inspection including Policy Filtering and Anti-Virus Scanning. After analysis, packet will be re-encrypted.

- **Application Tunneled Protocol Identification**

NGFW can detect the protocol in use by the application as the only protocol or the application is masking another protocol with the upper protocol.

- **Application Signatures**

Application signatures such as context based signature offers identification of application regardless of port and protocols.

VoIP PBX

An IP PBX is a telephone switching system that switches calls between VoIP users on local lines while allowing all users to share a certain number of external phone lines and provides internal communication for a business.

VoIP Gateway

A VoIP Gateway (Voice over IP Gateway) is a network device, which act as a gateway for VoIP traffic. It helps to convert voice and fax calls between an IP network and Public Switched Telephone Network (PSTN) in real time. Various protocols, such as MGCP, SIP, or LTP can help to control a gateway

Content Filter

A content filter is an extraordinary device, which can be configured to block some documents based on content that might be objectionable. The content filter helps decide which content is suitable for screening and accessing through a given system.

Functions

- Different types of content filters are based on the type of content they filter e.g, Application-layer content filtering is configured to be more sensitive than Network filtering
- Application-layer content filters can be configured in such a way that the user can disallow the website that contains inappropriate data or graphics
- Control filter is controlled by the software commonly known as web-filtering program or censorware

Applications

- Control filter is usually used in public Wi-Fi access points and places that promote BYOD policy
- It is often used in schools, colleges, and libraries to protect from offensive websites or harmful images
- It can be used in employer's wireless networks to protect from illegal activities
- Control filtering on wireless networks can also help in providing sustainability and increase productivity in many organizations by blocking time-wasting websites such as Twitter, Facebook, etc.

Web Usage Control

IronPort Web Usage Control offers Dynamic Content Analyzes to provide enhanced security in efficient manner. Cisco Web Usage Control feature is available in S-Series Cisco Web Security Appliance which ensures the advanced, next level security solution for URL Categorization. It monitors, analyze, and block the objectionable content over 50 percent ratio.

Dynamic Content Analysis Engine

Dynamic Content Analysis Engine controls all web access request by categorizing the URL dynamically. This categorization is done by inspecting the web traffic received as a response of web request from the web server. It is not possible to take action and block the content when a request is just sent or before receiving of a response. Once URL is inspected and validated by Dynamic Content Analysis engine, it stores it into a temporary cache, which provides quick revise response for the next requests.

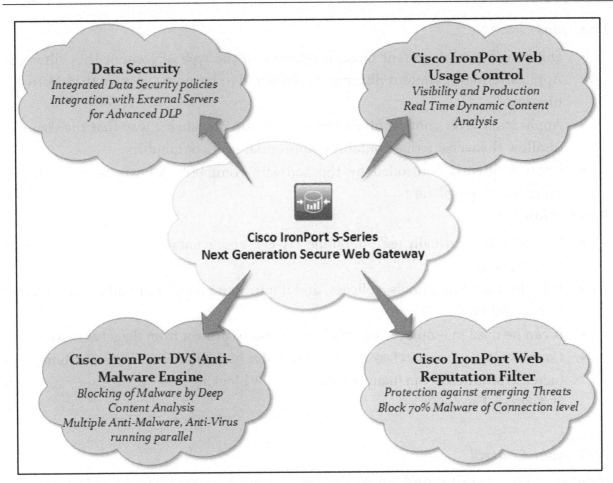

Figure 2-22: Cisco IronPort S-Series Web Security Gateway

To be effective, content filtering has to be deployed across all content channels. The most common channels include:

- Web
- Email
- Executables
- Documents

Application Visibility and Control (AVC)

Cisco Application Visibility and Control or AVC feature offers integrated solution at Application Layer. Cisco AVC offers State-full Deep Packet Inspection (DPI). This integrated Service Management Solution with Cisco ASR 1000 (Aggregation Service Router) performs Stateful deep packet inspection at layer 7 of every application. Cisco AVC can handle and control thousands of various types of Applications like Voice, Video, mailing, gaming and others. AVC can integrate with Cisco IOS/IOS XE devices as well as external tools.

Application Visibility and Control (AVC) ensures controlled access over the Web. Website offering features and service can be allowed with enhanced and more controlled manner.

Using Application Visibility and Control AVC engine, websites such as Social Media Websites, which are more popular nowadays can be allowed in a controlled manner by blocking desired services for granular control.

Data Loss Prevention

Configuring Data Loss Prevention polices keep your personal, secret, and confidential information secured. It ensures that this information will not leave the network based on the pre-configured policies or user defined custom polices. Cisco Email Security DLP engine configured with DLP policies make few false positives. The DLP engine monitor classifies violations by severity, offering application of different levels of remediation action. Remediation action can also be configured to be taken in cases of violation.

Packet Shaper

A packet shaper is mainly a hardware device that can investigate traffic at a granular level. Initially, it analyses the traffic flow to pass through it and classifies all traffic with minimum assistance from a network administrator.

Functions

- The shaping functionality is usually built-in routers and some switches to deal with times when the network requirement outpaces the ability of a device or its port
- Packet shapers control the inbound and outbound traffic flows when congestion occurs

Applications

- Provides bandwidth management solution that efficiently works on applications running over WANs and the internet
- Provides management to the web-connected application such as cloud applications, social media, audio/video communication
- Provides smart QoS tools for safe, superior application and web content varieties while containing the influence of unacceptable traffic

Mind Map of Networking Devices

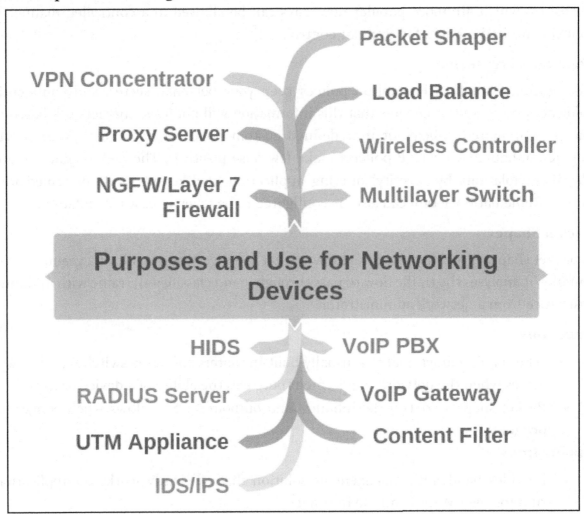

Figure 2-23: Mind Map of Networking Devices

The Purpose of Virtualization and Network Storage Technologies

Virtualization is the procedure of using powerful, special software running on a PC to generate a full environment that virtualizes all of the hardware. Virtualization consists specialized programs that act like physical devices. Almost anything can be virtualized, including CPU, RAM, hard drives, NICs, switches, routers, and even firewalls. Storage (hard drives) tends to be either highly under- or over-utilized on individual hosts.

Virtual Network Components

In computing, virtualization means to create something that is not an actual or virtual version of a device or resource like servers, storage devices or operating systems.

Virtual Switch

A Virtual Switch (vSwitch) is a software application that allows communication between virtual machines. A vSwitch provides more than just forwarded data packets; it intelligently directs the data packets by checking it before moving them to a destination.

Virtual switches are usually embedded into installed software, but they may also be included in a server's hardware as part of its firmware. The vSwitch combines physical switches into a single logical switch. It helps to increase bandwidth and create an active mesh between servers and switches.

Virtual Firewall

A Virtual Firewall is a firewall device or service that provides network traffic filtering and monitoring for virtual machines. A virtual firewall is installed, executed and operated from a virtual machine.

Virtual NIC

A Virtual NIC that is linked to a physical NIC is a true Ethernet link in the firmest sense. Its packets are sent on the wire with its own unique MAC address. A virtual NIC that is connected to a virtual network does not require an Ethernet interface on the host.

Virtual Router

A Virtual Router is a software-based routing structure that enables the host machine to perform as a typical hardware router over a local area network.

A virtual router can enable a computer/server to have the abilities of a complete router by performing the network and packet routing functionality of the router through a software application.

Hypervisor

The utilization of amazing host machines providing shared resource pools to expand the number of guests is both a basic explanation of virtualization and the supporting of cloud computing. In fact, cloud computing would not be conceivable without virtualization. The most convincing arguments for the utilization of virtualization are:

- Increasing the efficiency and agility of hardware by sharing resources
- A reduction in personnel resourcing and maintenance, leading to easier management
- Virtualization also allows the abstraction from the hardware via the use of a hypervisor

There are two types of hypervisors within virtualization:

1. Type 1
2. Type 2

Type 1 Hypervisors: Type 1 Hypervisor is native execution that runs tied directly into the basic hardware. It also enables tighter security and control because there are no extra applications or utilities running inside the hypervisor, other than those to satisfy its intended mission.

Type 2 Hypervisors: Type 2 Hypervisor varies from type 1 hypervisor in the sense that it runs under a host operating system as opposed to directly tied into the basic hardware of the virtual host servers. With this type of execution, additional security and architecture concerns become possibly the most important factor as the interaction between the operating system and the hypervisor turns into a basic connection. It implies that any security concerns within the basic operating system can affect the hypervisor as well.

Network Storage Types and their Connections

There are two types of network storage, which are discussed below.

Network Attached Storage (NAS)

Network Attached Storage (NAS) is a dedicated file server that has its own file system and typically uses hardware and software designed for serving and storing files. Whereas, a Storage Area Network SAN shares a fast, low-level interface that the OS can treat just as it was a disk. The simplicity and low price of a NAS make it attractive for some users. NAS is easier than SAN and uses TCP/IP. It offers file level access, and a client sees the shared storage as a file server.

Storage Area Network (SAN)

A Storage Area Network (SAN) consists of networked/shared storage devices. Consumers can use multiple devices to increase performance, with clustered storage. SANs are subsets of LANs and offer block-level information storage that appears within the OS of the connected devices. SAN can be costly and difficult to implement and maintain.

Connecion Type

When it comes to the infrastructure to connect a SAN, options include Fiber Channel (FC)/Fiber Channel over Ethernet (FCoE), Internet Small Computer System Interface (iSCSI), and InfiniBand.

FCoE

Fiber Channel over Ethernet (FCoE) encapsulates Fiber Channel frames over Ethernet networks. This allows Fiber Channel to use 10-Gigabit Ethernet networks (or higher speeds) while preserving the Fiber Channel protocol.

Fiber Channel

Fiber Channel is another technology that can be used to transfer data from the SAN. It uses either fiber-optic cables and switches, or a 10-Gbps network with particular cards. Fiber

Channel uses a special type of address called a World Wide Name (WWN). Each node in the Fiber Channel network has its own specific WWN.

iSCSI

Internet Small Computer Systems Interface (iSCSI) is a storage transport methodology that is fast and reliable and can help organization leverage the network cables, switches, and connections that they already have in place. It is used on 10-Gbps networks to leverage bandwidth. If any network has 10-Gbps bandwidth, the network can be served for storage purpose by installing iSCSI cards on the servers.

Infiniband

InfiniBand (IB) is a communication standard that features very high throughput and very low latency to interconnect both among and within computers. InfiniBand is also used as either a direct or switched interconnect between servers and storage systems, as well as an interconnect between storage systems.

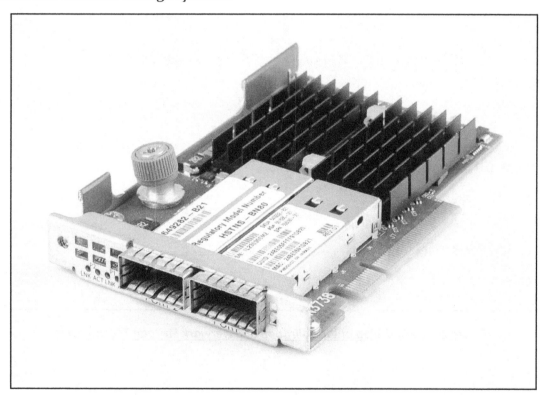

Figure 2-24: HP 10/40GB InfiniBand FDR/EN Dual Port PCI-E X8 Ethernet Adapter Card 656090-001

Jumbo Frame

One of the networking's biggest problems is that data of various sizes is crammed into packets and sent across the medium. Each time this is done, headers are generated, along with any filler required, creating additional overhead. To get around this, the concept

of jumbo frames is used to enable large Ethernet frames; by sending several information at once, the amount of packets is reduced, and the information sent is less processor intensive.

Mind Map of Network Storage Technologies

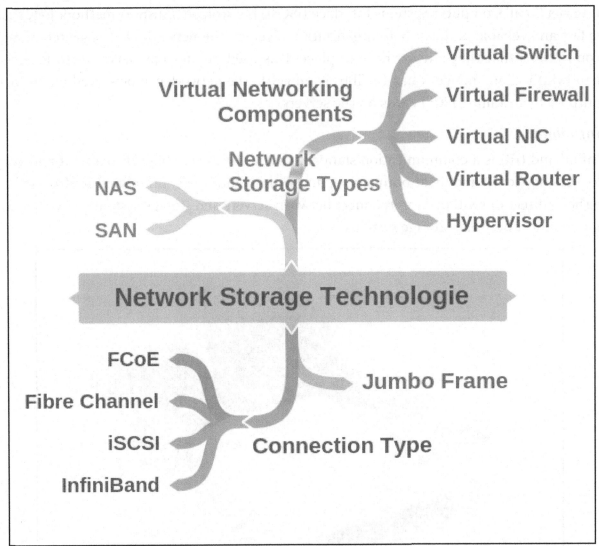

Figure 2-25: Mind Map of Virtualization and Network Storage Technologies

Compare and Contrast WAN Technologies

Nowadays, organizations use many WAN technologies according to their needs. It is important to know the attributes and benefits of these technologies for better deployment of the network.

WAN Services

Many network environments of today are not restricted to a single location or LAN. Instead, many networks span great distances, becoming Wide Area Networks (WANs). Various types of WAN services are discussed below.

Integrated Service Digital Network (ISDN)

Integrated Service Digital Network (ISDN) is a combination of digital telephony and data transport services delivered by telephone carriers. It handles the digitization of telephone network, which offers voice, data, text, video, etc. over existing telephone lines.

The two most important aspects of ISDN include; ISDN BRI, ISDN PRI. ISDN BRI service offees two B channels and one D channel (2B+D). B channel operates at 64 Kbps and is used to carry user data. D channel operates at 16 kbps used for control and signaling information. ISDN PRI offers 23 B channels and 1 D channels, both of which operate at 64 kbps.

Metropolitan Ethernet

Metro-Ethernet is an extension of Ethernet to Metropolitan Area Network. It is defined as a network that connects geographically isolated enterprise LAN and WAN networks that are usually held by service providers. Metro-Ethernet can increase network capacity and coverage area in a flexible, economical and scalable manner.

Broadband/Baseband

The baseband and broadband are types of signaling techniques. These terms were developed to categorize different types of signals depending on the particular type of signal representation or modulation technique.

The main difference between baseband transmission and broadband transmission is that in the baseband transmission, the whole bandwidth of the cable is consumed by a single signal. On the other hand, in the broadband transmission, multiple signals are sent on multiple frequencies simultaneously using a single channel.

Basis for Comparison	Baseband	Broadband
Type of Signaling	Digital	Analog
Signal Range	Signals can travel over short distances	Signals can travel over long distances without being attenuated
Encoding Technique	Manchester and Differential Manchester encodings	PSK encoding

Transmission	Bidirectional	Unidirectional
Application	Best used in a bus topology	Used with a bus and tree topology

Table 2-04: Baseband Vs. Broadband

Leased Lines

Leased lines are a private two-way circuit between two or more geographically distant areas, provided in exchange for a monthly lease. The services of leased lines include telephone and internet. The network of leased lines is deployed in a WAN environment.

T1/T3

T-carriers are the first digital trunk carriers used by the telephone industry. There are different versions of T-carriers, and the most common and most basic is the venerable T-carrier level 1 (T1). T1 lines are used in the United States and offer 1.54 Mbps dedicated bandwidth divided into 24 channels.

A T3 line supports about 45-Mbps data rate on a dedicated telephone connection. It consists of 672 individual DS0 channels. T3 lines are mainly used by regional telephone companies and ISPs connecting to the internet.

E1/E3

E1 lines are used in Europe and offer 2.048-Mbps connection that are divided into 32 channels. E1 and T1 lines can interconnect for international use. There are also E3 lines, which carry approximately 17 E-1 lines with a bandwidth of about 34 Mbps.

Carrier	Channels	Speed
T1	24	1.544 <bps
T3	672	44.736 Mbps
E1	32	2.048 Mbps
E3	512	34.368 Mbps

Table 2-05: T-Carriers

OC-3/OC-192

Optical Carrier (OC) is the standardized unit to measure transmission bandwidth of the data carried by SONET and fiber optics. The original speed of an OC trunk is approximately 50 Mbps, and was known as OC1. Therefore, OC3 is a multiple of OC1 that has 150-Mbps speed; OC192 delivers 9.955-Gbps line speed. The fastest considered standard is OC-7144F, which offers an exciting speed of 300 Gbps.

Broadband Cable

Broadband cable is a special type of cable that is connected to deliver high bandwidth services such as internet access, TV channels, telephony cable and other electronic interactive services.

Broadband cables are a coaxial cable that are connected to the cable modem. Service providers configure the cable modem for connecting to the internet and then connect users to their central offices.

Broadband cable provides great bandwidth speed, 30 Mbps for downstream, and greater than 1 Mbps for upstream.

Digital Subscriber Line (DSL)

Digital Subscriber Line (DSL) is an advancement in copper wire technology, usually used to achieve high-speed digital transmission, over standard copper public telephone network lines. It is specifically used for high-speed internet connection.

Asymmetric Subscriber Line (ADSL)

Asymmetric Subscriber Line (ADSL) is the most common type of DSL. In ADSL, the total capacity of the high-speed digital subscriber line is divided asymmetrically between the downstream and upstream way of transmission. The speed of downloading is 20 times greater than the uploading speed.

Dial-up

Dial-up technology is a wired communication technology also known as Public Switch Telephone Network (PSTN) or Plain Old Telephone Service (POTS). A dial-up connection is a regular phone line, used in homes, which are connected by the RJ11 jacks from the central office to the local exchange.

Dial-up connection offers painfully slow 56-kbps lines. Although, it is highly available and cost-effective. That is why it is used in business as a backup for a management connection for a router, switch, or computer.

PRI

PRI is a form of ISDN that generally is carried over a T1 line and can provide transmission rates of up to 1.544 Mbps. PRI is composed of 23 B channels, each providing 64 Kbps for data/voice capacity, and one 64 Kbps D channel, which is used for signaling.

Transmission Mediums

Besides copper and fiber cables, there are also satellite and wireless transmission mediums. Each medium comes with advantages and disadvantages.

Satellite

Satellites are the peak of modern communications technology. They provide worldwide access to information, by transmitting radio waves from orbit about the earth. The satellite communication is located in geostationary orbit. Satellite communications provider gets satellite signals from the antenna, this signal is used for downloading, and uploading purposes, they provide traditional telephone dial-up connections. Satellite communication providers offer high data rates as compared to their competitors.

Copper

Transmissions over copper wires (for example, using T1, T3, and ISDN lines) have fallen out of favor due to quicker and more practical types of mediums, like fiber and wireless.

Fiber

The optical fiber is an advanced technology in the network cable; it transmits light waves between the two ends of fiber along the long distance with high data rates.

Optical fiber consists of surrounding part cladding and central part core, through which the light is propagated by following the phenomenon of total internal reflection. Optical fiber provides flexibility and speed of 150 Mbps with less attenuation as compared to electrical cables. Optical fiber is mostly used for long distance communication where ordinary cable wires cannot be installed. However, its installation and maintenance are quite difficult. Common implementations of fiber include SONET, DWDM, and CWDM.

Synchronous Optical Networking (SONET)

Synchronous Optical Networking (SONET) is a standardized protocol in optical communication that is used to push data at 150 Gbps over fiber optic medium. SONET adds synchronization of time in multiple digital data flows, transmitted over fiber optic using lasers and LEDs. It usually provides an STS-1 link of 50-Mbps bandwidth and multiples of it, so STS-3 provides approximately a 150-Mbps bandwidth.

Dense Wavelength Division Multiplexing (DWDM)

Dense Wavelength Division Multiplexing (DWDM) is an optical technology used to increase the bandwidth of the existing fiber-optic backbones. It multiplexes the multiple transmitted signal, at different wavelengths on the same fiber. After the implementation of DWDM, a single fiber can transmit data at the speed of 400 Gbps.

Coarse Wavelength Division Multiplexing (CWDM)

Coarse Wavelength Division Multiplexing (CWDM) follows DWDM, but it is used in the small coverage area and uses fewer channels as compared to DWDM.

CWDM is appropriate for small businesses and regional areas. It can provide wider spacing of 20 nm and can bear higher temperature fluctuations as compared to DWDM.

Wireless

When wireless is discussed in terms of transmission mediums, it is being referred to data travelling over cellular networks and using cellular technologies.

Characteristics of WAN Services

The telephone industry came up with types of packets that operate on T-carrier and OC lines to carry information from one central office to another. These packet-switching protocols are functionally identical to routable network protocols such as TCP/IP. WAN connections traditionally used two different types of packet switching: Frame Relay and ATM. Other characteristics of service from concepts related to MPLS, PPPoE, PPP, DMVPN, and SIP trunks.

Multiprotocol Label Switching (MPLS)

Multiprotocol Label Switching (MPLS) offers an efficient encapsulation technique. It uses 'Label' attached to packets before transportation of data. MPLS packet can run on layer 2 technologies such as ATM, PPP, Ethernet. MPLS is responsible for the delivery of IP services. It provides greater flexibility in network planning and preference of traffic.

Asynchronous Transfer Mode (ATM)

Asynchronous Transfer Mode (ATM) is the transfer mode in which information is organized into 53 bytes of fixed cells for multiple services like voice, video, or data. ATM network is connection oriented; it handles multiple applications by integrating multiplexing and switching functions at different data rates. ATM technology is much faster and able to transfer voice, data, and video signals up to 500 Mbps.

Real World Scenario

Background

Asynchronous Transfer Mode (ATM) was a network technology originally designed for high-speed LANs in the early 1990's. ATM only saw limited success in the LAN world but became extremely popular in the WAN world.

When it comes to ATM exploits, however, credit card skimming understandably gets all the media attention: it accounts for more than 80 percent of ATM frauds.

Challenges

A German savings bank, Sparkasse has started patching its ATMs and self-service terminals after a researcher found that the machines can be tricked into revealing many sensitive data during software updates.

The problem was discovered by Benjamin Kunz-Mejri, CEO and developer of Germany-based security firm Vulnerability Lab. The researcher was using a Sparkasse terminal when the machine suddenly ejected his card, and changed its status to "temporarily not available".

Software updates are normally conducted in the background, but as Kunz-Mejri discovered, the progress and details of the update process can be made visible by interacting with the device. The researcher defined his interaction with the machine as a "timing attack", but he did not want to disclose additional details in order to avoid abuse.

When he discovered the vulnerability, Kunz-Mejri recorded a video of the data displayed on the terminal's command prompt screen. After reviewing the recording, he determined that the update process exposed many data, including the bank's main system branch usernames, serial numbers, firewall settings, network information, device IDs, ATM settings, and two system passwords.

In this scenario, the attacker records the data displayed on the screen during the update process and uses it to perform a Man-in-the-Middle (MitM) attack on the local network of the targeted bank.

Solution

The data disclosure and hardware misconfiguration flaws were first reported to Security and Data Protection team of Sparkasse in May, and the existence of the problem was confirmed shortly after the vulnerability report reached the Finance Security Center of the bank in Frankfurt, as Vulnerability Lab reported. The organization has already rolled out updates that address the vulnerabilities to some of its ATMs in the German city of Kassel (Hessen) as part of a pilot program.

Conclusion

Sparkasse thanked Kunz-Mejri for his effort and awarded him an undisclosed amount of money, according to documents viewed by SecurityWeek show. Kunz-Mejri declared that it was the first time a German bank acknowledged a security researcher for finding vulnerabilities in self-service terminals and ATMs.

Incidents involving hacked ATMs are not unheard of in Germany. Berlin Police announced that they have been looking for a man who illegally withdrew cash from two ATMs using a USB stick that he connected to the devices after unscrewing the front panel. This technique has been known for several years.

Frame Relay

Frame relay is a powerful WAN technology that operates at physical and data link layer of the OSI model. It is the simplified way of packet switching as it follows the principle of X.25 in which data frames are routed to various destinations, as described in the header information.

Frame relay was designed to be used over Integrated Service Digital Network (ISDN) interfaces. Frame relay does not guarantee the integrity of data, but its switching speed is much faster.

Point-to-Point Protocol (PPP)/Multilink PPP

Point-to-Point Protocol (PPP) is the standard remote access protocol that provides methods for authentication, error checking and multiple protocol support. PPP deals with different network layer protocols such as IP, IPV6. PPP offers several authentication methods including PAP (Password Authentication Protocol), CHAP (Challenge Authentication Protocol), and EAP (Extensible Authentication Protocol).

PPP follows three steps to establish a session:

1. Framing rules are set between the client and server that covers the size of frames where data rates are acceptable.
2. Authentication of the client by the server using authentication protocol is done.
3. Network Control Protocols (NCPs) are enabled for the remote clients for different network layer protocols.

After following these steps, PPP is able to interchange data. If it requires multiple physical links, multilink PPP could be used to send frames. This improves the throughput of the connection.

PPPoE

PPPoE is a point-to-point link over a shared medium. As we know, PPP can be used for serial link. As PPP can assign IP addresses to remote ends & due to its authentication features, ISPs often use PPP over broadband connections. As Ethernet link do not natively support point-to-point protocol, PPPoE was created to overcome this problem.

For the exam, users must be aware of the client side only. There are various technologies for Broadband Internet Access that normally ISP uses like the Datalink Protocol Point-to-Point (PPP) to form a connection. PPP can utilize all serial links as well as links created with dial-up analog and ISDN Modems.

The reason that ISP uses PPP as data Layer 2 Data-Link Protocol over a broadband connection is it supports the ability to assign an IP address to the remote end device of PPP links. Another main reason is PPP supports CHAP Authentication; this authentication is used for the authentication of clients. As the Ethernet does not support the native PPP Encapsulation, Point-to-Point Protocol over Ethernet (PPPoE) was created because of the ease and availability of Ethernet Connections. PPPoE allows PPP frame to be encapsulated into the Ethernet frame.

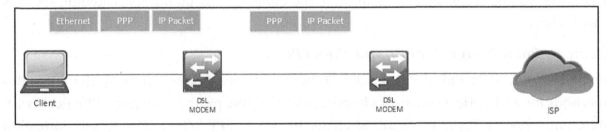

Figure 2-26: PPPoE

DMVPN

Extending VPN access across a company with different locations can generate some logistical issues. A traditional VPN located at the center location would become a bottleneck for traffic. A Dynamic Multipoint VPN (DMVPN) fixes this issue by allowing direct VPN connections between various locations directly.

As the Site-to-Site VPN solution is primarily used for connecting the main office with multiple branch offices for unique IP subnet, the configuration for network administrator gets complex as the number of branch offices increases. By defining static configurations like crypto-maps and pre-shared keys on each device, maintaining such network topology becomes a full time job as well.

In such situations, DMVPN comes to the rescue by providing same output while keeping low cost, less configuration complexity and increased flexibility of the overall network design.

In DMVPN, one device acts as central part of whole VPN topology while the remaining ones acts as clients to the central device for fetching information regarding VPN connection and destination address for intended connections. The central device is known as HUB while remaining devices are called SPOKE. Normally headquarter edge device is configured while branch office's device is configured as SPOKE.

Deployment of DMVPN consists of two main design considerations:

➢ **DMVPN Hub and Spoke**- Used for interconnecting headquarters with branch offices. In this mode of deployment, traffic between branch offices flow through hub as there is not direct communication between different spokes.

➢ **DMVPN Spoke to Spoke**- Used for branch to branch direct communication. It should be noted that Hub-and-Spoke topology is initially generated. Full or partial mesh network will be created once traffic from one spoke to some other spoke is generated.

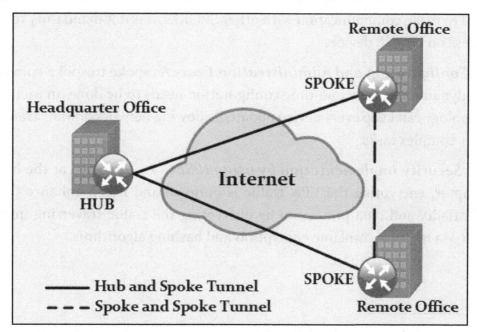

Figure 2-27: DMVPN Design Overview

From the diagram, we can see that only one interface needs to be created on a HUB device while each SPOKE device will connect to this interface that is shared with each branch office device. Static IP will always be assigned to HUB interface while SPOKE devices' interface can have static or dynamic IP address assignment.

As discussed earlier, DMVPNs have cleaner and less complex configuration than standard site-to-site VPNs. This benefit of DMVPN is just because of the shared interface known as multiple GRE (mGRE) tunnel.

mGRE tunnel interface along with Next Hop Resolution Protocol (NHRP) helps SPOKE devices to communicate with HUB or any other SPOKE. NHRP is a layer 2 protocol and works exactly like Address Resolution Protocol (ARP). The HUB device holds special database known as NHRP database and contains the public IP addresses of configured spoke. Whenever a SPOKE wants communication with some other SPOKE, it queries the NHRP database from HUB for intended public IP address.

Benefits of using DMVPN

The most prominent benefits of DMVPN that makes it a popular and recommended solution for site-to-site VPN implementation are:

➤ *Simplified HUB Configuration*- Unlike standard site-to-site VPN solutions, only one tunnel interface (mGRE) needs to be created. No matter how many SPOKE device there are, the HUB configuration remains the same.

➤ *Dynamic IP Addressing Support for SPOKE Devices*- As SPOKE devices use NHRP protocol to make communication with other SPOKEs, it is not mandatory to have static IP address on SPOKE devices.

➤ *Lower Configuration and Administration Cost*- As spoke to spoke communication is done dynamically, only one-time configuration needs to be done on each device and VPN topology can keep every device updated, allowing network administrators to focus on other complex tasks.

➤ *Option Security Implementation by using IPSEC*- As discussed at the beginning of this chapter, encrypting the VPN traffic is optional and it can enhance the network confidentiality and data protection by encrypting the traffic traversing mGRE tunnel interface via multiple available encryption and hashing algorithms.

DMVPN Deployment Models

The most commonly found DMVPN deployment models found in different network topologies around the globe are:

➤ Single DMVPN Network - Single Tier Headend Architecture

➤ Single DMVPN Network - Dual Tier Headend Architecture

➤ Dual DMVPN Network– Single Tier Headend Architecture

➤ Dual DMVPN Network– Dual Tier Headend Architecture

Independent from which model is implemented, DMVPN creation always involves the following components or control planes:

> mGRE Tunnels

> Next Hop Resolution Protocol-based Dynamic Routing

> IPSec-based mGRE Tunnel Protection

Single DMVPN Network - Single Tier Headend Architecture

The simplest implementation of DMVPN is by using single HUB device and connecting SPOKE devices to it as shown below:

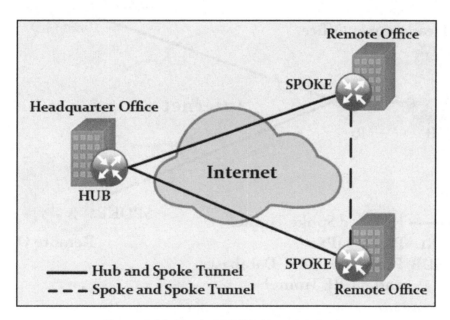

Figure 2-28: Single DMVPN Network Design

Single Tier Headend means that every single component will be performed and controlled via a single HUB device. The central device, HUB maintains NHRP database to be aware of every SPOKE in VPN topology.

During the initial configuration, each SPOKE is configured with static NHRP mapping and it dynamically knows every other SPOKE device in the VPN network.

The Single DMVPN-Single Tier Headend architecture is suitable for limited budget DMVPN deployment as HUB acts a single point of failure in the whole design. If the internet or mGRE tunnel interface gets down due to any reason, it will tear down the whole VPN network.

Let Your Career Flow

Single DMVPN Network - Dual Tier Headend Architecture

In the previous design, the CPU processing limitation of single HUB device also poses a serious threat to the overall VPN network. In order to facilitate the DMVPN topology, a dual tier headend design is used in which control planes or DMVPN components are performed mutually between two devices that is shown below:

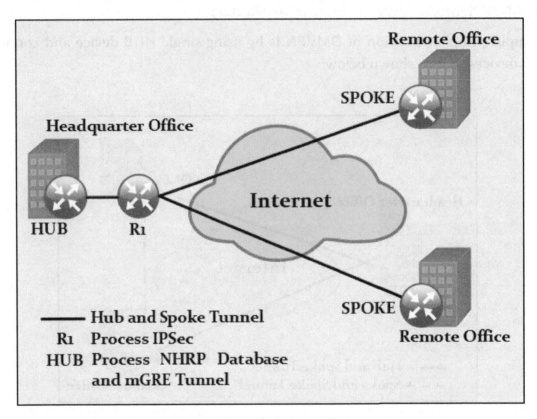

Figure 2-29 Single DMVPN Network - Dual Tier Headend Architecture

Apart from the distribution of processing tasks, the only real advantage of using this design is support for large number of spokes. Such design also has a limitation of not supporting SPOKE to SPOKE communication directly.

Dual DMVPN Network– Single Tier Headend Architecture

One of the most critical errors stated in the previous designs is the single point of failure in case HUB gets down. To cater to such problems, Two HUBs with two independent DMVPN networks can be established. Each HUB will process its own control planes. Similarly SPOKE to SPOKE communication will be done via respective tunnels of each DMVPN network. For auto failover mechanism, a dynamic routing protocol like EIGRP or OSPF needs to be enabled so that if HUB1 gets down the secondary DMVPN network (HUB2) takes over.

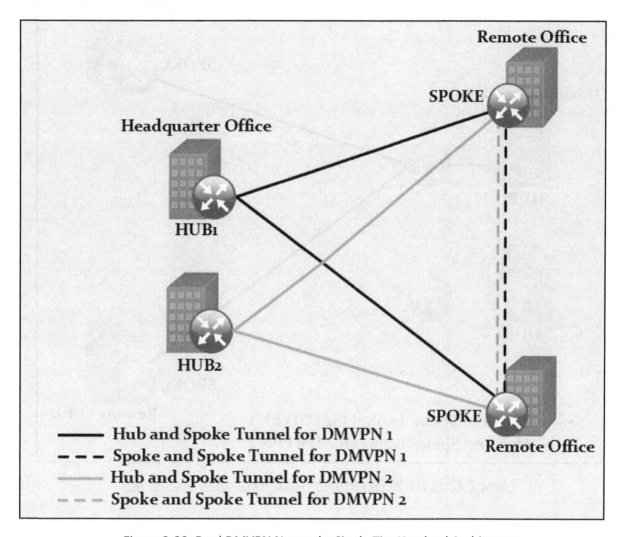

Figure 2-30: Dual DMVPN Network– Single Tier Headend Architecture

Dual DMVPN Network– Dual Tier Headend Architecture

In order to relieve the HUB 1 and HUB2 routers with some of their duties, as shown above, Dual Tier Headend design introduces two frontend routers to perform encryption while HUB1 and HUB2 maintain their respective NHRP databases and mGRE tunnels. In order to ensure auto-failover capability of DMVPN network, dynamic routing protocol (EIGRP or OSPF) needs to be enabled over DMVPN network.

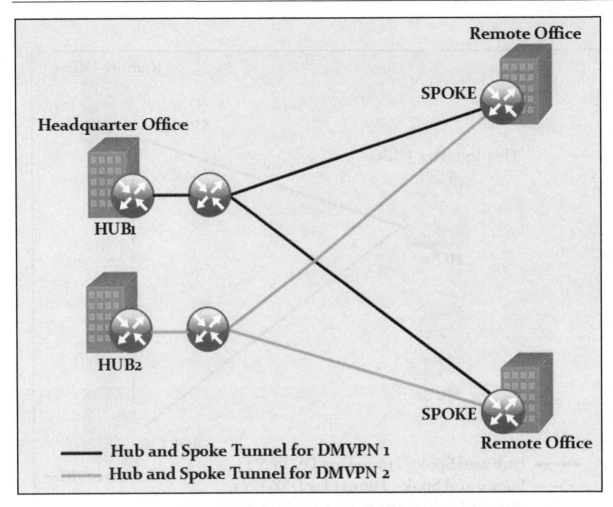

Figure 2-31: Dual DMVPN Network– Dual Tier Headend Architecture

SIP Trunk

Session Initiation Protocol (SIP) and H.323 handle the initiation, setup, and delivery of VoIP sessions. VoIP requires many special features that are not very common in many other Internet protocols. Multicasting is the biggest one. Users do not ever really use multicasting unless they want to show a video to a number of people or want to make a conference call. SIP and H.323 both have multicast handling techniques.

Termination

Network termination points are those points on the network where provider's equipment handovers the network link to customers' devices. Following are some important terminologies related to network termination.

Demarcation Point

The Demarcation Point or Point of Demarcation (POD) in telecommunication is the connection point at which the public network ends and connects with the customer's on-

premises network. For example, in telephony, the demarcation point is the point at which the public switched telephone network ends and connects with the customer's on-premises wiring.

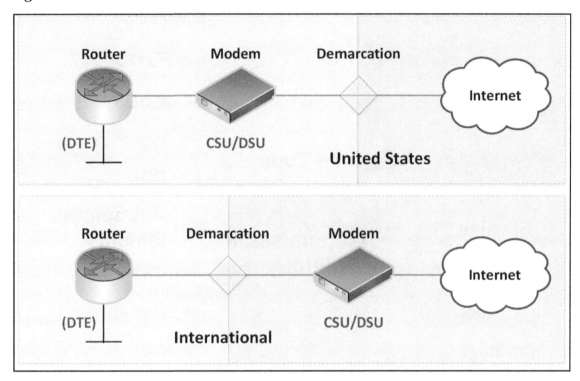

Figure 2-32: Demarcation Point

CSU/DSU

Modems are a type of Channel Service Unit/Data Service Unit (CSU/DSU) typically used for converting analog signals into digital. In this scenario, the CSU handles communication with the network provider, while the DSU handles communication with the internal digital equipment. Modems typically operate on Layer 2 of the OSI model.

Smart Jack

Smart jack is an intelligent device placed right between telephone company's demarcation and customer premises.

Smart jacks or Intelligent Network Interface Devices (INIDs) are intelligent device and used for complicated telecommunication services such as T1 lines. Smart jacks are capable of:

- Signal Conversion
- Conversion of codes and protocols (framing types)
- It may buffer or regenerate signals
- It may provide diagnostic capability
- Loopback capability
- Alarm indications

Mind Map of WAN Technologies

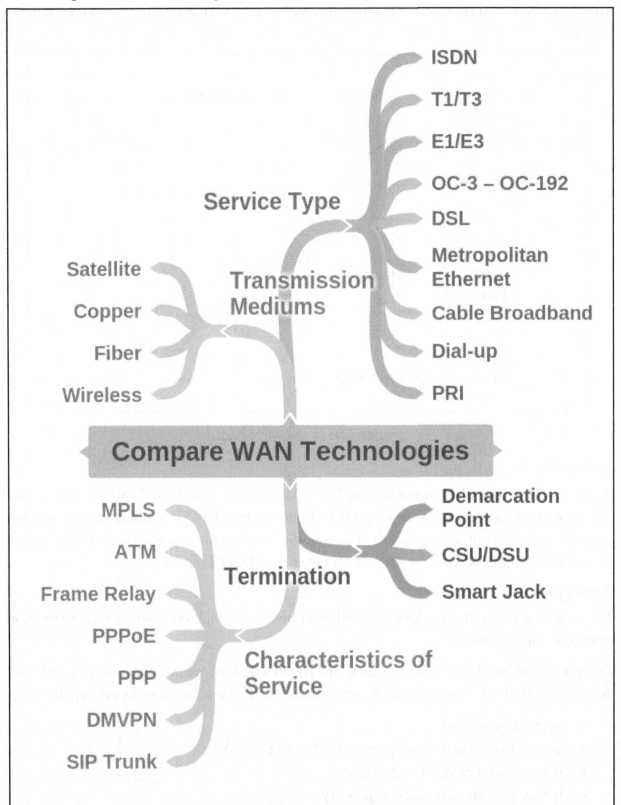

Figure 2-33: Mind Map of WAN Technologies

Summary

Deploy the Appropriate Cabling Solution

- SC connectors are used with fiber-optic cable
- RJ-45 connectors are used with UTP cable
- F-type connectors are used with coaxial cables. They are not used with fiber-optic, UTP, or STP cabling
- BNC is a connector type used with coaxial cabling. BNC is not used for fiber-optic cabling as a connector

Determine the Appropriate Placement of Networking Devices on a Network and Install/Configure them

- Firewalls block malicious packets from either entering or exiting networks and devices
- A media converter is used to link two different forms of network media
- Hubs are inefficient devices that send information packets to all connected devices

Purposes and Use Cases for Advanced Networking Devices

- Multilayer switches and DNS servers can serve as load balancers
- An Intrusion Prevention System (IPS) is a device that continually scans the network, looking for inappropriate activities
- A content filter is any software that controls what a user is allowed to peruse and is most often associated with websites

The Purpose of Virtualization and Network Storage Technologies

- A hypervisor that operates on top of a host OS is a Type-2 hypervisor
- InfiniBand allows for very high throughput with very low latency, competing with Ethernet, Fiber Channel, and other technologies

Compare and Contrast WAN Technologies

- A T1 line has a 1.544-Mbps transmission capability and is considerably cheaper than a T3 line
- MPLS is a technology that uses short path labels instead of longer network addresses to direct data from one node to another
- Metropolitan Ethernet is nothing more than an Ethernet-based MAN
- DMVPN provides the capability to generate a dynamic-mesh VPN network without having to pre-configure all the possible tunnel endpoints
- PPP is a data link protocol that is used to establish a connection between two nodes

Practice Questions

1. Which of the following connector types is associated with fiber-optic cable?
    A. RJ-45
    B. BNC
    C. ST
    D. RG-58

2. Which Cat standard is the latest standard approved by TIA/EIA?
    A. 5e
    B. 6
    C. 6a
    D. 6e

3. Which of the following connections would require a crossover cable?
    A. Router to Switch
    B. Switch to Switch
    C. PC to Switch
    D. Switch to Router

4. What do routers use to forward packets?
    A. Source IP Address
    B. Destination IP Address
    C. Source MAC Address
    D. Destination MAC Address

5. Which device(s) can notify a firewall about an intrusion so that the firewall can take action?
    A. Just an IDS
    B. Just an IPS
    C. Both an IDS and an IPS
    D. Neither an IDS nor an IPS

6. Which one of these is not part of AAA security?
    A. Authentication
    B. Authorization
    C. Auditing
    D. Accounting

7. What type of hypervisor runs on top of an existing operating system?
   A. Type-1
   B. Type-2
   C. Bare Metal
   D. Oracle

8. MPLS labels are located between which two layers?
   A. Layers 1 and 2
   B. Layers 2 and 3
   C. Layers 3 and 4
   D. Layers 4 and 5

9. Which of the following circuit-switching strategies does ATM use? (Choose 2)
   A. SVC
   B. VCD
   C. PVC
   D. PCV

10. Which of the following technologies requires a logical connection between the sending and receiving devices?
   A. Circuit Switching
   B. Virtual-Circuit Packet Switching
   C. Message Switching
   D. High-Density Circuit Switching

11. What kind of cable would you associate with an F-type connector?
   A. Fiber Optic
   B. UTP
   C. Coaxial
   D. ST

12. Which of the following fiber connectors uses a twist-type connection method?
   A. ST
   B. SC
   C. BNC
   D. SA

13. Which device reduces the traffic by spontaneous segmentation of a network?
   A. Modem

B. Switch

C. Router

D. Hub

14. On which two layers of the OSI model does multilayer switch operate?
    A. Layer 1 and Layer 2
    B. Layer 1 and Layer 3
    C. Layer 2 and Layer 3
    D. Layer 1 and Layer 4

15. Which physical device or software defends an internal network or system from unauthorized access by performing as a filter?
    A. HIDS
    B. IPS/IDS
    C. Content Filter
    D. Firewall

16. Which of the following is not a Fiber Optic protocol or technology?
    A. SONET
    B. CWDM
    C. DWDM
    D. Frame Relay

17. Which method is used by the router to make routing decisions?
    A. Route Aggregation
    B. Hop Count
    C. Routing Metrics
    D. HSRP

18. What term describes technologies that can deliver voice communications over the internet?
    A. SDN
    B. VoIP
    C. SAN
    D. Jitter

19. Which of the following statement is correct about Straight Through Cable?
    A. Both ends with TIA-568A standard

B. Both ends with TIA-568B standard

C. Either A or B

D. Neither A nor B

20. Which of the following cable issues is caused by signal bleed from wires running next to each other in a cable?

A. Short

B. Open

C. Crosstalk

D. EMI

Chapter 03: Network Operations

Technology Brief

In the previous chapter "Infrastructure", we have discussed about cabling solutions, placement and installation of network devices, virtualization concepts and WAN technologies. Now, in this chapter, we will discuss about network operations and processes, their standard documentation and mangement, business continuity planning, disaster recovery concepts, monitoring of different processes, and best practices of policies in an information system.

Appropriate Documentation and Diagrams to Manage the Network

In order to run a project, an operation or a process, it is mandatory to manage the processes running under different domains. With proper management, it becomes easy to oversee the performance and root causes of events as well as to plan how to boast the results. Furthermore, documentation also plays an important role while managing a process. Documentation helps to record the workflow of each process, provider better visibility, enhances security, and gives support for backup and disaster recovery.

Diagram Symbols

Network and topology diagrams are the most basic and important part of documentation. Implemented network topology must be properly documented. It helps to oversee the entire topology, demonstrate the network among different security and administrative teams to take actions. Symbolic representation helps to design, demonstrate and understand the network diagram on an information system. There are different ways to draw the diagram of a system. Software tools are also available for this purpose. These software tools include Microsoft Visio, Computer-Aided Design (CAD), and Smart Draw. Diagrams can be simple sketches drawn by brainstorming or troubleshooting the system infrastructure.

Standards Operating Procedures/Work Instructions

Standard Operating Procedures (SOP) is a "set of instructions used to describe a process or procedure that performs an explicit operation or explicit reaction to a given event".

In simpler words, SOP is a documented instruction from an organization for their employees to run complex routine operational processes. SOP is aimed to achieve efficiency, quality outcomes, and uniformity by reducing the miscommunication and failures.

A SOP must contain the following items:

1. Title
2. Scope
3. Equipment, Materials and Reagents
4. Procedures
5. Report Generation, Review and Approval
6. Calculations
7. Limitations
8. Safety
9. References
10. SOP Approval

Logical vs. Physical Diagrams

Network topologies can be defined on a physical or a logical level. The physical topology refers to how a network is physically constructed (how it looks). The logical topology refers to how a network looks to the devices that use it (how it functions).

Physical Network Diagrams

Networks are dynamic, and modifications can occur regularly, which is why the physical network diagrams also need to be updated. Networks have different policies and procedures on how often updates should occur. Best practice is that the diagram should be updated whenever significant modifications to the network happen, such as the addition of a switch or router, a change in protocols, or the addition of a new server. These modifications impact how the network operates, and the documentation should reflect the changes.

Physical network diagrams can operate from simple, hand-drawn models to complex models created by software packages like SmartDraw, Visio, and AutoCAD.

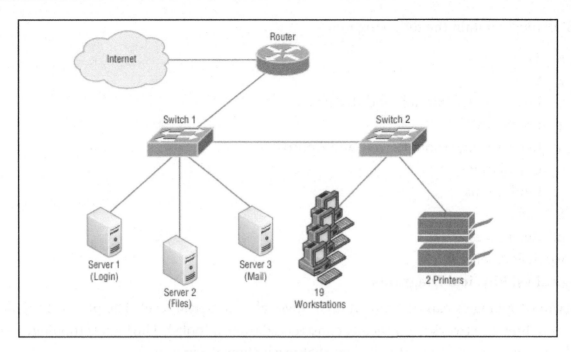

Figure 3-01: Physical Network Diagram

Logical Network Diagrams

Logical network diagram involves things like protocols, settings, scheme addresses, access lists, firewalls, application types, all logically applicable to the network.

The logical network relates to the direction in which information flows on the network within the physical topology. The purpose of a logical diagram is not to focus on the network hardware but rather on how information flows through that hardware. The physical and logical topologies can be the same in practice. In the case of the bus physical topology, information travels from one computer along the length of the cable to the next. Therefore, the diagram for the physical and logical bus would be the same.

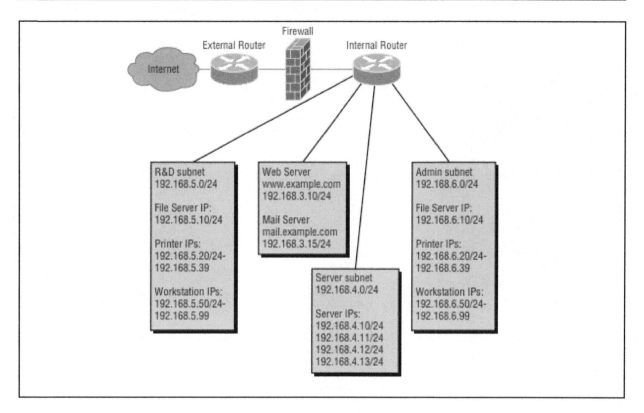

Figure 3-02: Logical Network Diagram

💡 **Exam Tip**

Be able to identify a physical and logical diagram. Readers need to know the types of information that should be included in each diagram.

Rack Diagram

Rack diagram is the graphical representation of rack equipped with servers, routers and other networking devices. Rack is a metal frame, which holds several hardware devices such as servers, routers, raid, UPS, modems and other electronic equipment. Several online tools are available for designing rack diagrams. Below is a rack diagram using the Smartdraw online tool.

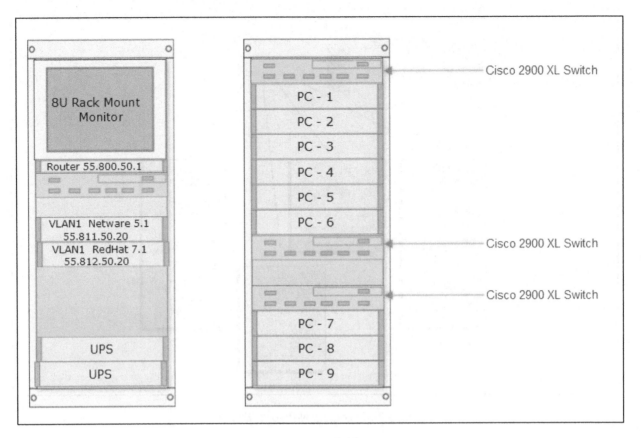

Figure 3-03: Rack Diagram

Cable Trays

Cable trays are metal trays used to organize the cabling neatly and keep it away from the heating areas. Cable trays are often used in today's networks to support insulated cables used for communication and power. They provide a physical management system that protect the cables, and leave them accessible for inspection and any necessary changes. Also, additional cables can be easily added to a tray by just dropping in another cable instead of having to pull it through a duct.

Rack Systems

Rack systems are used to hold and arrange the servers, routers, switches, firewalls, and other rack-ready equipment. Rack system provides a cleaner appearance and easier management, better airflow, redundant power supplies, and so on. These racks can place switches, routers, UPSs, and other equipment as well. They are typically 19 inches wide to accommodate all of the equipment that is specifically made to fit that width. Devices that are made to fit these are referred to as rack-mounted devices. The height of the devices is measured in rack units that are each called a U; a standard rack stands 42-U tall. A U is approximately 1¾ inches. Rack systems provide a great amount of flexibility in their design.

Server Rail Racks

Server rail racks are used to hold servers in one of the types of racks (two-post racks or four-post racks). They are designed to hold the server while allowing it to be slid out from the rack for maintenance.

Two-Post Racks

Two-post racks provide just two vertical posts to which devices can be attached from the front and back. They are especially good for installation of telecommunication equipment that is generally lighter and requires less maintenance.

Four-Post Racks

Four-post racks have four vertical posts that allow the installation of rails and the support of heavier devices such as servers, switches, routers, and so on. They are generally more expensive than two-post racks.

Free-Standing Racks

A freestanding rack is one that does not reach the ceiling and stands on its own.

Rack Monitoring

Racks should contain monitoring devices that can be operated remotely. These devices can be used to monitor the following issues:

- Temperature
- Humidity
- Physical Security
- Water Leaks
- Vibration
- Smoke

Rack Security

Rack devices should be secured from robbery. There are several locking systems that can be used to facilitate this.

These locks are typically implemented in doors on the front of a rack cabinet:

- Swing handle/wing knob locks with common key
- Swing handle/wing knob locks with unique key
- Swing handle with the number and key lock
- Electronic locks
- Radio-frequency identification (RFID) card locks

Change Management Documentation

Documentation is always needed when we make configuration changes in the future. Therefore, these documents should be changed with the system changes. In this section, we will discuss documenting the reason for the change, change requests, approval processes, maintenance windows, notification, and final documentation of the change.

Document Reason for the Change

Every change in a network should be properly documented. Although, it is not an easy task to update the document concerning any changes that occur in the network. For this, many organizations hire people to perform the responsibility. Some use software to update the track.

Change Request

A change should start its process as a change request. This request will move through various stages of the approval process and should include certain parts of information that will guide those tasked with approving or denying it.

Configuration Procedures

The particular steps required to implement the change and the particular devices involved should be detailed. Complete documentation should be produced and submitted with a formal report to the change management board.

Rollback Process

Changes always carry a risk. Before any changes are implemented, plans for reversing the changes and recovering from any opposing effects from the change should be known. Those making the changes should be completely briefed in these rollback process, and they should show a clear understanding of them before implementing the changes.

Potential Impact

One of the benefits of performing this process is that it can identify systems that may need to be more closely monitored for their reaction to the change, as the change is being implemented.

Notification

When all systems that may be affected by the change are identified, system owners should be notified of all changes that could potentially affect them.

Approval Process

The actual approval process will depend on the organization. Some organizations may approve by a verbal statement of the change, while others may require documentation. The

main factor is that the change should reflect the overall goals of the company regarding network connectivity, disaster recovery, fault tolerance, security, and so on.

Maintenance Window

A maintenance window is an amount of time a system will be down or unavailable, during the implementation of changes. Before this window of time is specified, all affected systems should be examined, with respect to their criticality in supporting mission-critical operations.

Authorized Downtime

When the time required to make the change has been compared to the maximum allowable downtime, a system can suffer and the optimum time for the change is identified, and the authorized downtime can be specified. These amounts help reach a final decision, on when the change will be made.

Notification of Change

When the change has been completed, and a sufficient amount of time has passed for issues to manifest themselves, all affected members should be notified that the change is complete. At that time, these affected members can continue to monitor the situation for any residual problems.

Documentation

The process is not complete until the paperwork is complete. In this case, the following should be updated to reflect the changed state of the network:

- Network Configurations
- Additions to Network
- Physical Location Changes

Wiring and Port Location

Rack management helps to design and install the devices into the rack(s) efficiently and easily. It also helps the administrator while troubleshooting the devices to connect or check the connection and cable. Following are some general best practices while setting up a rack:

- Determine the routes for data cables and power lines from either top or bottom of the rack. Separate the power lines from data cables and copper cables from fiber cable. This identification and separation helps in handling, installing and troubleshooting cable issues
- Make sure all cables are easily recognizable, using different color schemes as well as labelling the cables; this helps in troubleshooting

- Cable ties and proper insulation help with the sharp edges or heated corners of the rack
- Avoid leaving loose cables on the floor as this could constitute as a major safety hazard. Instead, use the vertical, horizontal, or overhead cable managers
- Use the patch cable of exact length, and leave some slack at each end for end device movements
- Use vertical and horizontal cable guides for routing cables within and between the racks
- Regularly maintain the cabling documentation, labeling, and physical or logical cabling diagrams

IDF / MDF Documentation

Intermediate Distribution Frame (IDF) is a distribution frame that connects several Intermediate Distribution Frame (IDF). Main Distribution Frame (MDF) typically distributes the telephone signals or cable rack to interconnect and communicate several IDFs. Each IDF manages the interconnection between users and MDF. Consider an example where IDFs are installed on each department building connected to MDF as shown in the figure below:

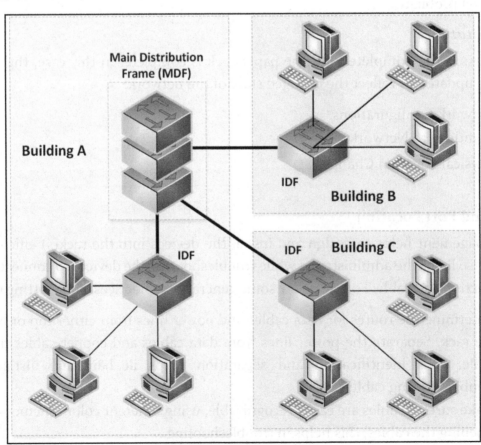

Figure 3-04: IDF/MDF Documentation

Labeling

In a data center/server room/wiring closet, correct and updated labeling of ports, systems, circuits, and patch panels help a lot in troubleshooting and configuration updates. Some types of labeling are discussed below.

Port Labeling

Ports on switches, routers, patch panels, and another systems should be properly labeled and resemble the wall outlets to which they lead. Port labeling has been done by considering an agreement with the naming convention, which is used because all technicians are operating from the same point of reference. They also should be updated in any case where changes are made that directive an update.

System Labeling

Other systems that are installed in racks, such as servers, firewall appliances, and redundant power supplies, should also be labeled with IP addresses and DNS names that the devices hold.

Circuit Labeling

Circuits arriving at the facility should also be labeled. Circuit labels can be done over electrical receptacles, circuit breaker panels, and power distribution units by circuit information, voltage and amperage, the type of electrical receptacle, and wherein the data center the duct terminates.

Naming Conventions

A naming convention guides and manages to label and ensure regularity. No matter what name or numbering system is used, be regular.

Patch Panel Labeling

The significant issue when labeling patch panels is to ensure that they are correct. In addition, users need to make sure that the wall outlet they are connected to is the same.

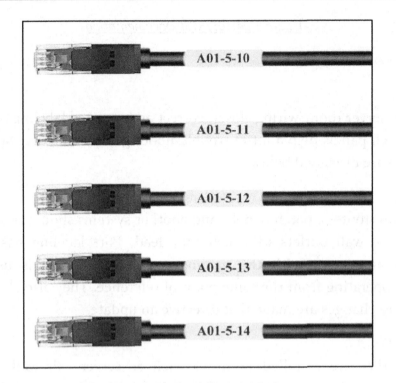

Figure 3-05: Patch Panel Labeling

Network Configuration and Performance Baseline

Network configuration and performance baselining is about performance of network devices to the standard level. Baseline refers to the standard level of performance that a certain device should achieve while operating in normal conditions. For example, consider a server in an organizational network. A server's baseline defines the normal factor like its processing capability and memory utilization and the required bandwidth. Normally, baselines include the following components:

- Memory
- Processor
- Hard-disk
- Network Utilization

Baseline monitoring enhances the performance and processes. Log reviewing, patching, troubleshooting and resolving general network issues helps to boast the process.

Inventory Management

According to NIST Special Publication 800-53 (Rev. 4), "Security Controls and Assessment Procedures for Federal Information Systems and Organizations", an organization must review and update the information system component inventory.

- An organization may choose to implement centralized system that includes components from all organizational system. The organization must ensure that the

resulting inventories include system-specific information required for proper component accountability

- Information deemed necessary for effective accountability of information system components includes, for example, hardware inventory specifications, software license information, software version numbers, component owners, and for networked components or devices, machine names and network addresses
- Inventory specifications include, for example, manufacturer, device type, model, serial number, and physical location

Mind Map of Documentation & Diagrams

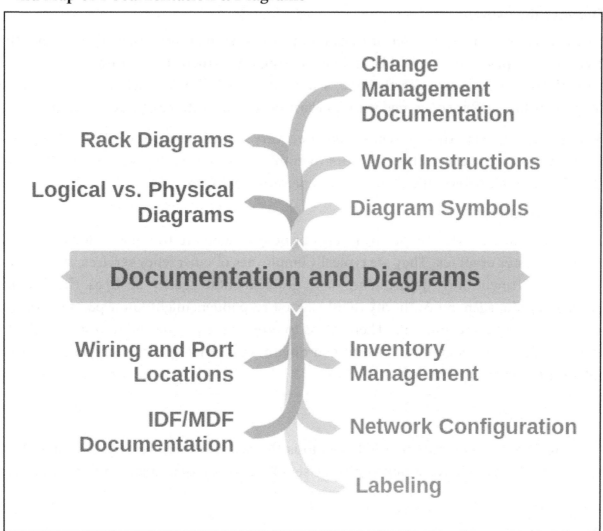

Figure 3-06: Mind Map of Documentation and Diagrams

Compare and Contrast Business Continuity and Disaster Recovery Concepts

The main idea to understand security is the assessment of risk. There is a risk in everything regarding networking, or anything else for that matter. The question is how much risk users are willing to take and how they will reduce that risk. Concepts to understand regarding the reduction of risk include are disaster recovery, business continuity, battery backups, first responders, data breach, end-user awareness and training, single point of failure, adherence to standards and policies, vulnerability scanning, and penetration testing. In the following sections, we will discuss all of these concepts and more.

Disaster Recovery

Disaster Recovery (DR) is a set of rules and procedures that are designed to enable the recovery or replacement of vital IT and networking infrastructure. The disaster could be a natural disaster such as an earthquake, a human-caused disaster such as a fire or just a human mistake. DR is concerned with how fast normal operations can be restored.

Key metrics related to this concept include Recovery Point Objective (RPO). RPO depends upon the measurement of the maximum tolerable data to lose. Recovery Time Objective (RTO) is used for determining how often to perform data backups.

First Responders

First responders are the people, or groups of people, who are the first to look after the natural disaster or attack. They are typically employees of emergency services, such as the police department, fire department, or a governmental agency such as the Federal Emergency Management Authority (FEMA). First responders might know paramedics and emergency medical technicians. Their role is to protect the people and to restore order to the site. They are generally trained to coordinate with other agencies to guarantee that relevant evidence is preserved.

 Exam Tip

During a recovery operation, a full backup is the fastest way to restore data of all the methods discussed here, because only one set of media is required for a full restore.

Business Continuity

Business Continuity (BC) involves strategies to make sure that an unplanned event or outage does not cause a disaster in the first place. BC includes concepts such as resilience, recovery, and contingency. Business continuity has a direct relation with redundant

servers, clustering, mirroring, and so on. BC attempts to make sure that the business itself remains workable no matter what happens to the network and servers.

Avaialability Concepts

Keeping a network up and running if something accidentally, maliciously, or just normally happens requires efforts in different areas. These areas encompass both hardware and software.

Fault Tolerance

Fault tolerance means that even if one component fails, users will not lose access to the resource it provides. Fault tolerance is defined as the uninterrupted functioning of a system despite the occurrence of fault. To implement fault tolerance, users need to employ several devices or connections that all provide a method to access the same resource(s). Data and services can be mirrored to ensure there is no disruption, so that if either one fails, there is still a copy of the data available. This can be a useful tool in servers because they are more critical to operations.

High Availability

High availability is a system design protocol that ensures during a specified period a certain quantity of operational uptime.

High availability is a system-design protocol that ensures a certain amount of operational uptime during a given period. It is the ability of a system to maintain space for data and operational services regardless of any disrupting events, or faults. High availability achieves the same goal as fault tolerance in ensuring the availability of data and services.

By deploying production workloads in multi-node clusters, it enables the data written to a node to be automatically replicated to other nodes within the cluster to achieve high availability.

Load Balancing

Load balancer automatically distributes incoming traffic across multiple instances or nodes. Using load balancing, users can provide an active/passive server cluster in which only one server is active and handling requests. For example, a user's favorite internet site might actually consist of 20 servers that all appear to be similar because owner of the site wants to ensure that its consumers always experience quick access. Users can accomplish this on a network by installing several redundant links to ensure that network traffic is spread across multiple paths and to maximize the bandwidth on each link.

It seamlessly provides necessary load balancing capacity required usually for application traffic distribution or network gateway traffic so that users can achieve greater levels of fault tolerance at bottleneck nodes.

NIC Teaming

Network Interface Card (NIC) Teaming allows the network administrator to setup one or more physical network adapters group into one or more software-based virtual network adapters. NIC teaming provides fast performance and fault tolerance in case of adapter failure. Single adapter in NIC team cannot provide load balancing and failover but can be used for separation of traffic for VLANs. Windows Server 2016 supports up to 32 team interfaces per team.

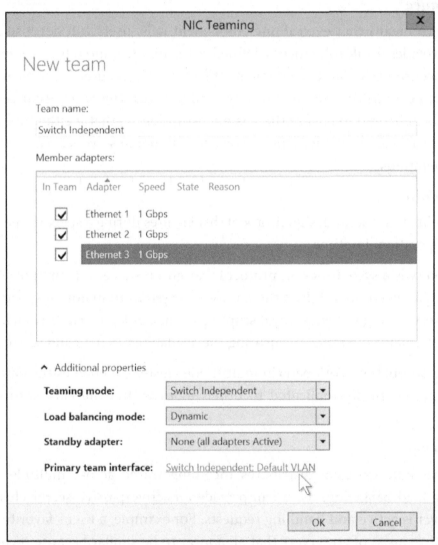

Figure 3-07: NIC Teaming

Port Aggregation

Port aggregation is an automated logical aggregation of Ethernet switch ports. Cisco offers its proprietary Port Aggregation Protocol (PAgP). A similar protocol known as Link Aggregation Control Protocol (LACP) is released by the IEEE and is also known as 802.3ad or 802.1ax recently.

All ports in every EtherChannel must be configured as either Layer 2 or Layer 3 ports. The number of EtherChannel is limited to 48. The EtherChannel Layer 3 ports are made up of routed ports. Routed ports are physical ports that are configured to be in Layer 3 mode by entering no switchport interface configuration command.

Users can configure an EtherChannel in one of these modes: Port Aggregation Protocol (PAgP), Link Aggregation Control Protocol (LACP), or Configure both ends of the EtherChannel in the similar mode:

When users configure one end of an EtherChannel in either PAgP or LACP mode, the system negotiates with the other end of the channel to determine which ports should become active. Incompatible ports are placed into an independent state and continue to carry data traffic, as would any other single link. The port configuration does not change however the port does not participate in the EtherChannel.

When users configure an EtherChannel in the on mode, no negotiations take place. The switch forces all compatible ports to become active in the EtherChannel. The other end of the channel (on the other switch) must also be configured in the on mode; otherwise, packet loss can occur. Users can configure an EtherChannel on a standalone switch, on a single switch in the stack, or on different switches in the stack (Referred as cross-stack EtherChannel).

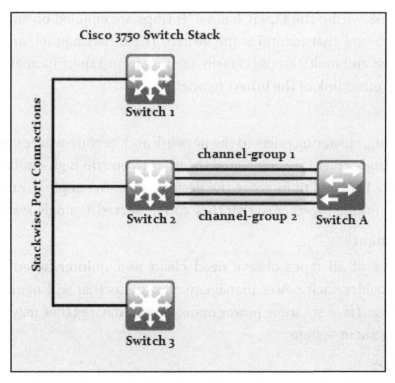

Figure 3-08: Single-Switch EtherChannel

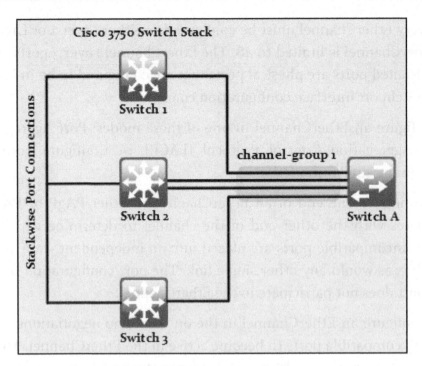

Figure 3-09: Cross-Stack EtherChannel

If a link in the EtherChannel fails, traffic previously carried over that failed link moves to the remaining links within the EtherChannel. If traps are enabled on the switch, a trap is forwarded for a failure that identifies the switch, the EtherChannel, and the failed link. Inbound broadcast and multicast packets on one link in an EtherChannel are blocked from returning on any other link of the EtherChannel.

Clustering

In cloud computing, clustering refers to the network architecture where multiple instances, such as storages and servers are connected together to ensure high availability. Clustering helps to distribute load and to improve the performance. In simple words, a cluster is the set of resources working together so that they can be served as single system.

Power Management

Electronic devices of all types always need clean and uninterrupted power. Network infrastructure provides such power management systems that will neither be fluctuated, nor face power loss. Here are some power management devices that may become a part of the power management system:

<u>Battery Backups/UPS</u>

As all of the networking devices run on electricity, the servers, routers, and switches have power supplies that convert the electricity from the power company to the power that they

can use to operate. All these network devices should have an Uninterruptible Power Supply (UPS) as a backup for each server or rack of servers. If the batteries in a UPS fails, it should be check periodically and replaced as needed.

Power Generators

A UPS allows users to shut down servers in an orderly fashion. It does not offer enough power for users to continue working. The device that manages the latter service is known as a power generator, which burns some petroleum product to generate electricity when the main grid goes dark.

Power Converters/Inverters

Regular electricity is not suitable for network devices or servers. Before supplying electricity to these devices, the current must pass through such converters that convert the AC power to DC power referred to as power Convertors.

There is also a special device that converts DC power to AC power. It produces no power and must be connected to a DC source referred to as power Inverters.

UPSs and Circuits

There are two main circuits to provide power when the power company is not providing it anymore, namely; inline UPS and offline UPS. In the case of an offline circuit, it is not commonly used in today's networks. It has a very fast switch that transfers power to the secondary source, as soon as it senses that the primary power source is down. Due to its fast switching, it is rarely used in today's network. On the other hand, in the inline circuit, the components are already running on power that is going through the battery system, which is constantly recharged by the power company. In the event that the power from the power company fails, the batteries continue to supply the power that the devices need, and often then, a diesel or natural gas engine kicks in and turns on a generator that recharges the batteries.

Dual Power Supplies

During a serious power outage, Keeping the lights on and the servers rolling, would be accomplished by connecting dual power supplies to the equipment room, such as two power generators.

Power Redundancy

Some large organizations whose role is to host computers and networks of the other organization and ensure that they will be operational 24/7, have a whole other power company or at least multiple power grids. It might also be used by utility companies,

government installations, and so on. The idea is that even if one grid goes down, the other will stay up.

Recovery

When companies have multiple data centers, they can often use one as the main data center and one another as a recovery site either a cold standby site or a warm standby site. An organization with 3 or more data centers can have a primary data center, a secondary data center (recovery site) and regional data centers. With the rapid development of public cloud capabilities, the public cloud provides more feasible, reasonable and most importantly cost effective solutions to backup data there.

Generally, applications and services were highly available within site such as a data center, but site resiliency was incredibly expensive and complex. Today, it is common for companies to have multiple data centers, and connectivity between the data centers is much faster and less expensive. Because of these approaches, many applications provide site resiliency with the ability to have multiple instances of an application spread across three or more data centers. In some cases, application vendors are recommending backup free designs in which an app and its data are stored in three or more locations, with the application handling the multisite synchronizing.

It is generally very late to start the procedure of a response when a disaster takes place. Therefore, it is necessary to build disaster recovery sites. For building a disaster recovery site, there are many options available like the hot site, warm site, and cold site.

Cold Site

A cold site is a similar type of disaster recovery service that provides office space, but the customer provides and installs all the equipment needed to continue operations. Users are required to bring these things with them, and it takes weeks to get the cold site to be in operational state.

Warm Site

A warm site is a compromise between hot and cold. These sites will have hardware and connectivity already established, though on a smaller scale than the original production site or even a hot site.

Hot Site

A hot site has everything a warm site has, but also contains recent backups. It is a site that is fully configured and duplicate of the operating environment. It takes no time or few hours to operate the hot site.

Backups

Having a backup of everything serves as the key factor in the disaster recovery of any organization. Backup can be made to tape, disk, optical drive, etc. For database backup, replication (online duplication) can be used.

Full Backup

In order to backup files in an OS, various strategies can be followed. One of them is full backup. In full backup, every time the backup process is performed, every single file is copied sequentially.

Differential Backup

Differential backups only backs-up the changes and modifications that are done after previous backup.

Incremental Backup

In incremental backups, those files are copied that have been modified since the last time incremental backup is performed.

 Exam Tip

A backup strategy must include offsite storage to account for theft, fire, flood, or other disasters.

Snapshots

Using snapshots is common to the backup operating system. A snapshot is a replicate of virtual machines at a definite moment in time. A snapshot is a generated by replicating the files that keep the virtual machine.

MTTR

MTTR stands for Mean Time to Repair. It is the time required to repair a given failure. Mathematically, MTTR is formulated below:

MTBF = Σ (start of downtime – start of uptime) / number of failures

Availability is defined as the time in which the system performs its intended function. It is expressed in percentage, and its mathematical formula is as follows:

Availability = MTBF / (MTBF + MTTR)

MTBF

MTBF stands for Mean Time between Failure, which is a measure of system's reliability, and its expression describes the average time between system failures. Mathematically, MTBF is defined as the arithmetic means of system failures set and expressed as:

MTBF = Σ (start of downtime – start of uptime) / number of failures

SLA Requirements

SLA stands for Service Level Agreement. It is a type of agreement that takes place between the client and the service provider. The SLA specifies performance expectations and often includes penalties if the vendor does not meet these expectations. As an example, many organizations use cloud-based services to rent servers. A vendor provides access to the servers and maintains them to ensure they are available. The organization can use an SLA to specify availability such as with maximum interruptions. Keep in mind, an organization should have a clear idea of their requirements when working with third parties and make sure the SLA includes these requirements.

R&S®Service Level Agreement	Warranty 1 year	Basic 1 to 4 years	Advanced 1 to 4 years	Premium 1 to 4 years
24/7 problem reporting: access to online ticketing system	●	●	●	●
Technical phone support during business hours	●	1 working day	4 hours	2 hours
24/7 emergency support technical support, even outside of business hours			4 hours	2 hours
Overview of your requests (service level agreement reporting)	●	●	●	●
Maintenance releases (software updates)	●	●	●	●
Remote error analysis	●	●	●	●
Remote system updates		●	●	●
Access to feature request system	●	●	●	●
Repair services	●		10 working days	5 working days
Hardware exchange service				shipped no later than the next working day
Managed local spare parts pool	optional	optional	optional	optional
On-site support	optional	optional	optional	optional
Regular maintenance of your Rohde & Schwarz system	optional	optional	optional	optional
Warranty extension to service level		1 year – optional	1 year – optional	1 year – optional

Figure 3-10: Service Level Agreement Template

Mind Map of Business Continuity and Disaster Recovery

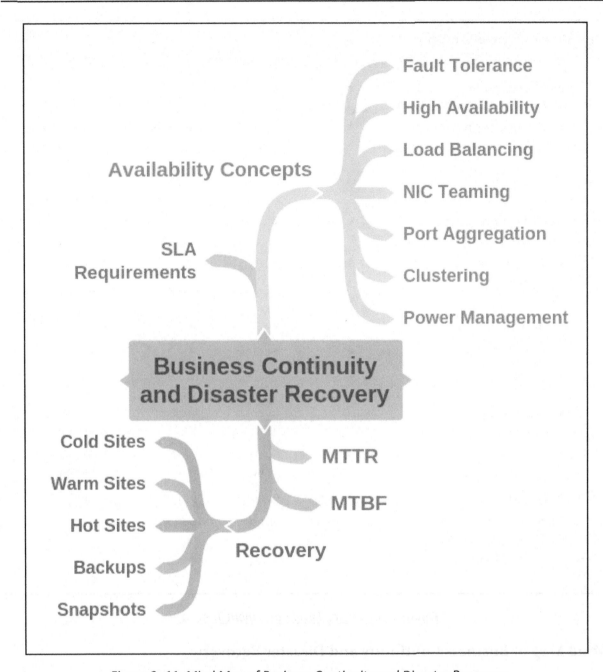

Figure 3- 11: Mind Map of Business Continuity and Disaster Recovery

Common Scanning, Monitoring and Patching Processes and their Expected Outputs

Without regular or irregular intervention from network technicians, a network does not behave properly. Technicians need to install network management tools and then deploy other tools to scan, monitor, and patch networks over time. There are different procedures and tools to accomplish these goals.

Processes

Collecting and analyzing data on a regular basis needs certain procedures to be in place before something occurs. Being proactive is imperative, and can be achieved with well-established and maintained processes.

Log Reviewing

Logging not only helps in auditing the network and system administrators about their activities on network infrastructure but also helps in viewing the systems events that may be generated by networking devices like routers, switches or firewalls etc. due to some failure or certain threshold like CPU or RAM is exceeded. Now there are different levels of logs generated by these devices.

As far as Cisco devices and Cisco IOS are concerned, it can send log output to the following destinations:

Console: A Router/Switch/Firewall can send log messages to the connected terminal. For example, an attached computer with terminal emulation program running like HyperTerminal.

VTY Lines: Whenever an administrator tries to connect remotely to Cisco devices, a *VTY line* is activated for that *exec session*. Depending on the device model, this number may vary. Terminal Monitor command also needs to be issued at privilege level 15 to see the logs on terminal.

Buffer: In order to save log messages for later analysis, a device's internal memory (RAM) can be used. Depending on the size of RAM dedicated for storing log messages, which is named as buffer, these messages are stored on first-in/first-out basis. As RAM is emptied on reboot, so is the buffer.

SNMP Server: Log messages can be sent to the SNMP server in the form of SNMP TRAPs if configured on devices. Normally, SNMPv3 is preferred due to its support for Hashing and Encryption.

Syslog Server: A Syslog server is a dedicated device, whose purpose is to store any kind of log messages directed to it. Depending on the nature of event, which generated the log message, an immediate action may be required by a responsible person otherwise situation may get worse. To categorize the events, Syslog uses eight severity levels from zero to seven with zero being the most critical one when system becomes severely degraded.

Name	Level	Description
Emergencies	0	System is unusable
Alerts	1	Immediate action needed
Critical	2	Critical Condition

Errors	3	Error Condition
Warnings	4	Warning Condition
Notifications	5	Normal but require attention
Informational	6	Informational messages
Debugging	7	Debugs messages with maximum details depending on number of processes for which debugging is enabled

Table 3-01: Syslog Severity Levels and their Descriptions

A Syslog, being the most suitable and usable option, is based on client server architecture. It means there will be a Syslog server and multiple Syslog Clients (different networking devices). Keep it in mind that more detailed log messages will be required than hard drive space for storage. Normally, a RAID technology is also considered where the log belongs to an important infrastructure.

As log messages contain important information, a leakage may result in very serious attacks on the network. The payload of Syslog messages, which may contain information like IP addresses, username/password of logged in users etc., should be in encrypted form when in transit over the network.

NTP Service: Another important feature of logging is the time stamp of an event. An attacker may want to change the time settings so that user may be unaware of an event. In order to synchronize the time over the network, *Network Time Protocol (NTP)* is used. Nowadays, NTP v3 is widely used due to its support for encryption.

NTP uses *UDP port number 123*. Although Cisco routers can be set to be the NTP Clients of publically available NTP servers, we can set a single device in network infrastructure to be NTP server and all the devices will synchronize their time according to the NTP server. One of the advantages we have by using NTP is to correlate different events. If time is tampered, it would be impossible to find the root cause of the problem.

Critical systems require at least daily log review; however, what types of logs/activities should we pay attention to?

1. Consecutive login failure especially in non-office hours.
2. Login at non-office hours.
3. Authority change, addition and removal. Check them against with authorized application.
4. Any system administrator's activities.
5. Any unknown workstation/server that are plugged into the network.
6. Logs removal/log overwritten/log size is full.
7. Pay more attention to the log reports after weekends and holidays.

8. Any account unlocked/password reset by system administrators without authorized forms.

Port Scanning

Scanning is a pre-attack phase. In this phase, an attacker scans the network through information acquired during the initial phase of reconnaissance. Scanning tools include dialers, scanners such as port scanners, network mappers, and client tools such as ping, as well as vulnerability scanners. During the scanning phase, attackers finally fetch the ports' information including port status, operating system information, device type, live machines, and other information depending on scanning.

<u>Scanning Tool</u>

1. Nmap

Another way to ping a host is by performing a ping using Nmap. Using the Windows or Linux command prompt, enter the following command:

nmap –sP –v *<target IP address>*

Upon successful response from the targeted host, if the command successfully finds a live host, it returns a message indicating that the IP address of the targeted host is up, along with the Media Access Control (MAC) address and the network card vendor.

Apart from ICMP echo request packets and ping sweep, Nmap also offers a quick scan. Enter the following command for a quick scan:

nmap –sP –PE –PA*<port numbers> <starting IP/ending IP>* For example: nmap –sP –PE –PA 2 1,23,80,3389 < 192. 168.0. 1-50>

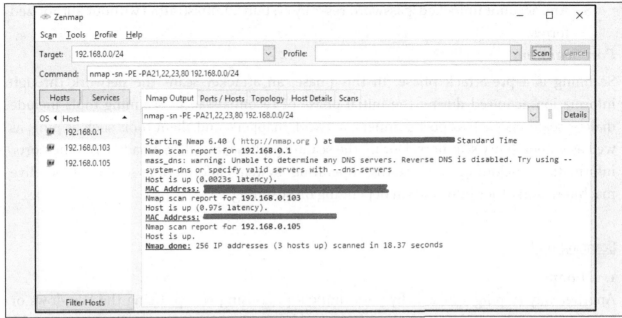

Figure 3-12: Nmap

Nmap, in a nutshell, offers host discovery, port discovery, service discovery, version information of an operating system, hardware address (MAC) information, service version detection, vulnerabilities, and exploit detection using the Nmap Scripting Engine (NSE).

Note
Nmap Scripting engine is the most powerful engine for network discovery, version detection, vulnerability detection, and backdoor detection.

Vulnerability Scanning

Vulnerability scanning is a security technique used to identify security weaknesses in a computer system. Vulnerability scanning can be used by individuals or network administrators for security purposes, or can be used by hackers.

No particular vulnerability scanner works for every aspect of the infrastructure. There are variety of vulnerability scanners used for the specific purpose of the organization. Some of them are described here:

Patch Management

Patches and Hotfixes are used to remove vulnerabilities, bugs, and issues in a software release. Hotfixes are updates that fix these issues, whereas patches are pieces of software specially designed for fixing an issue. A hotfix is referred to as a hot system, specially designed for a live production environment where fixes are made outside normal development and testing is done to address the issue.

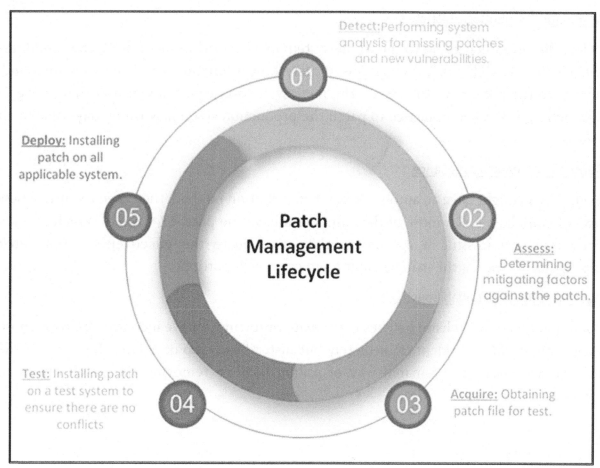

Figure 3-13: Patch Management

Patches must be downloaded from official websites, home sites, and application and operating system vendors. To receive alerts about the latest issues and patches, registering or subscribing is recommended.

These patches can be downloaded in the following ways:

- Manual Download from a Vendor
- Auto-Update

Patch management is an automated process that ensures the installation of necessary patches on a system. The patch management process detects the missing security patches, finds a solution, downloads the patch, tests the patch in an isolated environment, i.e., testing machine, and then deploys the patch onto the system.

Automatic Detection and Download of New Patches

Detection and downloading should occur at least once per day. The system should be monitored by the detection of patches so that it is notified if detection or downloading is not functional.

Automatic Distribution of Patches

Before distributing patches to the whole system in a lab environment, first, check and test the releases of patches on a few systems. If everything is functional and no issues are found, distribute the patches to the rest of the non-production environment and then move to production. It is a good practice to patch the production systems within 7 days of a patch release.

Reporting on Patch Compliance

Even if users might have an automatic patch distribution method, they need a way to assess overall compliance. Do 100% of the computers have the patch? Or 90%? Which specific computers are missing a specific patch? To evaluate the effectiveness of a patch management system, the management team can use Reporting.

Automatic Rollback Capabilities

Sometimes, vendors release patches that create problems or have incompatibilities. Those issues might not be evident immediately but instead show up days later. Ensure that the environment has an automated way of rolling back or removing the patch across all systems.

Reviewing Baselines

The only way to know when an issue is brewing on the network is to know how things work when all is well with the network. The facility to create a baseline is a part of any proper performance monitor: a log of performance indicators, also known as metric, such as CPU usage, network usage, and other values is used to give a picture of the network and servers when they are working properly. Reviewing baselines allows discovering any major modification in these values, which can point to issues on a server or the network as a whole.

Microsoft Baseline Security Analyzer (MBSA):

MBSA is designed to test individual systems. It is old technology, but still does a great job of testing Microsoft Windows system for vulnerabilities.

Procedure:
MBSA is capable of scanning a local system, remote system, and range of the computers.

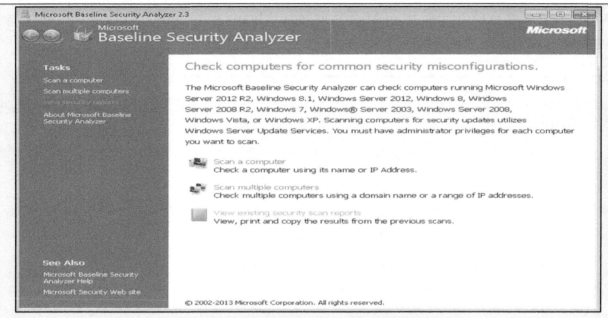

Figure 3-14: Microsoft Baseline Security Analyzer

Select the scanning options as required.

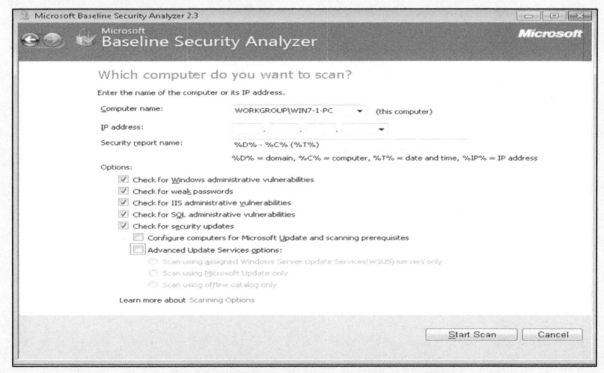

Figure 3-15: Scanning Local System Using MBSA

MBSA will first get updates from Microsoft, scan them, and then download the security updates.

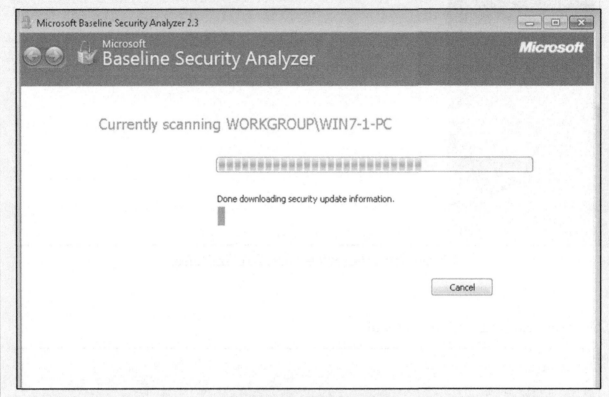

Figure 3-16: MBSA Scanning

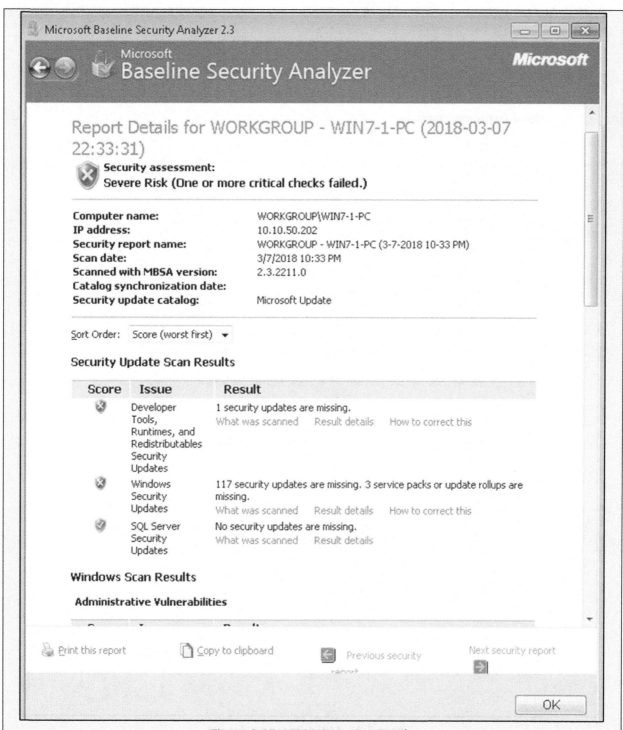

Figure 3-17: MBSA Scanning Results

In the above figure, the MBSA scanning shows **Security Update Scan Results**. Security update scan results are categorized by issue and the results show a number of missing updates.

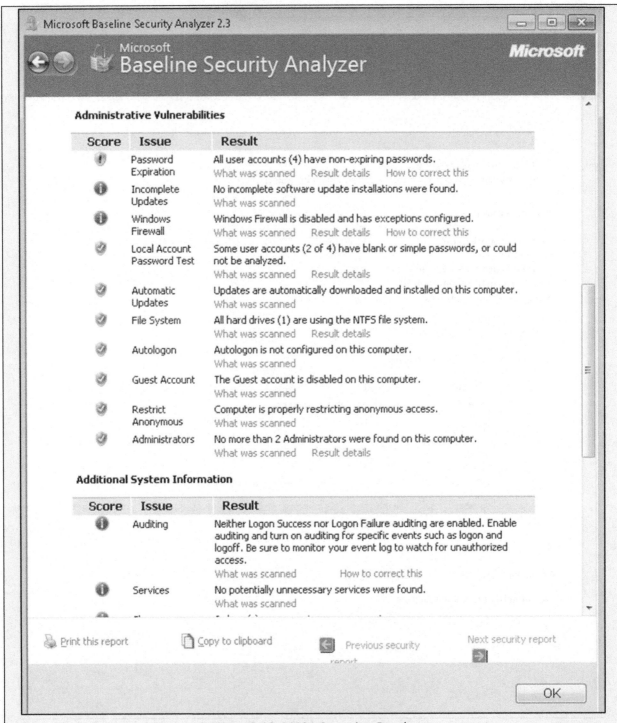

Figure 3-18: MBSA Scanning Results

In the figure above, the MBSA Scanning results shows **Administrative Vulnerabilities**. Vulnerabilities can be password expiry, updates, firewall issues, accounts, etc.

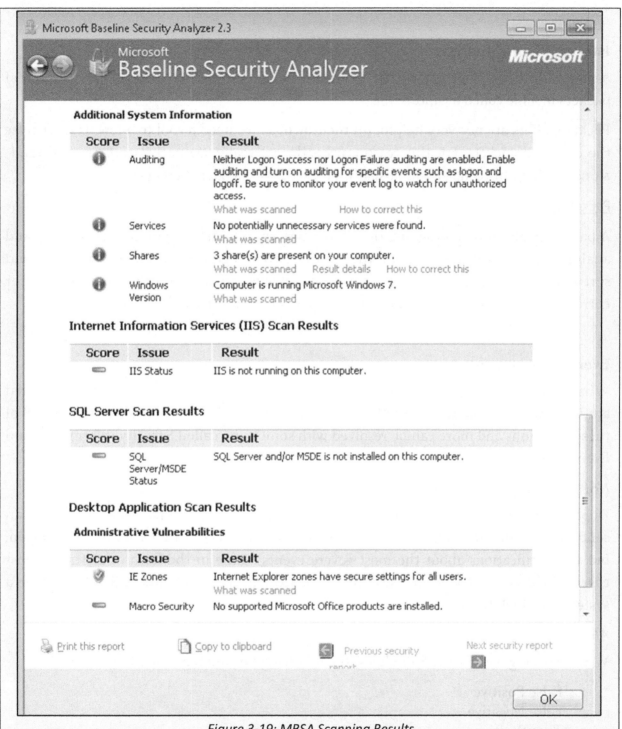

Figure 3-19: MBSA Scanning Results

In the above figure, the MBSA scanning results show **System Information; IIS Scan Results, SQL Server Results, and Desktop Application Results**.

Packet / Traffic Analysis

A packet sniffer is a program that queries a network interface and collects (captures) packets in a file called a capture file.

Packet sniffers are not very helpful on their own, as we need a tool to allow us to analyze the captured packets. For this reason, users do not really see packet sniffers as a stand-alone product. Instead, they are usually packaged with a packet analyzer.

Packet Analyzers

A packet analyzer is a program that processes capture files from packet sniffers and analyzes them based on the monitoring requirements. A good packet analyzer can file and sort a capture file based on almost anything and generate an output to assist us monitor correctly. In other words, a packet analyzer performs packet/traffic analysis.

Event Management

What happened on the network? Where do we have to look? Can we be notified automatically the next time something like this happens? What will trigger an alert? All of these questions and more can be resolved with something called Security Information and Event Management (SIEM).

Notifications

Depending on the severity of analyzed and correlated events, SIEM systems can send notifications and alerts. Notifications can inform users of various events that happen, but the notifications about the most severe events, come in the form of alerts. In most cases, when an alert comes in, a user must acknowledge it, before proceeding to work on a system on which the alert came.

Alerts

When working with IPS/IDS modules, the following terminologies are often used:

1. False Positive
2. False Negative
3. True Positive
4. True Negative

False Positive

A false positive is a situation when the sensor generates an alert about the traffic, which is not malicious, but requires serious attention as long as security is concerned. False positive

can be easily identified, as immediate alerts are generated for this and they can be easily viewed.

False Negative

A false negative is a situation when something malicious is introduced in a network and IPS/IDS sensor cannot generate any alert due to some unforeseen reasons. In this case, some extra tools and techniques are required to get updates related to such situations like Syslog messages from routers.

True Positive

A true positive means that a malicious activity is detected by the IPS module or sensor and an alert has been generated for this. Depending on the configuration of IPS, it may be dropped at the first place.

True Negative

A true negative means that general traffic, i.e., without having anything malicious has been detected by IPS/IDS sensor and no alert has been generated for this.

The Security Information and Event Management (SIEM) is the primary tool used to comfort the correlation of data across dissimilar sources. Correlation of security-related data is the primary utility provided by the SIEM. The goal of data correlation is to understand the context better to arrive at a greater understanding of risk within the organization due to activities being noted across various security platforms. While SIEMs typically come with some built-in alerts that look for particular correlated data, custom correlation rules can typically be created to enhance the built-in capabilities. Since many companies deploy a SIEM solution to centralize the log data and make it simpler to work with. For example, suppose users were looking for failed logon attempts on web servers. They could individually look through the logs on each web server. However, if users have a SIEM solution, they can go to a portal and look across all web servers with a single query. A SIEM is a vital technology in large and security- conscious organizations.

Some popular SIEM options include:

- ArcSight Express

- McAfee ESM (Enterprise Security Manager)

- IBM Security QRadar

- Splunk Enterprise Software or Virtual Machines

- LogRhythm's appliance, Software and Virtual Machines

Some common features offered by SIEM are:

Logging Device

SIEM is a centralized logging device.

Common Database

Collects data from all the devices and brings it to a single database.

Security Alerts

It can also provide security alerts as the user is getting real-time information.

Storage

The storage of SIEM is long term.

Data Correlation

SIEM also includes additional feature of data correlation.

SIEM provides reports on security-related events and incidents like failed and successful logins, malicious activities, etc. It sends alerts if analysis shows any that activity runs against pre-determined rule sets and thus indicates a potential security issue.

Challenges

One of the most occurring challenge during log collection against all the devices that are connected to a network like switches, workstations, routers, servers, etc. is *Time Synchronization*.

Every device has its own clock, and if the user wants to synchronize all the devices to a single clock, then a standard protocol is required that is NTP (Network Time Protocol). This allows all the devices to automatically synchronize all the clocks to one single clock. It is a flexible and accurate method.

Log Transfer

It is a standard method to transfer logs between devices to gather log data from the devices. There is a central receiver, which is often integrated into a SIEM.

An organization that is focused on the security of logs and needs storage method that cannot be changed uses WORM device technology which, in short, protects important security logs. *Example*: DVD-R

SNMP Monitors

Some management of network devices requires the use of the Simple Network Management Protocol (SNMP). SNMP is commonly used to remotely manage (configure and/or monitor) a remote networking device.

SNMP is made up of three components:

- **Network Management Station (NMS)-** This device manages agents, and sometimes referred to as the manager

- **Agent-** This is a device managed by an NMS

- **Management Information Base (MIB)-** This defines how information (configuration, operational, and statistical) is stored on an agent

The interaction is between the NMS and the agent, which can involve two types of connections:

- NMS sends "get" or "set" commands to the agent; get commands are used for retrieving MIB information, and set commands are used to change MIB information

- The agent sends "traps" or "informs" to the NMS, which are a form of log message, indicating an important condition on the device

Information stored on an agent is located in an MIB. Each MIB is uniquely identified with an object identifier (OID). Get, send, and trap messages are based on the MIB information identified by a particular OID.

SNMP Versions

There are three main versions of SNMP: versions 1, 2c, and 3. SNMPv1 and v2c use community strings for security: read-only and read-write. The read-only community string is used to restrict the reading of MIB information, and the read-write community string is used to change MIB information. The main problem with community strings is that they are sent in clear text and thus are susceptible to eavesdropping attacks. SNMPv2c also added the support of inform requests, which allows acknowledged notifications, and get bulk requests, which then allows a management station to access multiple MIBs in one request.

SNMPv3 is an enhancement of SNMPv2c. Besides supporting the same MIB structure and gets, sets, and traps, SNMPv3 also supports authentication, message integrity, and payload encryption. Message integrity is used to ensure that SNMP messages have not been tampered with and are coming from a legitimate source; this is accomplished with the MD5 or SHA-1 HMAC function. Payload encryption is used so that a man in the middle cannot examine the get, set, and trap command information. A man in the middle is basically a

device that sees traffic flowing between the source and destination. Encryption can be used to defeat man-in-the-middle attacks: the attacker can still see the packets, but the content is encrypted from eavesdropping. Encryption is accomplished with the DES, 3DES, or AES encryption algorithms.

SNMP Version	Level	Authentication	Encryption	What Happens
1	NoAuthNoPriv	Community string	NO	Authentication with community string match
2c	NoAuthNoPriv	Community string	NO	Authentication with community string match
3	NoAuthNoPriv	Username	NO	Authentication with a username
3	AuthNoPriv	MD5 or SHA	NO	Provides MD5/SHA for authentication
3	AuthPriv	MD5 or SHA	DES,3DES or AES	Provides MD5/SHA for authentication and encryption via DES/3DES/AES

Table 3-02: SNMP Versions

Metrics

Metrics are the measure of performance by quantitative assessment of the process. In computer networking, route metrics are used for best path selection and preference. Routing decisions are based on metrics. A router metric is typically based on information such as path length, bandwidth, load, hop count, path cost, delay, Maximum Transmission Unit (MTU), reliability and communications cost.

Error Rate

In digital transmission, Bit Error is the number of altered bits in a bit stream due to interference, distortion or bit synchronization. Bit Error Rate (BER) is the number of bit errors per unit time.

Error detection is the process of detecting the error during the transmission between the sender and the receiver.

Types of Error Detection

- Parity checking
- Cyclic Redundancy Check (CRC)
- Checksum

Utilization

Network utilization is measure or ratio of current and maximum network traffic or load. For example, the ratio of current and maximum traffic on a port determines the utilization of port capacity. With network utilization monitoring, a network administrator determines the busy, normal or idleness of the network. It is also an important aspect to troubleshoot congestion and bottlenecks in the network to improve network performance.

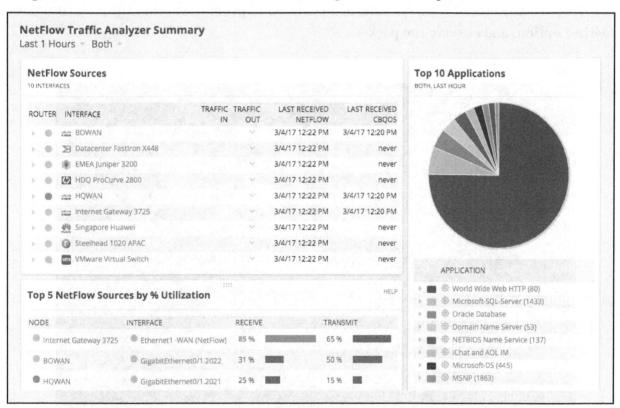

Figure 3-20: Solarwinds NetFlow Traffic Analyzer

Following are some network traffic analyzers:

- Solarwinds Network Traffic Analyzer
- Solarwinds Real-Time Bandwidth Monitor
- PRTG Network Monitor
- ManageEngine
- nTop-Ng
- Cacti

- BandwidthD

Packet Drops

Packet loss is the condition of the network when it is dropping the packets while transmission. Packet loss reduces the reliability of the link and becomes the most important task for the network administrator. The primary cause of packet drop is insufficient network bandwidth and congestion in the network. Solarwind offers "**Packet Loss Monitoring Tool**" for monitoring baseline network performance. Similarly, there are several tools available for network monitoring and performance assessment. Apart from software-based tools, there are some network commands that helps users to identify the packet loss between source to destination.

In Windows based operating systems, open command prompt, execute the ping command with -t option, and observe the packets.

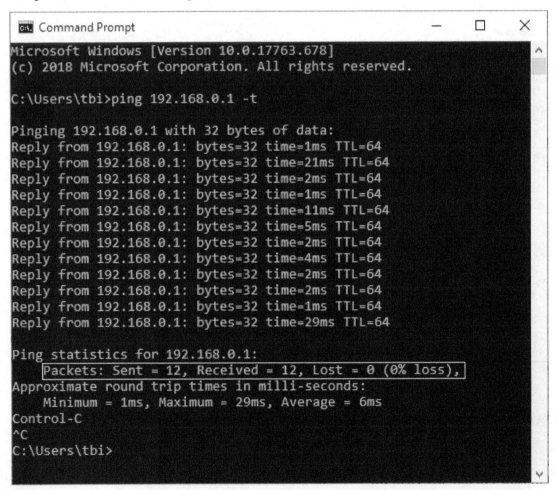

Figure 3-21: Executing the Ping Command with "-t" Option

Bandwidth/Throughput

There are several bandwidth-monitoring tools for comprehensive network bandwidth analysis and performance monitoring. These tools helps to detect and diagnose the issues, response time tracking, uptime of network devices, observation of network traffic pattern and much more.

Mind Map of Scanning, Monitoring & Patching

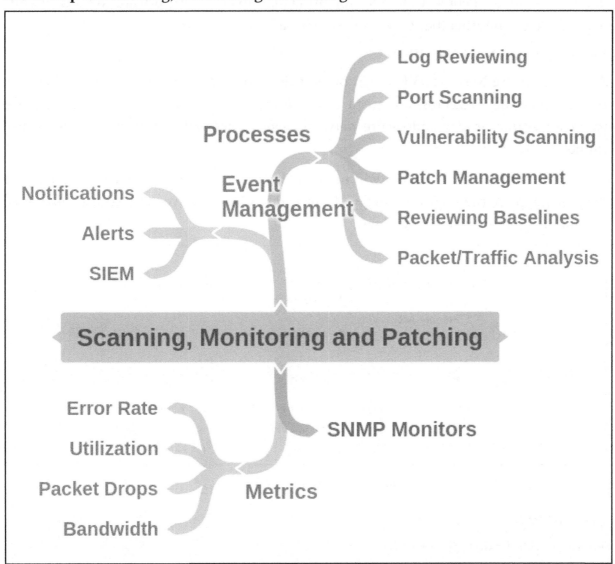

Figure 3-22: Mind Map of Scanning, Monitoring and Patching Processes

Remote Access Methods

Remote connections have been around for a long time, even before the internet existed. The greatest drawback to remote connections was the cost to connect. The only connection option was a telephone, when users were on one side of the continent and had to connect to the LAN on the other side of the continent. Alternatively, if users required connecting two LANs across the continent, they ended up paying outrageous monthly charges for a private connection. Internet introduction gave individuals an alternative to connect to their home or work networks, but there was one issue, the entire internet was (and still is) open to the public. People wanted to stop using dial-up and costly private connections and instead use the internet, but they wanted to be able to do it securely.

Virtual Private Network (VPN)

A Virtual Private Network (VPN) can be best described as an encrypted tunnel between two computer devices across an insecure network such as the internet. A VPN is designed to create virtual private and secure networks using encapsulation protocol, also called tunneling protocol.

VPNs provide impressive flexibility in network infrastructure and a reduced total amount of ownership in the WAN topology. It provides cost-effective and secure encrypted communication upon the leased lines.

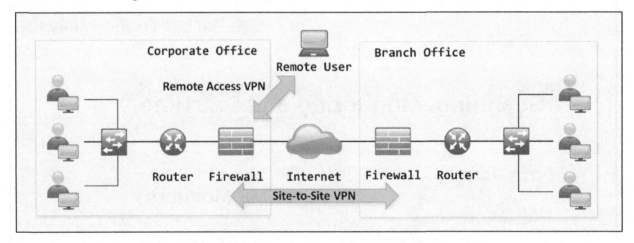

Figure 3-23: Virtual Private Network

Types of VPNs

There are two basic types of VPNs:

1) Remote Access VPN
2) Site-to-Site VPN

<u>Remote Access VPN</u>

Remote access VPN allows the users to connect to a private network and access its services remotely. The connection is secure and private between the user and the private network even though it is built on the internet. It is useful for business and home users.

<u>Site-to-Site VPN</u>

A Site-to-Site VPN is also called a Server-to-Server VPN and is mainly used in corporate fields. Enterprises with branch offices in different geographical locations use site-to-site VPNs to connect the network of one branch office to another branch office. Site-to-site VPNs practically provide a virtual bridge between the enterprises and their geographically distant site offices.

<u>Client-to-Site VPN</u>

A client software is used to link a single faraway computer to a remote network. This generates a typical host-to-site or client-to-site connection.

In a client-to-site case, individual clients (such as telecommuters or travelers) link to the network remotely. Each client must have VPN client software installed, because each client makes a direct connection to the network.

VPN Protocols

The types mentioned above of VPNs are based on different security protocols. Each of these has individual features and security levels.

<u>IPSec</u>

Internet Protocol Security (IPSec) provides secure internet communication over an IP network. Practically, IPSec can be used to provide secure communication on all TCP/IP related communications.

IPSec provides three main security services:

- **Data Verification**: Verifies whether the data received is surely from the intended receiver
- **Protection from Data Manipulating**: Protects the data from being changeable during the transmission
- **Privacy of Transactions:** Ensures the transmitted data is readable only by the intended receiver

IPSec has two main modes:

1) **Transport Mode:** Used to send and receive encrypted data packets among same networks.
2) **Tunneling Mode**: Used to send and receive encrypted data among different networks.

GRE

Generic Routing Encapsulation (GRE) is a protocol used to encapsulate many network layer protocols that have to be sent on point-to-point links in IP network.

It encapsulates the original payload into an outer packet that is sent through the tunnel. GRE is a flexible tool that can be used to send multicast and IPV6 packets.

SSL/ TLS/DTLS

Secure Socket Layer (SSL) protocol is used to provide secure authentication and communication privacy over the Internet. SSL protocol uses cryptography technique and is usually used in e-commerce for online shopping websites and service providers. SSL connections appear with "https" instead of "http" in the URL.

Clients connect to the VPN server using a standard Web browser, with the traffic secured using Transport Layer Security (TLS). TLS replaced SSL several years ago, but the SSL VPN stuck. The two most common kinds of SSL VPNs are SSL portal VPNs and SSL tunnel VPNs.

With SSL portal VPNs, a client who accesses the VPN is presented with a secure web page. The client gains access to anything related on that page, be it emails, information, links to other pages, and so on.

Datagram TLS (DTLS) VPNs optimize connections for applications that are sensitive to delay, such as voice and video over a VPN. After generating a traditional TLS tunnel, DTLS VPNs use UDP datagrams instead of TCP sections to communicate. This improves some kinds of VPN traffic. Cisco AnyConnect DTLS VPN is the prototype instance of this kind of VPN application.

PTP/PPTP

Point-to-Point Tunneling Protocol (PPTP) is used to create a secure tunnel between the two points on a network. It is implemented on other protocol specifically on Point-to-Point Protocol (PPP).

PPTP cannot authenticate some tunnels, but Layer 2 Tunneling Point (L2TP) can. That is why it has been highly replaced by L2TP.

Remote Access Service (RAS)

Remote Access Service (RAS) is a remote access solution that is compatible with MS Windows server products. RAS enables users to access the same service at the same time from remote locations, yet sometimes the access is very slow.

RAS has been implemented in Windows NT server as RAS server but in Windows server 2000, 2003, and 2008, it is implemented as Routing and Remote Access Server (RRAS). It can provide dial-up connections using the modem as well as VPN connections using WAN mini ports.

Remote Desktop Protocol (RDP)

Citrix made a product breakthrough — so powerful that Microsoft licensed the Citrix code and created its own Windows Terminal Services product. Microsoft then created its own standard called Remote Desktop Protocol (RDP) without wanting to pay Citrix any more money.

A server and a client are required for remote terminal programs. The server is the PC to be controlled. The client is the PC from which users do the controlling. Citrix created a standard called Independent Computing Architecture (ICA) that describes how terminal data was passed between the server and the client.

Consider a scenario where the network administrator having the IP address 192.168.0.132 has to access the remote user's laptop having IP address 192.168.0.126. Firstly, the administrator has to allow the RDP connection from the user's machine.

Enabling Remote Desktop Connection on User's PC

Open the properties of user's PC as shown in the figure below:

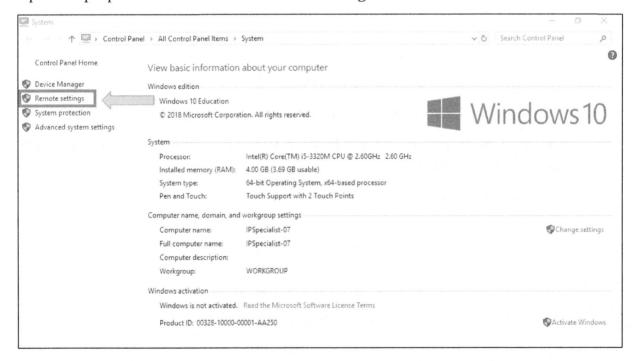

Figure 3-24: Enabling Remote Desktop Connection on User's PC

Now enable the remote access connection to this PC. Remote Desktop protocol also offers network level authentication by specifying users.

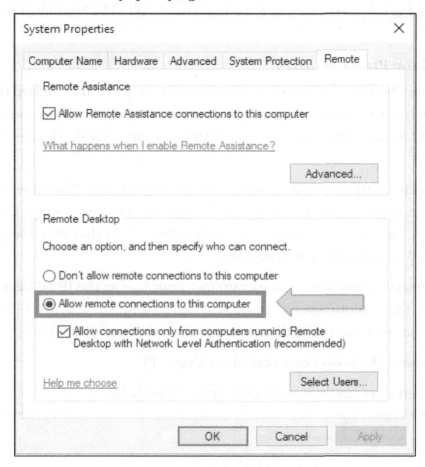

Figure 3-25: System Properties' Tab

Connecting Remote Desktop from Administrator's PC

Now, go to start menu and search for Remote Desktop Connection application. This application is built-in Windows.

Enter the User's IP address.

Figure 3-26: Remote Desktop Connection

Then, click the "**Show Options**" dropdown.

Figure 3-27: General Tab

Enter the Username of target's PC and click the "**Connect**" button.

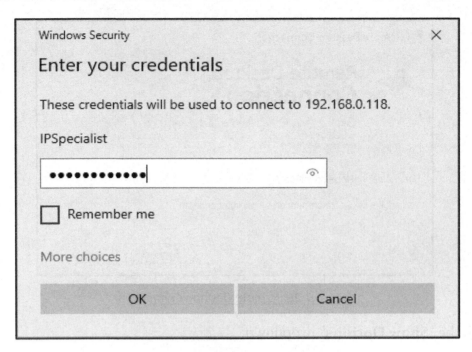

Figure 3-28: Windows Security

Enter the password and click the "OK" button.

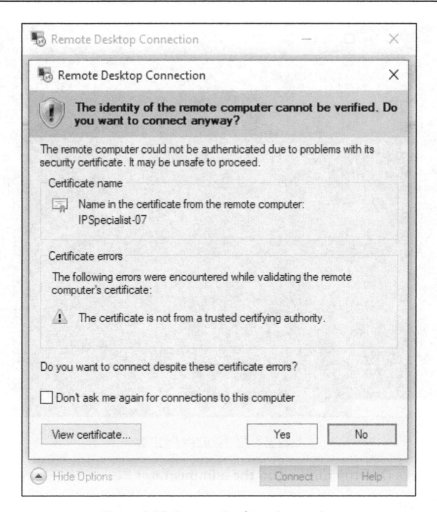

Figure 3-29: Remote Desktop Connection

If there is no certificate from the trusted authority, it will ask you whether proceed or not. Click "Yes" to continue.

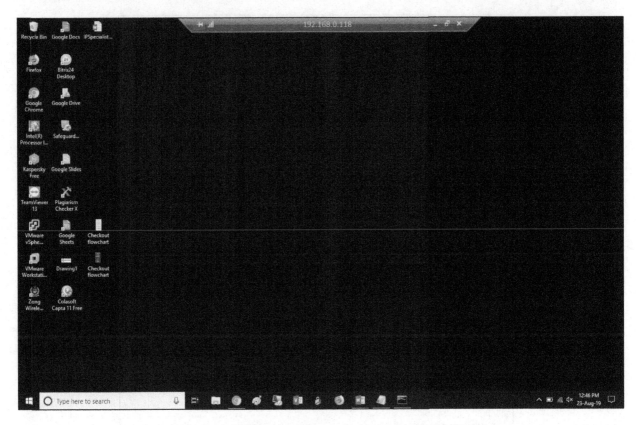

Figure 3-30: Target's Desktop

This is the target's Desktop running on the administrator PC.

Secure Shell (SSH)

SSH was originally created as a tunneling protocol for UNIX/Linux systems. It uses encryption to set up a secure connection between two systems and gives alternative, security-equivalent applications for utilities such as Telnet, File Transfer Protocol (FTP), Trivial File Transfer Protocol (TFTP), and other communications-oriented applications. It is the preferred way of security for Telnet and other clear-text-oriented programs in the UNIX/Linux environment, although it is available with Windows and other operating systems. SSH uses port 22 and TCP for connections.

Let's implement SSH on the Cisco router shown in the topology diagram below.

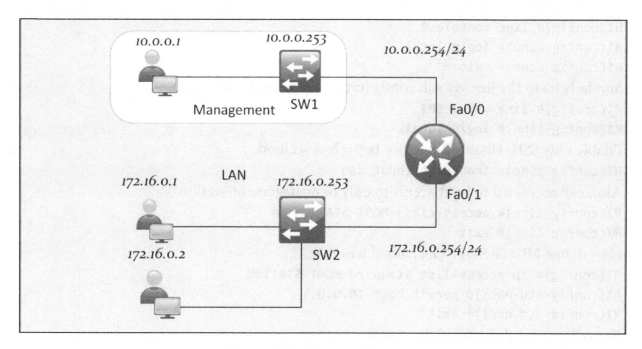

Figure 3-31: Topology Diagram

Let's assume that management station has an IP address of *10.0.0.1*. As Cisco devices come with no configurations, we need to access the device via console port for the first time to implement the concepts defined above.

R1:
Enter the level 15 by entering enable on user privilege mode.

```
R1> enable
```

Enter configure terminal to enter the global configuration mode.

```
R1# configure terminal
```

Use enable secret command to set the level 15 password.

Use long string of password with multiple character types.

```
R1(config)# enable secret P@$$word:10
```

Define a username and password with associated privilege level.

```
R1(config)# username IPSpecialist privilege 1 secret P@$$word:10
```

Set the hostname of your choice.

```
R1(config)# hostname R1
```

Set the domain name and RSA for SSH.

```
R1(config)# ip domain name IPSpecialist.net
R1(config)# crypto key generate rsa general-keys modulus 1024
```

Set the SSH version to 2.

```
R1(config)# ip ssh version 2
```

Go to the line console sub configuration mode to set authentication.

```
R1(config)# line console 0
R1(config-line)# login local
R1(config-line)# exit
```
Similarly go to the line vty sub configuration mode to do the same.
```
R1(config)# line vty 0 903
R1(config-line)# login local
```
Enable only SSH. Disable Telnet for being less secured.
```
R1(config-line)# transport input ssh
```
Also, call access list to limit access to only to management-station.
```
R1(config-line)# access-class MGMT-STATION in
R1(config-line)# exit
```
Now define MGMT-STATION named based ACL.
```
R1(config)# ip access-list standard MGMT-STATION
R1(config-std-nacl)# permit host 10.0.0.1
R1(config-std-nacl)# exit
```
Go to line aux sub configuration mode.
```
R1(config-line)# line aux 0
R1(config-line)# login local
```

Verification:

Open PuTTY on management PC. Enter router's IP address. Management PC should be able to access the router through SSH.

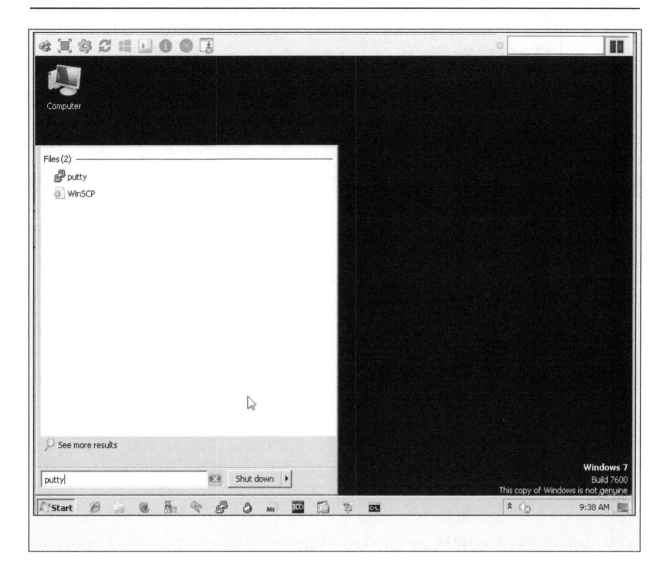

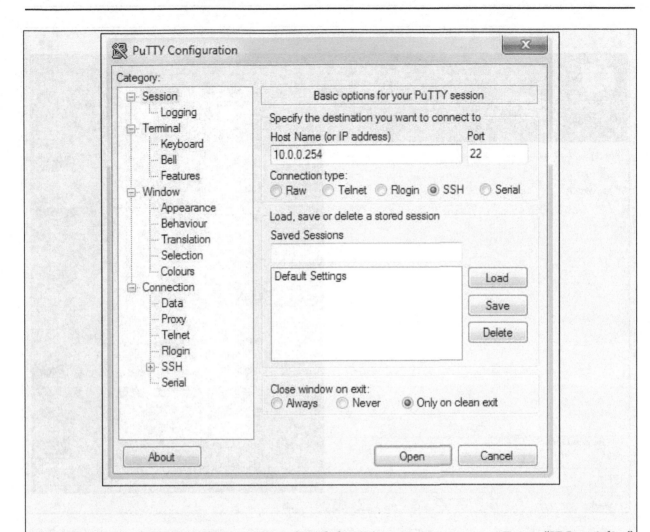

Click "Open" and users will be prompted with login username prompt. Enter "IPSpecialist" as username and "P@$$word:10" as password. Users will also be prompted with Putty security alert. Click "Yes" to continue.

After entering the username and password, you should get Level 1 access. Enter Level 15 by entering "enable command" and providing the above-defined password.

```
10.0.0.254 - PuTTY

login as: IPSPecialist
Using keyboard-interactive authentication.
Password:

R1>en
Password:
R1#
```

VNC

Virtual Network Computing (VNC) allows remote login, in which clients can access their own desktops while being physically away from their PCs. By default, it uses port 5900 and it is not considered overly secure. It works in Secure Shell (SSH) tunnels for great security, by default it comes with every copy of MacOS and almost every Linux distro.

VNC server application must be installed on the system users want to access whereas, VNC viewer application is to be installed on the machine that the users are accessing from.

Once the VNC server is successfully installed on target server, the application should look like the figure below:

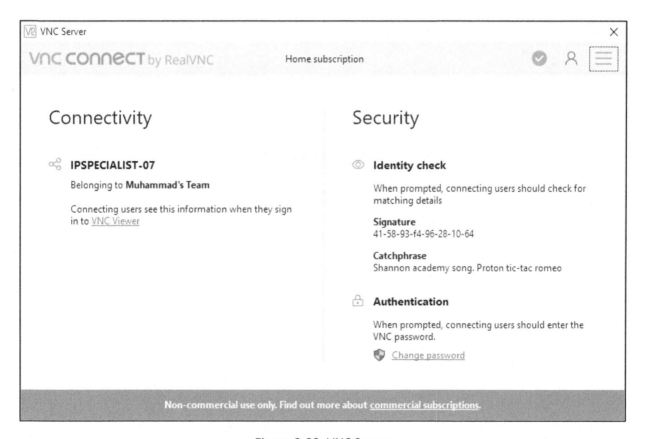

Figure 3-32: VNC Server

Now, login to PC. Open VNC viewer application to connect it to remote PC.

Figure 3-33: VNC Viewer

Sign in to the VNC viewer with the same login credentials used for VNC server application.

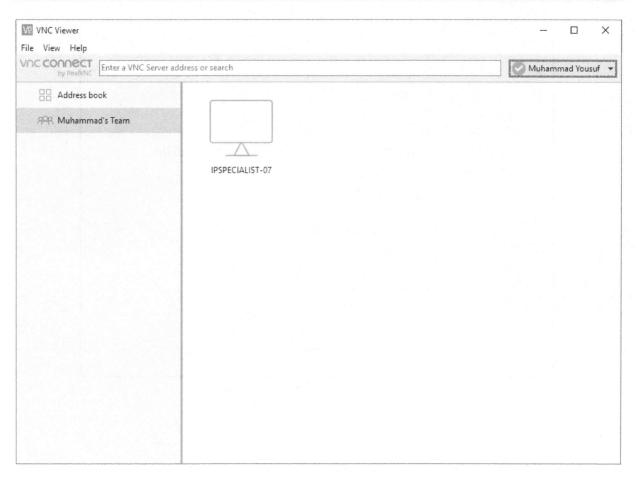

Figure 3-34: VNC Viewer

If you have logged in successfully on VNC Server and Viewer application, it will automatically detect the server(s). Now click on the server detected.

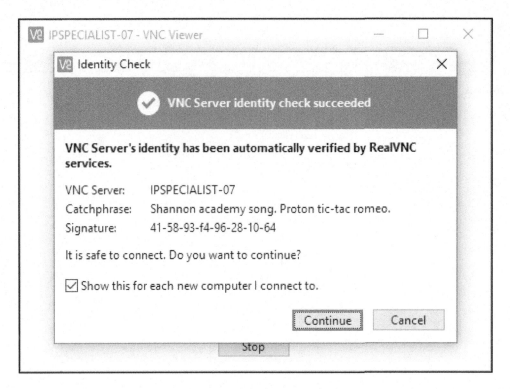

Figure 3-35: VNC Server

Click "Continue".

Figure 3-36: Authentication

Enter the login password you had setup while installing the VNC server. Upon successful login, target machine will be on the desktop.

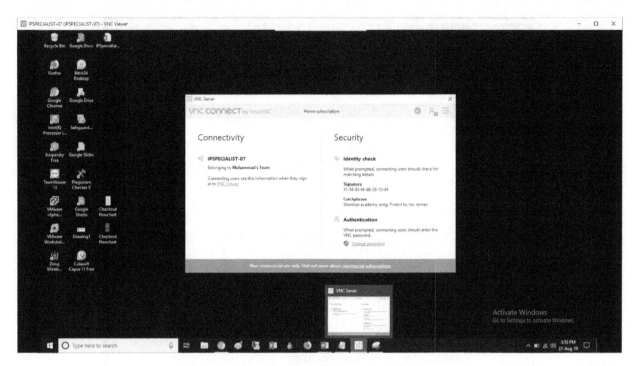

Figure 3-37: Successful Login to Target Machine

Telnet

Telnet allows sessions to be opened on a remote host and is one of the oldest TCP/IP protocols still in use today. Telnet is blocked due to the issues with security on most systems, and SSH is considered a secure option to Telnet that allows secure sessions to be opened on the remote host.

To connect a device using Telnet connection, Putty can be used as for SSH. All users have to do is set connection type as Telnet.

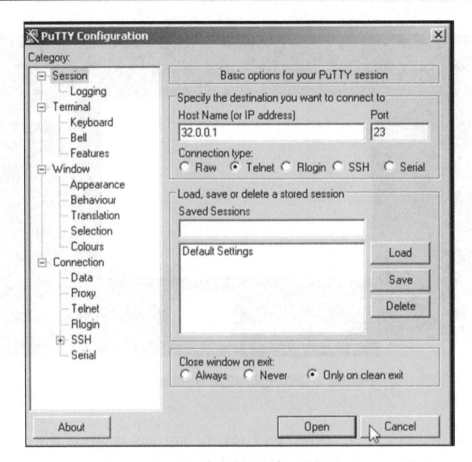

Figure 3-38: Putty Configuration

By putting the correct login username and password, users will be able to get access to the CLI of the remote device.

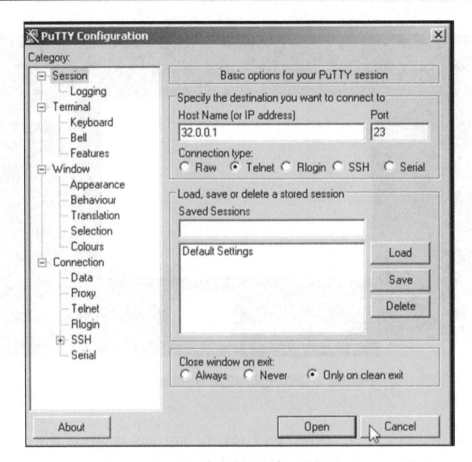

Real World Scenario

Background

Telnet is a protocol developed in 1969 that provides a command-line interface for communication with a remote device or server. Telnet is sometimes used for remote management or the initial setup of network hardware. It can also be used to test or troubleshoot remote web or mail servers, as well as for accessing remote MUDs (multi-user dungeon games) and trusted internal networks. Telnet is used in modern PCs to connect remotely to another computer via the command line Telnet runs on TCP port 23, enabling users to connect to a Telnet server and run commands on that server.

Challenges

Telnet, a TCP/IP protocol for accessing remote computers, remains one of the most dangerous services that users can expose to the internet. In fact, Cisco released Cisco Security Advisory: Cisco Telnet Denial of Service Vulnerability on Aug. 27, 2004.

This advisory stated that a remote attacker could send packets to TCP 23 (Telnet port) or reverse Telnet ports TCP 2001 to 2999, 3001 to 3099, 6001 to 6999, and 7001 to 7099. These packets would cause a denial-of-service condition and cause network devices to refuse any further connection attempts to the Telnet, reverse Telnet, SSH, SCP, RSH, and HTTP remote management services.

Solution

Cisco Systems has released Security Advisory 61671, "Cisco Telnet Denial of Service Vulnerability," to address the vulnerability and recommends that affected users immediately apply the appropriate patch available via normal update channels.

Conclusion

Telnet is not secure; it passes all data in clear text. If you must use Telnet to manage network devices, then you should at least add an access list to the router to restrict access to the virtual terminal (vty) lines.

HTTPS/Management URL

Hypertext Transfer Protocol Secure (HTTPS) is the protocol used for "secure" web pages that should be seen by customers when entering private information such as credit card numbers, passwords and other identifiers. It combines HTTP with SSL/TLS to provide

encrypted communication. The default port is 443 and instead of http://, the URL begins with https://.

This is the common protocol used for management URLs to perform tasks such as checking server status, changing router settings, and so on.

Following are some characteristics of HTTPS:

- Hypertext Transfer Protocol Secure (HTTPS) is an extension of the Hypertext Transfer Protocol (HTTP)
- It is used for secure communications
- In HTTPS, the communication protocol is encrypted using Transport Layer Security (TLS)
- It protects against man-in-the-middle attacks
- The bidirectional encryption of communications between a client and server protects against eavesdropping and tampering of the communication
- X.509 certificates are used to authenticate the server
- HTTPS URLs begin with "https://" and use port 443 by default, whereas HTTP URLs begin with "http://" and use port 80 by default

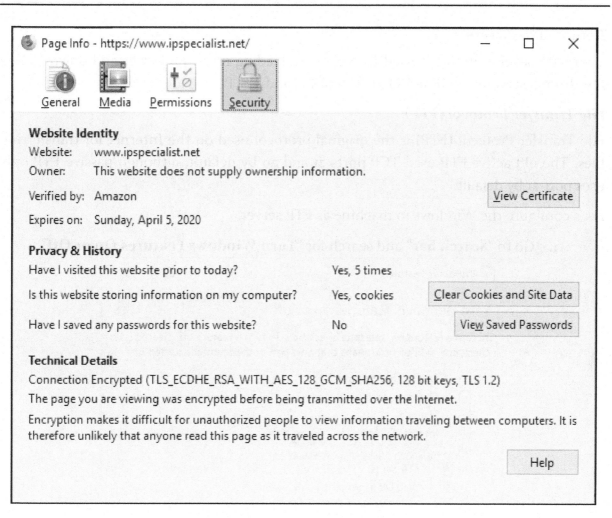

Figure 3-39: Management URL

Remote File Access

There are several protocols used for simply uploading files to a server and downloading files from a server, including FTP, FTPS, SFTP, and TFTP.

File Transfer Protocol (FTP)

File Transfer Protocol (FTP) is the original protocol used on the Internet for transferring files. The old active FTP used TCP ports 21 and 20 by default, although passive FTP only uses port 21 by default.

Let's configure the Windows 10 machine as FTP server.

1. Go to "**Search bar**" and search for "**Turn Windows Features On or Off**".

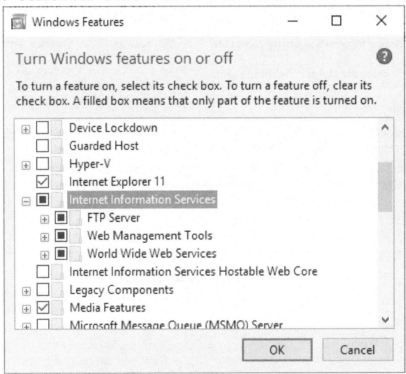

Figure 3-40: Windows Features Tab

2. Select "**Internet Information Services**" enable "**FTP Server**".
3. Now, go to "**Control Panel**" > "**System and Security**" > "**Windows Defender Firewall**" > "**Allows App**". Allow the FTP Server application on firewall.

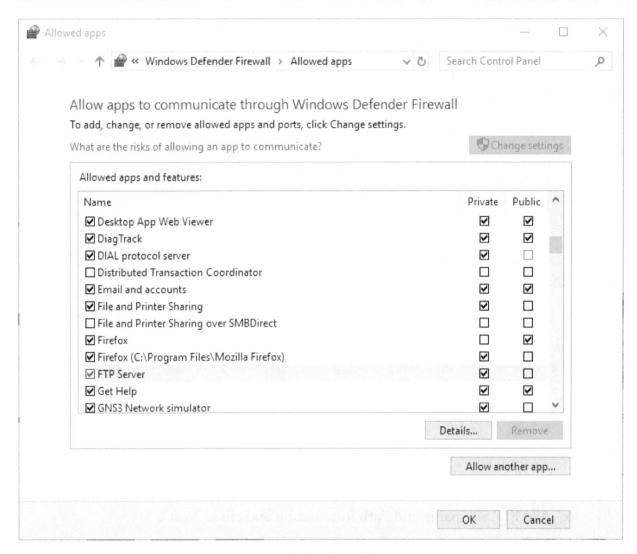

Figure 3-41: Allowed Apps

4. Now, search for "**Internet Information Services (IIS) Manager**".
5. Go to "**Connections**" > "**Sites**" > "**Add FTP Site**".

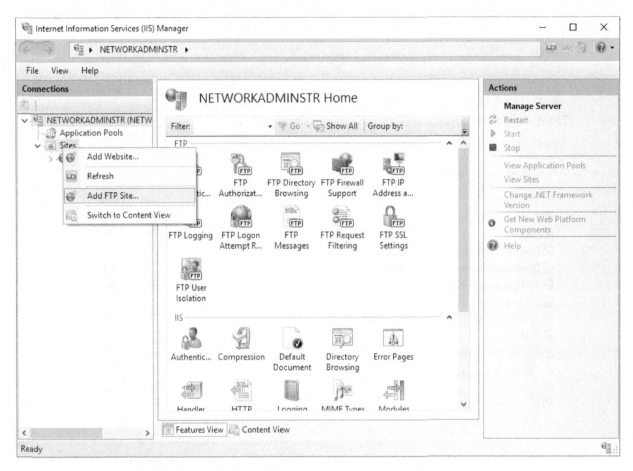

Figure 3-42: Internet Information Services (IIS) Manager

6. Add FTP Site name and Path information and click "Next".

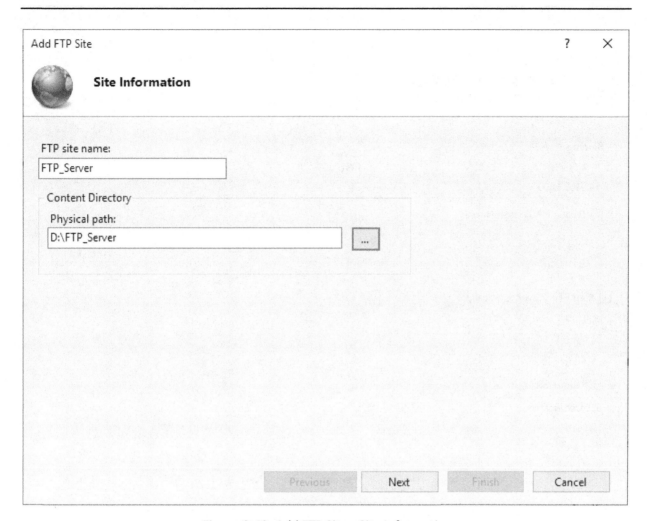

Figure 3-43: Add FTP Sites, Site Information

7. Assign an IP address and associated port details. Virtual Host Name and SSL certificates can be setup here.

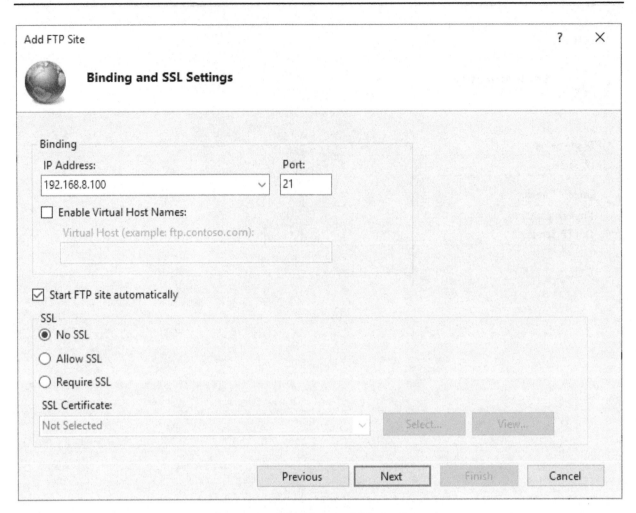

Figure 3-44: Binding and SSL Settings

8. Now, if authentication is required, select "users allowed to access FTP Server". Or else, "anonymous" logins can also be permitted.

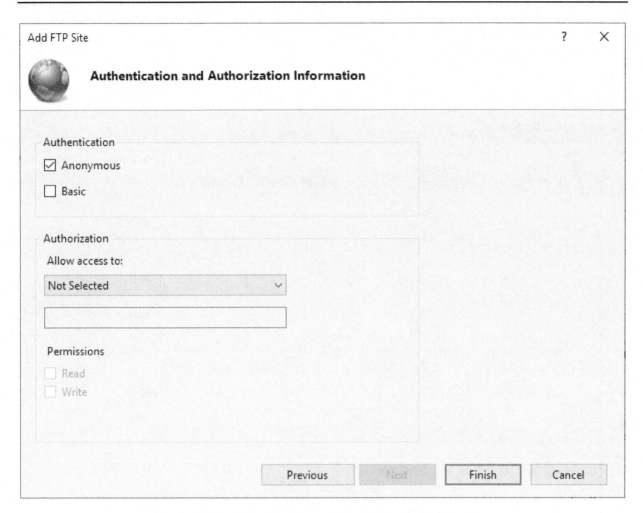

Figure 3-45: Authentication and Authorization Information

9. As shown in the figure below, FTP site is running.

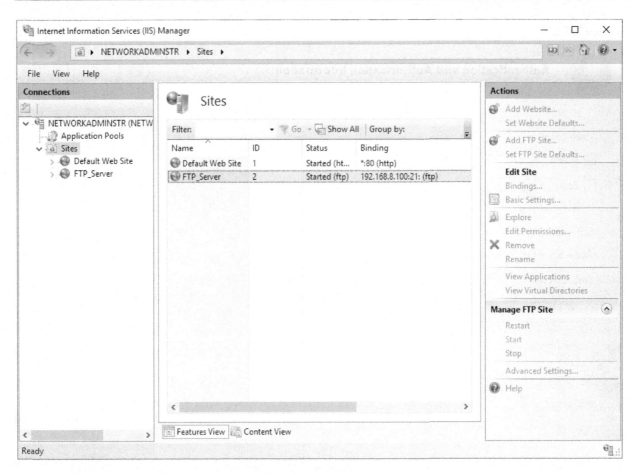

Figure 3-46: FTP Site

10. Now, open FTP application such as WinSCP as shown below to access FTP server.

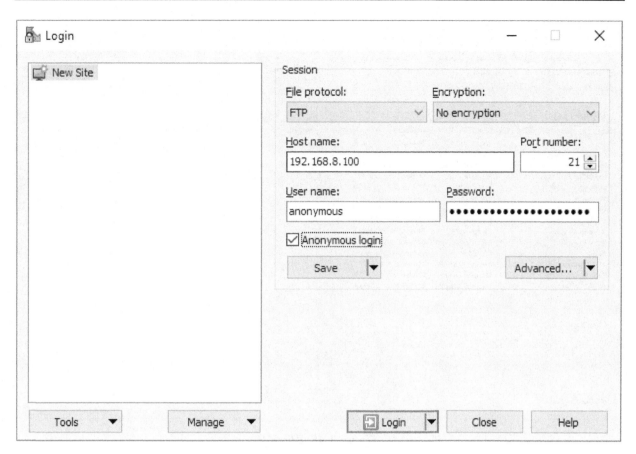

Figure 3-47: Login Tab

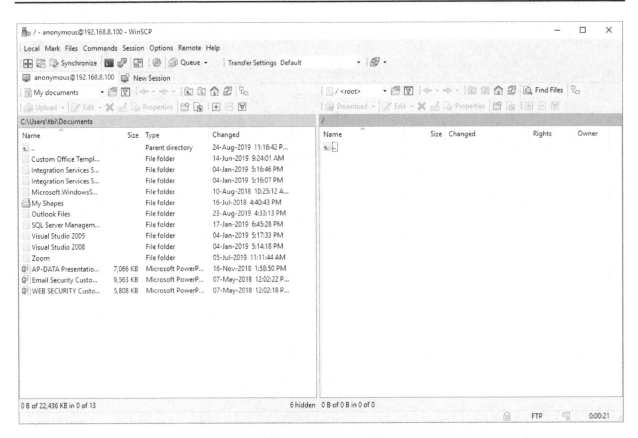

Figure 3-48: WinSCP

Secure File Transfer Protocol (SFTP)

Secure FTP (SFTP), also known as SSH FTP, was designed to replace FTP after discovery of many of the inadequacies of SCP (such as the inability to see the files on the other PC). Although SFTP and FTP have similar names and perform the same task of transferring files, they differ greatly in the manner they do that task.

The introduction of SSH made it simple to secure most TCP applications just by using them in an SSH tunnel. However, FTP is another case. FTP, at least active FTP, uses two ports, 20 and 21, to create a two-session communication. This makes FTP a challenge to operate in its original form over SSH as only one session per tunnel can be handled by SSH. To fix this, a group of programmers from the OpenBSD organization created a sequence of secure programs called OpenSSH. One such program was SFTP. With servers and clients, SFTP looks like FTP but relies on an SSH tunnel. If users are on Windows and would like to link with an SFTP server, WinSCP and FileZilla are two great client options.

Out-of-Band Management

When a dedicated channel is established to manage network devices then it is called out-of-band management. A connection can be set up through a console router, or modem, and this can be used to guarantee management connectivity independent of the status of

in-band network connectivity (which would include serial port connections, VNC, and SSH). Out-of-band management allows the administrator to monitor, access, and manage network infrastructure devices remotely and securely.

Modem

At the back of a router or switch, there is an AUX (short for auxiliary) port close the console port. This port can be used in conjunction with a dial-up modem to provide command-line interface access just as console and SSH connections do.

Console Router

There are several different techniques to establish a connection, but one of the oldest (yet still very common) techniques is to use a special serial connection through a console port of the router.

This sort of connection is unique to Cisco-brand routers, but massive market share of Cisco makes this kind of connection a requirement for anyone who wants to know how to configure routers. There is often some sort of configuration interface for both switches and routers. Both routers and these advanced switches are referred to as managed devices.

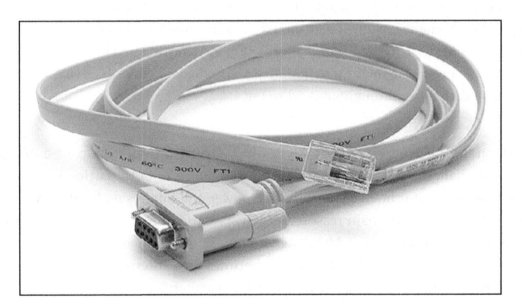

Figure 3-49: Classic Cisco Console Cable

Security Policies

Security policies should be designed and acceptable by the concerned authority members. While designing security policies, it should be kept in mind that the authorized person will have permission to enter the organization and use assets while unauthorized persons will

not have permission to do this. Security policies can be done by locks, cameras, timers, guards, dogs, and so on.

Network Policies

A good network security policy should be, setting a standard of security by establishing access of users to resources, with the least privilege that each user of the network needs to do their job, and that includes the administrators. It will establish local controls and logging mechanisms that can be used in the event of a breach. It will also establish security checks on access to the network from a remote location.

Standard Business Documents

Standard Business Documents do not relate to the security policies but instead, relate to the business. These documents should be easy to understand for the customer that makes the business viable.

The business-related documents that you should understand are the following:

Service Level Agreement (SLA)

A Service-Level Agreement (SLA) is the part of a service contract between a service provider and the customer that fully defines what services are expected and how they are to be accomplished. It might include a contracted delivery time for initial services and then an expectation of Mean Time Between Failures (MTBF) and Mean Time to Repair (MTTR) when a failure occurs. It might also identify a specified quality of service that could be measured by data rates, throughput, and so on.

MOU

A Memorandum of Understanding (MOU) is a formal interpretation of a gentleman's agreement or handshake. It establishes expectation levels of both parties, so as to prevent future arguments, but it holds no enforceable power and implies no legal commitment on behalf of either party. The main reason an MOU is sometimes used is that the two parties are in different countries. An MOU agreement is established to avoid time wasting documents and legal fees. MOUs are also sometimes used internally in an organization to establish the specific responsibilities of various departments regarding a project.

MLA

A Master License Agreement (MLA) is a document created by a software company that defines how their product can be used. It defines the proper use of the software and the liabilities associated with its improper use. It may also define how the software may be modified and who should benefit or be compensated for any profits related to its use. Large software vendors with their customers commonly use MLAs.

SOW

A Statement of Work (SOW) is a formal document that defines the work activities, what is to be delivered, and the timeline associated with its delivery. It usually includes pricing information and payment terms as well. Also, it may include compensation terms to the customer, if the work is not done on time or in a satisfactory manner. A SOW is generally drawn up by an attorney and is a legally enforceable document.

End User Awareness and Training

End users are possibly the main source of security problems for any organization. IT administration must increase end-user awareness and training, so they know how to look after their systems and how to act to avoid attacks. The following training policies are helpful to develop end-user awareness.

Security Policies: End Users need to read, understand, and sign all appropriate security policies when required.

Passwords: Make sure users understand necessary password skills, such as sufficient length and complexity, refreshing passwords regularly, and password control.

System and Workplace Security: Users need to understand how to keep their workstations secure through screen locking and not storing written passwords in plain view.

Social Engineering: Users need to be able to identify typical social-engineering strategies and know how to counter them.

Malware: Users need to be able to recognize and deal with malware attacks.

Single Point of Failure

A Single Point Of Failure, (SPOF) is any component of a system that causes the whole system to stop working if it fails.

Critical Assets - Redundancy

Every organization has assets that are critical to the operation of the organization. Critical assets can include patents/copyrights, corporate financial data, customer sales information, human resource information, proprietary software, scientific research, schematics, and internal manufacturing processes. Critical assets can be identified by using different methods, including risk assessments, asset tracking through a service or hardware inventory, and network traffic monitoring that discloses the most frequently used network and system components.

Critical Nodes

Identifying critical nodes is generally much clearer than identifying critical assets because of the IT nature of critical nodes and the fact that the IT department is always going to be responsive of what nodes are critical.

Critical nodes are unique to IT equipment. Some examples of critical nodes are:

- A file server that contains critical project files
- A single web server
- A single printer
- An edge router

Redundancy

Redundancy means that another component can handle the event when one component fails. This component might be SPOF. A well-designed system will attempt to reduce all single points of failure by redundancy. Redundancy is relatively easy to do, but the trick is to determine where the redundancy is needed to avoid single points of failure without too much complexity, cost, or administration. Redundancy performs this by identifying two things: critical assets and critical nodes. It is beneficial to have redundancy on any critical node, or critical asset.

Adherence to Standards and Policies

Given the importance of company policies and standards; it is also vital for an organization to adhere to standards and policies strictly. For company policies, this can often be a challenge. Standards can be found on the websites maintained by the International Organization for Standardization (ISO) at www.iso.org as well as many others. If users are the decision maker, they can review these standards and then decide what will be done for the specific organizational needs.

 Exam Tip

The protocols described in this chapter enable access to remote systems and enable users to run applications on the system, using that system's resources. Only the user interface, keystrokes, and mouse movements transfer between the client system and the remote computer.

Mind Map of Remote Access Methods

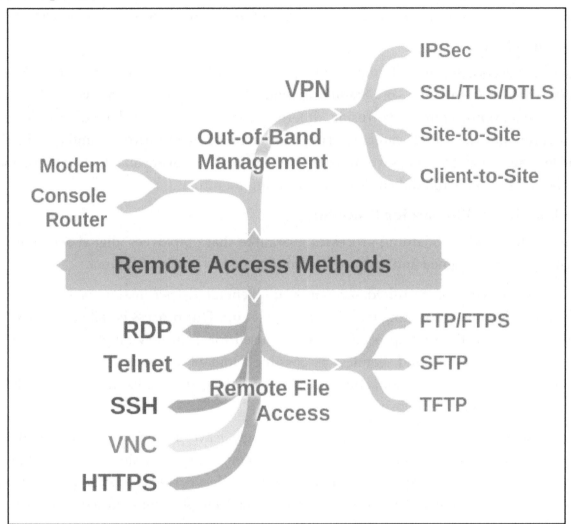

Figure 3-50: Mind Map of Remote Access Methods

Identify Policies and Best Practices

In a scenario where users are in charge of implementing the policies and procedures in the organization, they should know the following information; policies and procedures should be clearly outlined in writing. These rules and procedures are written and authorized by the management. Policies may include security policies, network policies, acceptable policy use, and standard business documents.

Privileged User Agreement

Users who have access to sensitive information or control over accounts must sign a privileged user agreement to indicate that they are aware of the power they have and will always act appropriately. A privileged user has access to resources just not as much of those

available to administrators. Anyone who has been granted one of those accounts should know the policies on what they can access without escalating a permission request.

Password Policy

Make sure users comprehend fundamental password skills, such as long password. In 2017, NIST (National Institute of Standards and Technology) moved two other past recommendations, complexity (using different character sets) and regularly changing passwords into the "don't" category. They have actually been proven counterproductive, causing users to write down, save, and create passwords far more available than they should be (because they are too difficult to remember and monitor).

On-boarding / Off-boarding Procedures

On-boarding and off-boarding processes guarantee that employees' digital accounts and permissions are assigned and revoked in a consistent and efficient manner.

When employees are recruited, accounts are generated, permission is granted, and authentication and accounting mechanisms are set up. This process is called on-boarding. If done properly, the same procedures will be used for each new employee, so that the process is as consistent and seamless as possible. Domain accounts, email accounts, file shares, resources authorization, and more are network-related items that require to be set up when hiring a new employee.

The same applies when employees either willingly leave a company or are fired. Off-boarding processes need to cancel any digital accounts and permissions before employees are terminated, and make sure employees do not leave the company with sensitive corporate data, or possess any privileges that would enable them subsequent access to networks they should no longer have access to.

Licensing Restrictions

Licensing restrictions must be strictly enforced through policies in relation to hardware and software. Some software licenses cover an entire site, enabling a company to simultaneously install software and use that software on several machines. Other software licenses enable the use of a single machine for just one installation.

On network computer systems, no outside software should be installed. The network administrator must approve all software installations. No software can be copied or removed from a site.

International Export Controls

Different countries have regulations in place for exporting hardware and software. For example, if users take the laptop to another country, there might be software on that laptop that uses encryption that cannot be exported and is subject to control. In addition, items

such as software and manuals on the laptop may also be restricted from moving from country to country. Policies need to enforce these controls.

Data Loss Prevention

Data Loss Prevention (DLP) software ensures that users do not enable the exfiltration of sensitive information from the network, either internationally or unintentionally. DLP can also be proactive, by defending private information from a potential data breach, for example through malware. Sensitive data can be monitored, detected, and blocked in the three common states of data in use, data in transit, and data at rest. There require to be well defined policies in place, to minimize DLP.

Remote Access Policies

Remote access policies deal with how corporate resources can be accessed from a remote, offsite location. VPNs, encryption, and other security features are included.

Incident Response Policies

When an incident occurs, it is the responsibility of all employees to lookout for incident and report it immediately to the appropriate party. The team may be responsible for things mentioned in an incident response policy, depending on the event type: deciding whether the event qualifies as an incident to be addressed, ignored, or escalated; evaluating the scope and cause of the problem; avoiding further disruption; resolving the cause; restoring order to impacted systems; and identifying methods to avoid recurrence. At this level, the incident response team handles most incidents. However, if an incident is so vast that the incident response team cannot stop it, then the disaster recovery comes into play.

Bring Your Own Device (BYOD)

The movement of Bring Your Own Device (BYOD) has stormed the corporate world, as employees are using their personal devices for work. These days, everybody seems to have a smartphone, a tablet, or both. In addition, these devices rival desktop computers in sheer computing power and functionality.

In fact, for a number of years, companies have included mobile devices into their networking experience. The issue is not so much with equipment, but rather with personal devices. How does an employee bring his/her Apple iPad to the office, take it on the road, and get access to the company's data at both locations? Simple. The network administrators could install Mobile Device Management (MDM) solutions (or have the employee install such on his/her iPad). Once the device connects to the network, the network administrator controls many private data.

Acceptable Use Policy (AUP)

An Acceptable Use Policy (AUP) is a simple set of rules that define how the computer equipment and network can be used. It is generally a small document that a new employee can read and understand quickly, so they know what they are signing. It may refer to other documents such as the larger security policy, but it should be concise and easy to understand. It should clearly define the expected code of conduct, what should be considered inappropriate or even illegal, and the concerns of violating the policy.

NDA

Any company with substantial intellectual property will require new employees—and occasionally even potential candidates—to sign a Non-Disclosure Agreement (NDA). An NDA is a legal document that prohibits the signer from disclosing any company secrets learned as part of his or her job

System Lifecycle

Most businesses and organizations have in place policies and best practices to deal with legacy systems. Each computer device has a system life cycle, from brilliant and new to patched and secure. System life cycle policies address disposal of assets with concept of reuse, repurpose, recycle. Users should not just throw old gear in the trash. Donate and take a tax write-off. For systems that do not need high speed, such as printers and multifunction systems, repurpose older WAPs as simple bridges.

Asset Disposal

Before disposing of any resources, such as PCs, routers or switches, all configurations and data should be destroyed, especially if there is sensitive client information on the devices. Government-grade erasure standards should be followed. To ensure complete data destruction, some companies use an accredited company that specializes in asset disposal. Writing zeros to hard drives enables the devices to be used again, while degaussing avoids storage media from being used again.

There should be a verification process after data is destroyed, to ensure that the data has been deleted and is fully unrecoverable.

Safety Procedure and Policies

The life of every individual has a worth taking and has its value, so management should always maintain safety standards that minimize the chance of danger to employees and damage to network equipment and servers. This might include electrical safety measures for people and devices, emergency procedures, fire-suppression systems, and so on.

Electrical Safety

IT administrators spend a lot of time in dealing with electrical devices. Therefore, electrical safety should be anxious in all procedures. In this section, we will look at key issues involved

with electrical safety, relevant to preventing injuries and for preventing damage to network equipment.

Grounding

Grounding is the electrical term for providing a path for an electrical charge to follow for returning to earth. When working with electric devices, it should be certain that the devices are grounded. This provides safety from harm and damaging electrical goods.

Electrostatic Discharge (ESD)

Electrostatic Discharge (ESD) is a sudden spark of electricity that sometimes happens when two materials are moved close to each other and have an opposite charge. ESD can be generated easily by walking across a carpeted floor.

To prevent ESD damage, always use mats, wearing a wrist strap, using antistatic bags, spray, and so on when working on electrical equipment.

Static

When ESD is created, it is a form of static energy. When computers are used in the area where extremely dry conditions, it makes the problem of static electricity worse. This is why the humidity of the area must be controlled so that it is not too humid; which causes corrosion of electrical connections. It must also not be too dry; which causes static build up and potential for damage.

Installation Safety

During prevention of electrical damage, the safety against installation is very important.

Lifting Equipment

When lifting heavy equipment, do not try to lift heavy loads that you cannot handle it. Lifting with your legs and not your back. If there is any question as to whether it is too heavy, get some help. Use tools such as a hand truck, to lower the load and make it safer.

Rack Installation

Follow the vendor recommendations when installing and securing the racks. The last thing that you want is for a rack to fall over while you are loading it up with very expensive equipment. Follow your organizational guideline for the correct installation of your server racks.

Placement

The main factor to consider in the placement of a rack is that it should be secure and stable. Some racks stand on the floor and some are attached to the floor. Others are made to stand

next to a wall and take their stability from wall mounts as well. Racks should be placed in such a way that you can easily reach the front and back of it to control the cables.

Tool Safety

Use the right tools for the right job in an appropriate manner for achieving safety.

Material Safety Data Sheet (MSDS)

A Material Safety Data Sheet (MSDS) is a document or web page that prescribes the correct way to use a product that could be dangerous if handled improperly. This document describes the safety instruction, room temperature, humidity, potential health risk and so on. An MSDS also describes what damage could be caused and how to treat the injury. You can get an MSDS while purchasing the product, or on the company's website.

Emergency Procedures

Every organization should be prepared for emergencies of all types. If possible, this planning should start with the design of the facility and its layout. This section will go through some of the components of a well-planned emergency system, along with some guidelines for maintaining safety on a regular basis.

Building Layout

Planning for emergencies can start with the layout of the building.

Here are some key considerations:

- All walls should have at least two-hour fire rating
- Doors must be of peaceful entry
- The location and type of fire suppression systems should be known
- Flooring in server rooms and wiring closets should be raised to help mitigate flooding damage
- Separate AC units must be dedicated to the information processing facilities
- Backup and alternate power sources should exist

Fire Escape Plan

The organization should develop such a plan that identifies the escape route in the event of a fire. They should create a facility map showing the escape route for each section of the building, keeping in mind that it is better to use multiple exits to move people out quickly. These diagrams should be pasted in all areas.

Safety/Emergency Exits

All escape routes on the map should have the following characteristics:

- Clearly marked and well ignited
- Wide enough to accommodate the expected number of people

- Clear of obstacles

Fail Open/Fail Close

Door systems that have electronic locks may lose power during a fire. When they do, they may lock automatically or fail to close and unlock automatically or fail to open. While a fail close setting may enhance security during an electrical outage, the effect of the departure and taking steps to ensure that everyone can get out of the building when needed should be considered.

Emergency Alert System

All areas of the building should be equipped with a system to alert employees when a fire or any other type of emergency occurs. It might be advisable to connect the facility to the Emergency Alert System (EAS).

Fire Suppression Systems

Fire extinguishers are important and should be placed throughout a facility when large numbers of electronic devices are present; it is worth the money to protect them with a fire-suppression system. Fire suppression systems generally come in two varieties: water sprinkler systems and gaseous agents. The gaseous agent is the best for your network equipment and servers. In gaseous agent, an inert gas is used that takes the oxygen away from the fire and puts it out. However, before any agents are released into an enclosed area, an alarm will generally ring that will alert when to leave the area.

Device Placement

A device should be placed in such a way that heavy devices are placed at the bottom, and lightweight devices are placed on the top of the heavy device. Therefore, switches go at the top, followed by routers, servers, and finally the UPS at the bottom of the rack. This is because the UPS generally has very heavy batteries in it and you do not want to make the rack top heavy.

Air Flow

Most networking devices and servers produce heat as a side effect of just being powered on. Airflow around the equipment is critically important to keep devices in operation. When hot air is not removed from the area and replaced with cooler air, the devices overheat and start doing things like rebooting unexpectedly, and maybe the high heat will shorten the life of the costly equipment.

The air flow between racks must be controlled to remove the heat. Some organizations use thermal dividers to create hot and cold zones that they can work with individually. Sometimes, heat is removed from the top of a hot zone by forcing the cooler air from the

cold zone into the hot zone air. The hotter air will then rise to the top and be collected and cooled or eliminated from the place.

 Exam Tip

Be sure that you know the types of information that should be included in network documentation. You should also be able to identify a physical and logical diagram. You need to know the types of information that should be included in each diagram.

Mind Map of Identify Policies and Best Practices

Figure 3-51: Mind Map of Identify Policies and Best Practices

Summary

Appropriate Documentation and Diagrams to Manage the Network

- A physical diagram shows how a network looks, while a logical diagram shows how the traffic flows on the network
- A baseline is a log of performance indicators such as CPU usage, network utilization
- Routers are usually represented as circular objects in networking diagrams

Compare and Contrast Business Continuity and Disaster Recovery Concepts

- High availability is when devices and systems keep working without interruption or downtime
- NIC teaming combines multiple physical interfaces on a router or switch into one logical interface
- Cold sites, warm sites, and hot sites allow an organization to continue to run after a disaster
- Snapshots save a virtual machine's state at that moment

Common Scanning, Monitoring and Patching Processes and their Expected Outputs

- Patch management includes regularly updating operating systems and applications to avoid security threats
- A packet sniffer is a program that queries a network interface and collects (captures) packets in a file called a capture file
- A packet analyzer is a program that reads capture files from packet sniffers and analyzes them based on the monitoring requirements
- Simple Network Management Protocol (SNMP) is the de facto network management protocol for TCP/IP networks

Remote Access Methods

- Common VPN protocols include IPsec, SSL, TLS, and DTLS
- VNC (Virtual Network Computing) is an open source alternative to RDP and can operate on any OS
- File Transfer Protocol (FTP) is the original protocol used on the Internet for transferring files
- SFTP (SSH FTP) is similar to FTP, with servers and clients, but relies on an SSH tunnel

Identify Policies and Best Practices

- The Acceptable Use Policy (AUP) describes what is and what is not acceptable to do on an organization's PC
- The system life cycle deals with a regular plan of pushing out old devices and moving in new ones
- One of the best methods to strengthen the password, is to make it longer, preventing a brute-force attack

Practice Questions

1. Which type of diagram represents a topology or map of how the network looks?

   A. Logical Diagram

   B. Physical Diagram

   C. Rack Diagram

   D. Change Management Diagram

2. Which of the following concepts combines multiple physical ports on a router or switch into one logical port?

   A. NIC Teaming

   B. Clustering

   C. Incremental Backup

   D. Redundant Circuit

3. Which one of the following sites represents the quickest way for a company to recover from a disaster?

   A. Hot Site

   B. Warm Site

   C. Cold Site

   D. Web Site

4. Which of the following devices provides only temporary power, to allow devices to shut down properly?

   A. UPS

   B. MTTR

   C. SLA

   D. Generator

5. Which one of these protocols is not used for VPNs?

   A. IPsec

   B. SSL/TLS

   C. DTLS

   D. FTPS

6. Which one of the following is not used primarily for file transfers?

   A. SFTP

   B. FTPS

   C. TFTP

   D. HTTP

7. Which one of the following password recommendations is viable?

   A. Longer is better

   B. Shorter is better

   C. Length does not matter

   D. Reuse a previous password

8. Which of the following defines what is and what is not acceptable to do on an organization's computers?

   A. NDA

B. AUP

C. VPN

D. BYOD

9. NetFlow is an example of _____.

    A. Port Scanner

    B. Network/Packet Analyzer

    C. Interface Monitoring Tools

    D. Packet Flow Monitoring

10. When employees bring their own devices to work, the administration can allow the devices to access the network. What is this called?

    A. On-loading

    B. On-boarding

    C. Off-boarding

    D. Off-loading

11. In CompTIA term, Link Aggregation Control Protocol (LACP) is also called _____.

    A. Port Mirroring

    B. Port Filtering

    C. Port Bonding

    D. Flooding

12. RTO and RPO metrics are related to which concept?

    A. Business Continuity

    B. Uninterruptible Power Supply

C. Disaster Recovery

D. Data Breach

13. A document or agreement that defines what services are expected and how they are to be accomplished is called _____.

   A. Standard Business Document

   B. Acceptable Use Policy

   C. Service level Agreement

   D. Memorandum of Understanding

14. Which component is used to arrange cable neatly and avoid heating areas?

   A. Cable Management

   B. Cable Trays

   C. IDF

   D. MDF

15. Which two types of backup methods clear the archive bit after the backup has been completed? (Choose 2)

   A. Full

   B. Differential

   C. Incremental

   D. GFS

16. Which of the following recovery sites might require the delivery of computer equipment and an update of all network data?

   A. Hot Site

   B. Warm Site

   C. Cold Site

   D. None of the above

17. Which type of recovery site mirrors the organization's production network and can assume network operations on a moment's notice?

    A. Hot Site

    B. Warm Site

    C. Cold Site

    D. Mirror Site

18. Which of the following are used to find weaknesses in your systems before others do? (Choose 2)

    A. Data Breachers

    B. Vulnerability Scanners

    C. Penetration Testers

    D. First Responders

19. By default, the automatic update feature on most modern operating systems is _____.

    A. Disabled

    B. Turned on

    C. Set to manual

    D. Ineffective

20. Which of the following prohibits employees from violating the confidentiality of any proprietary and sensitive company-related information?

    A. NDA

    B. AUP

    C. VPN

    D. BYOD

Chapter 04: Network Security

Technology Brief

Network security is one of the most challenging areas of IT to be dealing with. It seems like new threats are surfacing on a regular basis and continually learning new technologies is just a half a step ahead of potential problems. The chapter "Network Security" focuses on some of the elements administrators use to make their networks as secure as possible.

Physical Security Devices

With an understanding of the secure protocols, encryption algorithms, and access lists, it is also important to have a general sense of physical security for servers and network components. Many types of physical components improve physical security, these include mantraps, network closets, video monitoring, door access controls, proximity readers/key fobs, biometrics, keypad/cipher locks, or even an outdated security guard. In this section, we will discuss all of these physical security components in detail.

Detection

Detection is a device and feature that provide help to detect when something is not going as usual. Technicians make use of these tools and features to impart themselves of issues that require their attention.

Motion Detection

Through either mechanical or digital methods, we can install motion detection devices that alert us when objects change position in a physical network location.

Video Surveillance

Video monitoring is a technology to enhance physical security. It has been made much easier with the development of IP cameras and closed-circuit TV systems that can be placed in key locations to find attackers and record their actions if they still proceed. It is more securable if hidden cameras are used to catch the attacker.

Asset Tracking Tags

We can use various wireless technologies to track the physical location of network objects and personnel by using tag technologies attached to the objects.

Tamper Detection

Devices including computers, routers, and switches should be locked with tamper detection devices that transmit alerts if the lock is removed. The physical security of these devices is even enhanced by the sight of these tamper detection devices.

Prevention

As the famous saying goes, "An ounce of prevention is worth a pound of cure". Even though nothing is guaranteed from a security perspective, we still have to do our due diligence and implement preventative mechanisms to keep our network assets secure.

Badges

Badges used to be a type of visual identification but now, badges with incorporated Radio Frequency ID (RFID) chips are queried by circuitry in a door frame, called a proximity reader, and checked against a database for authentication. If the authentication verifies, the door will slide open electromechanically.

Biometrics

A biometric access is the best way to build physical security by using a unique physical characteristic of a person to allow access to a controlled IT resource. These physical characteristics include fingerprints, handprints, voice recognition, retina scans, and so on. The biometric is stored in the database to implement any security measures that the vendor recommends for protecting the integrity of the metrics and the associated database.

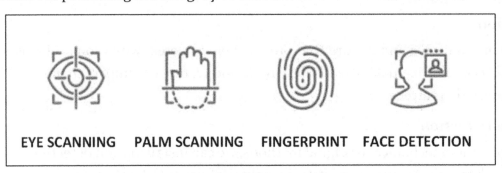

Figure 4-01: Biometric Authentication

Smart Cards

Today, smart cards use microprocessor circuitry to enable authentication, among different things. They can certainly be used to gain access, but also to make transactions and more.

Proximity Readers/Key Fob

A proximity card and reader system are often used to allow an authenticated person to enter an enterprise or a secure area in a building. It is a fast and suitable method for the people who want security, but it can often be cheated with piggybacking techniques. The best way to prevent that type of behavior and still use the proximity reader and card is to train people to use the card properly and enforce the fact that piggybacking is not allowed.

Keypad/Cipher Locks

Keypads and cipher locks are often used to control access to secured areas. The most secured types of keypads scramble the number locations on the pad each time they are used, so no one can follow the code that a person is entering while they enter it. A cipher lock is a door unlocking system that uses a door handle, a latch, and a sequence of mechanical push buttons. When the buttons are pressed in the correct order, the door unlocks and operates.

Mantraps

A mantrap typically consists of a two-door system that requires an authentication to open each door. It is an entry path with two successive locked doors and a small space between them providing one-way entry or exit. After a person enters the first door, the second door cannot be unlocked until the first door is closed and secured. This means that if someone wants access to an environment without authentication and thinks that they can hack the system, then they better be absolutely sure about both the hacks because otherwise they will be stuck in the mantrap giving time for an authoritative figure to trace them.

Network Closets

In small to medium-sized environments, a simple room with a lock on the door can be used to store sensitive computer and network equipment. This room might contain racks of computers, routers, switches, UPSs, and so on. Typically, there is additional physical security such as cameras or guards, and there may be more than one closet with additional equipment and connections for redundancy.

Door Access Controls

Door access controls are generally directed by something that is in possession of someone who has the authorization to enter a locked place. That something may be a key, a badge, a key fob with a chip, or some other physical token.

Security Guard

Security guards are great as they are responsible for protecting assets, building access, secure individual room, and office access, they also perform facility patrols. The guard station can serve as a central control of security systems such as video surveillance and key control. Like all humans, security guards are subject to attacks such as social engineering. However, for flexibility, common sense, and a way to take the edge off of high security, professional security cannot be beaten.

Exam Tip

Physical security is a recent addition to the Network+ exam. Ensure that you are familiar with all the topics discussed here.

Authentication and Access Control

Authentication, Authorization, and Accounting (AAA) is a framework designed to control access to computing resources, enforce policies, and audit usage. As its name implies, AAA defines fundamental security building blocks that are the basics of network management and security.

Authentication, Authorization and Accounting

Authentication, Authorization, and Accounting (AAA) allows a network to possess a single database of user credentials. A network administrator can then, for example, supply the same credentials to log in to various network devices, e.g. routers and switches. RADIUS and TACACS+ are most commonly used protocols to communicate with a AAA server.

RADIUS

Remote Authentication Dial in User Service (RADIUS) is a UDP-based protocol developed to communicate with a AAA server. Unlike TACACS+, RADIUS does not encrypt an entire authentication packet, but only the password. However, RADIUS offers more robust accounting features than TACACS+. Today, RADIUS is an authentication and accounting service that is used for verifying users over various types of links, including dialup. Many ISPs use a RADIUS server to store the usernames and passwords of their clients in a central location through which connections are configured to pass authentication requests. RADIUS servers are client-server-based authentication and encryption services maintaining user profiles in a central database.

 Exam Tip

RADIUS is a protocol that enables a single server to become responsible for all remote-access authentication, authorization, and auditing (or accounting) services.

Terminal Access Controller Access Control System (TACACS/TACACS+)

Terminal Access Controller Access Control System (TACACS) primarily represents two evolutions of the protocol. TACACS, developed in the early ARPANet days, possesses limited functions and uses UDP (connectionless protocol). Its architecture is based on Authentication, Authorization, and Accounting (AAA).

TACACS+ is a service that is similar to RADIUS but uses TCP (connection-oriented protocol) between the RAS and TACACS+ server for their communication because TCP has

several advantages over UDP. TACACS+ also follows the AAA architecture, but it separates their functions and adds encryption to them.

Kerberos

Kerberos is a protocol for authenticating service requests between trusted hosts across an untrusted network, such as the internet. Kerberos was a three-headed dog who guarded the gates of Hades. The three heads of the Kerberos protocol represent a client, a server and a Key Distribution Center (KDC), which acts as Kerberos' trusted third-party authentication service. Users, machines, and services using Kerberos need only to trust the KDC, which runs as a single process and provides two services: an authentication service and a ticket granting service. KDC "tickets" provide mutual authentication, allowing nodes to prove their identity to one another in a secure manner. Kerberos authentication uses conventional shared secret cryptography to prevent packets moving across the network from being read or changed and to protect messages from eavesdropping and replay attacks. Kerberos is built into all major operating systems, including Microsoft Windows, Apple OS X, FreeBSD, and Linux.

Single Sign-on

The ability to log in only one time and use the same token to access any resource that is allowed on the entire network is called single sign-on.

Local Authentication

Local authentication refers to the network device authenticating the user with a database of user account information stored on the device itself. When users authenticate to their computer, the authentication can be either to a domain or to the local machine. When local authentication is performed, the user's local account and password are verified with the local user database. This local user database is called Security Accounts Manager (SAM) and is located in C:\windows\system32\config\. In Linux, the database is a text file, /etc/passwd (called the password file), which lists all valid usernames and their related information.

Lightweight Directory Access Protocol (LDAP)

The Lightweight Directory Access Protocol LDAP is an open standard, application protocol. LDAP is for accessing and maintaining distributed directory information services. A directory service plays an important role by allowing the sharing of information like user, system, network, service, etc. throughout the network. LDAP provides a central location to store usernames and passwords. Applications and Services connect to the LDAP server to validate users.

LDAP functions by default on TCP and UDP port 389, or on port 636 for LDAPS (LDAP over SSL). LDAPS is the non-standardized "LDAP over SSL" protocol that in contrast with StartTLS (LDAP with TLS).

Note:

The primary goal of the SSL protocol is to provide privacy and reliability between two communicating applications. Symmetric cryptography is used for data encryption. SSL link ensures using SSL certificate that all data passed between the web server and browsers remain private and integral.

Certificates

A certificates is a form of digital credentials that validates users, computers, or devices on the network. It is a digitally signed statement that relates the credentials of a public key to the identity of the person, device, or service that holds the corresponding private key.

Auditing and Logging

Auditing is the process of monitoring events and keeping a log of the events that has occurred on a system. A system administrator identifies which events should be audited. Tracking events and attempts to access the system helps prevent unauthorized access and provides a record that administrators can analyze to make security changes where necessary. It also provides administrators with strong evidence if they need to look into improper user action.

The first step in auditing is to identify which system events need to be monitored. After the system events are identified, in a Windows environment, the administrator can choose to monitor the success or failure of a system event. For example, if "logon" is the event being audited, the administrator might choose to log all unsuccessful logon attempts, which might indicate that someone is attempting to gain unauthorized access. Inversely, the administrator can choose to audit all successful attempts to monitor when a particular user or user group is logging on. Some administrators prefer to log both events. However, extremely challenging audit policies can reduce overall system performance.

Multi-Factor Authentication

Multi-factor Authentication means to authenticate the user by above two factors along with something they are. For example, authentication by a smart card that has pin numbers along with biometric verification such as thumb scanned, iris scanned, and others belong to multifactor authentication.

Two-Factor Authentication

Two-factor Authentication means to authenticate the user by something they have or something they know. For example, authentication by a smart card that also has pin numbers usually belongs to two-factor authentication.

Something You Know

A user name, a password, a passphrase, or a Personal Identification Number (PIN).

Something You Have

A physical security device that authenticates users, such as a smart card, badge, or key fob.

Something You Are

Some distinctive, specific characteristic, such as a biometric.

Somewhere You Are

Some location factor that requires users to be in a place to authenticate. It is somewhat based on geolocation.

Something You Do

Some actions that users must take to complete authentication, such as typing on the keyboard.

> **Exam Tip**
>
> Ensure that you understand that two-factor authentication is a subset of multi-factor authentication.

Access Control

After authentication, the time has come to determine what privileges are given to which type of users. Access control is determined with 802.1X, NAC, port security, MAC filtering, captive portal, and access control lists.

802.1x

802.1x is a standard developed by the Institute of Electrical and Electronics Engineers (IEEE), it defines a method for access control by authentication. This authentication will get access when client computer requests access to a network through a device such as a network appliance or an authenticator (WAP), this authenticator passes the request to the authentication server. The authentication based on the decision of authentication server either accepts or rejects by following the databases. The authentication server plays an important role while the authenticator just follows the authentication server's instructions.

Network Access Control (NAC)

Network Access Control (NAC) is an evolution in security protocols and methods. In recent days, NACs are available in high processing CPU with high bandwidth connection. When a new computer wants to connect to the network, it first examines the network access control. If approved, then it allows to connect to the network. NAC prevents the computer from viruses and unwanted threats.

Port Security

The switch port security feature is a key implementation of the network switch security. It provides the ability to limit what addresses will be allowed to send traffic on individual switch ports within the switched network. Switch port security starts with understanding potential vulnerabilities and then addressing them through correct configuration. This address may include DHCP snooping, ARP inspection, MAC address filtering, and VLAN assignments.

DHCP Snooping

DHCP snooping is a method of controlling IP address assignment to prevent the possibility of attacks related to ARP spoofing. It uses a series of switches and ensures that only specific hosts with specific MAC addresses will receive specific IP addresses. It can consequently ensure that the recorded MAC address associated with an IP address will not approach the network. Furthermore, it can ensure than only authorized DHCP servers are added to the network.

ARP Inspection

ARP inspection is similar to DHCP snooping, it confirms IP to MAC assignments of packets based on the trusted list. It can be used to fight against man-in-the-middle attacks and ARP poisoning attacks.

MAC Address Filtering

MAC address filtering is a method that creates a table of "accepted users" list called Whitelisting that limits access to the wireless network. A table stored in the WAP lists the MAC addresses that are allowed to participate in the wireless network. MAC address filtering can also create a table of "blocked users" list called Blacklisting that denies specific MAC addresses from logging onto the network. A MAC address can easily be a spoof by a hacker, making the NIC report an address other than its own and then accessing the network, in order to disturb blacklisting. For this reason, if MAC address filtering is used as part of network security, then it should be a single part of it, and additional physical security and Layer 3 security measures should also be used.

VLAN Assignments

VLANs on switches allow you to create network segmentation by creating multiple virtual subnets while maintaining a flexible network that is easy to modify when required. Alternatively, an improper VLAN assignment on a port will effectively place clients in a subnet that will not be controlled by the administrator. It is not only a connectivity problem, but it could also create security issues. While assigning a VLAN, it should be done with great care as to which client computer is connected to which VLAN interface.

MAC Filtering

MAC Filtering is applied on switches working at Data-Link Layer of the OSI model. It focuses on source MAC address and destination MAC address in the packet and can be configured in such a way as to allow only specific MAC addresses through an interface on the switch. MAC filtering is usually applied at the access layer of a computer network, where the host computers are connected to the switches.

Captive Portal

Many public places like airports employ a captive portal to control access to their public Wi-Fi networks. When users attempt to connect to the network, they must deal with a web browser that insists them to follow the acceptable use policy. Because it is an additional step in internet connectivity, that captive portal can result in a seemingly slow connection. Higher security standards in web browser can also block such content and thus users access to the network.

Access Control Lists

An Access Control List (ACL), in the current section, is nothing more than a clearly defined list of permissions that specifies what an authenticated user may perform on a shared resource. During the past few years, the way to assign access to resources has changed dramatically. To help understand these changes, the security department likes to use the idea of ACL access models. There are three types of ACL access models: mandatory, discretionary, and role based.

Mandatory Access Control

In a Mandatory Access Control (MAC) security model, every resource is assigned a label that defines its security level. If users lack that security level, they do not get access. MAC is used in many operating systems to define what privileges programs have over other programs stored in RAM. The MAC security model is the oldest and least common among the three.

Discretionary Access Control

Discretionary Access Control (DAC) is based on the idea that a resource has an owner who may at discretion assign them to access to that resource. DAC is considered much more flexible than MAC.

Role-based Access Control

Role-based Access Control (RBAC) is the most popular model used in file sharing. RBAC defines a user's access to a resource based on the roles the user plays in the network context.

Securing Basic Wireless Network

Wireless communication has become popular with each passing year. Therefore, it is essential to understand such protocols and procedures that can secure wireless networks. This section will discuss WEP, WPA, WPA2, TKIP/AES, 802.1x, TLS/TTLS, and MAC filtering.

WEP

Wired Equivalent Privacy (WEP) was the first attempt to secure wireless connections. It was secured by encrypting only the data transfer. However, WEP was found not to be equivalent to wired security because the security mechanisms that were used to establish the encryption were not encrypted. It used a key length that was originally 64-bit and then later upgraded to 128-bit. WEP also operates only at the lower layers of the OSI model and therefore cannot offer end-to-end security for applications.

WPA

Wi-Fi Protected Access (WPA) was designed to improve on WEP as a means of securing wireless communications. WPA is an upgradation on the system that currently uses WEP.

WPA offers two distinct advantages over WEP:

- Improved data encryption through the Temporal Key Integrity Protocol (TKIP), which scrambles the keys using a hashing algorithm.
- User authentication using the Extensible Authentication Protocol (EAP) and user certificates. These ensure that only authorized users can gain access to the network.

WPA2

Wi-Fi Protected Access version 2 (WPA2) further improves on WPA, offering additional advantages such as the following:

- Uses Advanced Encryption Standard (AES) mode of encryption for much stronger security and longer security keys. It is usually installed in enterprise environments.
- Implements Counter Mode Cipher Block Chaining Message Authentication Code Protocol (CCMP), which is based on the 802.11i standard and offers an enhanced

data cryptographic encapsulation mechanism that replaces TKIP completely with a much stronger security method.

WPA Enterprise

WPA Enterprise is a wireless protocol that enhances security using IEEE 802.1x standard to enable you to set up a network with some seriously secured authentication using a RADIUS server and passwords encrypted with Extensible Authentication Protocol (EAP). WPA is used in medium to large sized organizations.

TLS

Transport Layer Security (TLS) provides secure communication among various network devices while avoiding eavesdropping, tampering, and message forgery. It is designed to allow end users to be sure about whom they are communicating with. To secure transmission of data, clients can exchange the keys.

TTLS

Tunnel Transport Layer Security (TTLS) is a protocol that allows each client to authenticate to a server that has created a tunnel for communication. The clients have to authenticate only the server that created and authenticated the tunnel. It can save resources and provide for a more flexible setup of secure tunnels.

TKIP-RC4

WPA works by using an additional layer of security, called the Temporal Key Integrity Protocol (TKIP), around the WEP encryption scheme. It is not, therefore, a complete replacement protocol for WEP and still uses RC4 for cipher initialization; thus the name TKIP-RC4. TKIP added a 128-bit encryption key that seemed unbreakable when first developed. Within four years of development, however, researchers expressed methods by which hackers could waltz through WPA security almost as quickly as through WEP security.

CCMP-AES

The IEEE 802.11i standard amended the 802.11 standard to add much-needed security features. 802.11i replaced TKIP-RC4 with the much more robust Counter Mode Cipher Block Chaining Message Authentication Code Protocol – Advanced Encryption Standard (CCMP-AES) a 128-bit block cipher, which is quite difficult to crack.

Wireless Authentication and Authorization

Saying you are someone (identification) is one thing, but proving it (authentication) is another. Based on the users account and associated privileges, they will be able to access certain resources, but not others, and they will be able to perform certain actions, but not others (authorization).

WEP networks use shared or open authentications. WPA networks, for authentication, use pre-shared keys and RADIUS servers. WPA2 networks, for authentication, like their WPA previous networks, use pre-shared keys and RADIUS servers. Devices can be authorized by their MAC address, while geo-fencing authorizes devices, based on their geographical location.

Extensible Authentication Protocol (EAP)

Extensible Authentication Protocol (EAP) is an open set of standards that allows the addition of new authentication methods. EAP use certificates from other trusted parties as a form of authentication. It is currently used for smart cards, and it is evolving in many forms of biometric verification using a person's fingerprint, retina scan, and so on.

PEAP

Protected Extensible Authentication Protocol, also known as Protected EAP (PEAP), is a protocol that encapsulates the Extensible Authentication Protocol (EAP) within an encrypted and authenticated Transport Layer Security (TLS) tunnel. It requires only a server-side PKI certificate to create a secure TLS tunnel to protect user authentication.

EAP-FAST

EAP-FAST works in two phases. In the first phase, a TLS tunnel is established. Unlike PEAP, however, EAP-FAST's first phase is established by using a pre-shared key called a Protected Authentication Credential (PAC). In the second phase, a series of type/ length/value (TLV)-encoded data is used to perform a user authentication.

EAP-TLS

EAP with Transport Layer Security (EAP-TLS) defines the use of a RADIUS server as well as mutual authentication, requiring certificates on both the server and client. On the client side, a smart card may be used in place of a certificate. EAP-TLS is very robust, but the client-side certificate requirement is an administrative challenge. However, the EAP-TLS is used mostly in all secure wireless networks. EAP-TLS is only used on wireless networks, but TLS is used heavily on secure websites.

Shared Authentication or Open Authentication

WEP uses two kinds of authentication, shared authentication and open authentication. If open authentication is used, a wireless client does not need the WEP key to connect to the access point, although the key would be needed for encrypting and decrypting data frames. If shared authentication is used, the client must encrypt a plaintext challenge from the access point with the WEP key. If the access point's decryption is successful, the client is authenticated.

Pre-Shared Key Authentication

The most common way to set up WPA2 encryption is to use a simple version called WPA2-PSK (pre-shared key) by creating a secret key that must be added to any device that is going to be using that SSID. There is no authentication with WPA2-PSK, other than the knowledge of the key.

WPA2 attacks can occur, especially with wireless networks using WPA2-PSK passwords. The attacks are attempted by using sophisticated methods that make a number of assumptions about the password, and the fact that certain passwords are used quite often. The most important thing to do to prevent these attacks from succeeding is to use long password (16 or more characters), thus making the network impossible to crack.

MAC Filtering

MAC address has 48-bits hexadecimal address present on all network host. MAC filtering is applied on switches working at Data-Link Layer of the OSI model. It focuses on source MAC address and destination MAC address in the packet and can be configured in such a way as to allow only specific MAC addresses through an interface on the switch. MAC filtering is usually applied at the access layer of a computer network, where the host computers are connected to the switches. Whether your network is wired or wireless, MAC address filtering is generally not used as the only means of security, because MAC addresses can easily be spoofed with the accurate software.

Exam Tip

Make sure that you understand the purpose of MAC address filtering and that this functions the same whether the network is wired or wireless.

Geo-fencing

Geo-fencing is the process of defining the area in which an operation can be performed by using global positioning (GPS) or Radio Frequency Identification (RFID) to define a geographic boundary. An example of usage involves a location-aware device of a location-based service user entering or exiting a geo-fence. This action could trigger an alert to the user's device and as well as sending messages to the geo-fence operator.

Real World Scenario

Burger King Trolls McDonald's

Background

Geo-fencing, a location-data service that creates a region around a specific geographic area for the purpose of advertisement targeting, is a relatively new but powerful

marketing strategy. Thanks to consumers' demand for deals and personalization, and marketers' desire to penetrate consumers' smartphones, geo-fencing is increasing exponentially. Geo-fencing is found across all areas, but travel, banking, retail and quick-service restaurants have jumped on the technology early and set the standard.

In a given scenario, Burger King trolls McDonald's by creating successful geo-fencing campaigns to attract shoppers and expand brand recognition.

Challenge

Trolling McDonald's appears to be one of Burger King's favorite interests of late. The stunt derives on the heels of another recent Burger King campaign, in which the fast-food chain hacked McDonald's previous marketing efforts.

Solution

Burger King rolled out a "Whopper Detour" stunt in December 2018, that used mobile geo-fencing to direct people away from McDonald's locations. When smartphone users went around 600 feet of most McDonald's brick-and-mortar locations, they were sent a mobile offer for ordering a Burger King Whopper for a penny from the chain's revamped BK App, which then navigated them to the nearest Burger King to pick up their food.

The risky promotion resulted in Burger King app being downloaded over 1,000,000 times and boosted from ninth to first place in the Apple App Store's food and drink category.

Conclusion

Brands hijacking another brand's marketing effort, is becoming a hallmark of Burger King's strategy. The stunts often get media attention and heighten engagement on social media, which help the brand stand out in the competitive fast-food space.

Mind Map of Network Security

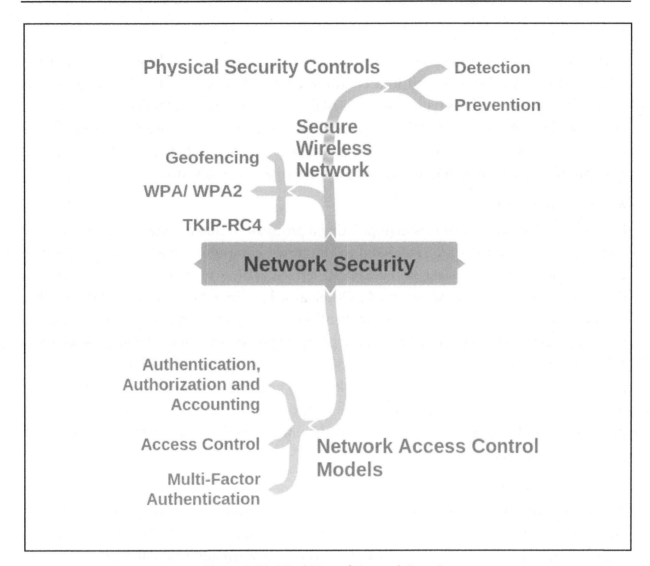

Figure 4-02: Mind Map of Network Security

Common Network Attacks

A network threat is any form of potential attack against the network. This threat in the form of a person sneaking into the offices and stealing passwords, or an ignorant employee deleting files that they should not have access to in the first place.

This section will discuss the most common network threats and the attacks that can be launched against the network.

Denial of Service (DoS)

A Denial-of-Service (DoS) attack is a targeted attack on servers that make the server site unable to process any upcoming request by providing some form of service on the internet such as a website.

Distributed DoS

A Distributed-Denial-of-Service (DDoS) attack occurs when multiple systems under the control of the attacker are used in a coordinated attack to create a traffic spike on the system. The purpose of this type of attack is to flood the resources so that they are no longer available for legitimate use. DDoS attack uses a group of computers connected in a coordinated manner for malicious activities which is termed as a botnet. Each computer in a botnet is called a bot. A botnet may also be known as a zombie army.

Reflective/Amplified

One type of DoS attack involves manipulating a protocol so that a request is sent from one computer, but all replies are redirected to the target computer. One such type of attack that uses ICMP echo request is the SMURF attack. These types of attacks are often a diversion that leads to a larger attack. Other attacks might target DNS, NTP, or other essential protocols. In smurfing, the attacker floods a network with ping packets sent to all target addresses. The return address of the pings is spoofed to that of the intended victim. When all the targeted addresses on the network respond to the initial ping, they send their response to the intended victim. The attacker then amplifies the effect of the attack by the number of responding machines on the network. Due to modern network management procedures, and controls built into modern Operating Systems, the danger of the smurf attack has been largely mitigated.

Friendly/Unintentional DoS

A different type of DoS event can be caused, not by an attack, but simply due to a sudden enormous spike in popularity that is not ready to handle the traffic. Sometimes an unexpected news event may cause a web server, that normally has sufficient amount of resources, to be completely overcome by a spike in traffic. This is normally a short-term event that tends to fix itself over time.

Exam Tip

To pass the Network+ N10-007 exam, understand that the reflective, amplified, and distributed are the characteristics of Denial-of-Service (DoS) attacks.

Social Engineering

Social Engineering in Information Security refers to the technique of psychological manipulation. This trick is used to gather information on different social networking and other platforms from people for fraud, hacking and getting information for being close to the target.

You can understand the social engineering is an art of extracting sensitive information from people. Social Engineers keep themselves undetected while people are unaware and careless and share their valuable information. This information is related to the type of social engineering. In Information Security aspects, Footprinting through social engineering gathers information such as:

- Credit Card Information
- Username and Passwords
- Security Devices and Technology Information
- Operating System Information
- Software Information
- Network Information
- IP Address and Name Server's Information

Insider Threat/Malicious Employee

The most exceptional hackers in the world are inside an organization, either physically or by access permissions. They do hacking much easily. Malicious employees are a huge threat because of their ability to destroy data, inject malware, and initiate attacks directly.

Logic Bomb

A logic bomb is a type of malware that executes itself when a particular event occurs. For example, that event could be a time of day or a specific date or it could be the first time users open notepad.exe. Some logic bombs execute when forensics are conducted, and in that case the bomb might delete all digital evidences.

Rogue AP

A Rogue Access Point (Rogue AP) is any wireless access point that has been installed on a network's wired infrastructure without the approval of the network's administrator thereby providing unauthorized wireless access to the network's wired infrastructure.

To prevent the installation of rogue access points, the users should know that these types of unsecured installations are not acceptable, and they also monitor their network for newly installed access points using wireless IDS/IPS systems that can detect changes in the radio spectrum indicating a new access point is installed and is operational.

Evil Twin

Wireless threats come in all sorts, from someone attaching to your WAP without authorization, to grabbing packets out of the air and decoding them by a packet sniffer.

An evil twin is a fake Wi-Fi connection that fools people into considering that it is an authentic connection for phishing attacks and exploitation of data transactions. Evil twins work best in unsecured networks such as those you see in airports and hotels that boast

"Free Wi-Fi here". They can affect you personally and professionally. You can protect yourself from Evil Twin by learning more about it and also by using Virtual Private Networks (VPNs) with SSL or TLS to certify that all email, passwords, and other sensitive information is encrypted during transmission.

WarDriving

WarDriving is a method of looking for wireless networks by using omnidirectional antennas connected to laptops or PDAs using wireless sniffing programs in a moving vehicle. WarDriving can be best described as a new form of hacking into the network.

Once the car is installed, the crackers start driving and log data as they go. The specialized software logs the latitude and longitude of the car's position as well as the signal strength and network name.

Phishing

Phishing is a type of social engineering attack that sends an email to the user appearing to be legitimate in an attempt to have that user enter authentic information, which is then captured. Often users receive a variety of emails offering products, services, information, or opportunities. This technique involves a bogus offer sent to hundreds of thousands or even millions of email addresses. Phishing can be dangerous because users can be tricked into disclosing personal information such as credit card numbers or bank account information. Today, phishing is performed in several ways like phishing websites and even phone calls designed to steal money or personal information.

Ransomware

Ransomware is a kind of malware that prevents or limits users from accessing their information or systems. In many cases, the data is encrypted and the decryption key is only made available to the user when the ransom has been paid.

DNS Poisoning

In DNS cache poisoning, an attacker targets a DNS server to query a malicious DNS server instead of the legitimate one, or simply changes existing cached records. The server can in turn tell the target DNS server spoofed DNS information. The DNS server will cache that spoofed information, spreading it to hosts and possibly other servers.

ARP Cache Poisoning

The Address Resolution Protocol (ARP) resolves IP addresses to MAC addresses. After the IP addresses are resolved, they are stored in a cache for further use. If an attacker can poison the cache, then the IP address will be incorrectly resolved to a different MAC address. This type of attack may be just the beginning of a larger attack. ARP cache poisoning attacks

target the ARP caches on hosts and switches. Every node on a TCP/IP network has an ARP cache that stores a list of known IP addresses with their MAC addresses.

To show ARP cache on a Windows system, use the arp –a command.

The result of typing arp –a on a given system:		
Interface: 192.168.0.25 --- 0x3		
Internet Address	Physical Address	Type
192.168.0.1	d4-6e-0e-b3-88-2e	dynamic
192.168.0.39	80-56-f2-7c-3f-4f	dynamic
192.168.0.46	5c-ac-4c-07-6f-5c	dynamic
192.168.0.255	ff-ff-ff-ff-ff-ff	static
224.0.0.22	01-00-5e-00-00-16	static
224.0.0.251	01-00-5e-00-00-fb	static
224.0.0.252	01-00-5e-00-00-fc	static
239.255.255.250	01-00-5e-7f-ff-fa	static
255.255.255.255	ff-ff-ff-ff-ff-ff	static

If a device wants to send an IP packet to another device, it must encapsulate the IP packet into an Ethernet frame. An attacker can send an unsolicited ARP and associate his/her MAC address with the gateway's IP address. Now all packets will pass through the attacker before the destination address.

Spoofing

Spoofing is the concept of a program masquerading as another one by falsifying data in an attempt to gain an illegitimate benefit. Attackers use many types of spoofing attacks because many of the protocols in the TCP/IP suite do not provide a tool for authenticating the source and destination of a message. IP spoofing and ARP spoofing may be launched by man-in-the-middle attacks. Other types of spoofing include email and even GPS spoofing. The network can be prevented from spoofing attacks by enabling authentication as much as possible and by disabling old or unusable protocols.

De-authentication

A wireless de-authentication attack is a form of a DoS attack in which the attacker sends a large number of management packets called de-authentication frames on the WLAN, causing area to be disconnected from the access point.

Brute Force

Brute force is a method of hacking passwords where an attacker guesses every possible password until the correct combination is found and then attacker gains access. Brute force attacks were successful in the past, but with the passage of time, as the complexity of protocols increases, the difficulty of brute force attacks has increased exponentially. Brute force attacks can be eliminated by limiting the number of wrong attempts for a password to a fixed amount, i.e., five attempts and then the account locks up.

VLAN Hopping

VLAN hopping is a method of attacking computer resources that are connected to VLANs. There are mainly two ways to finish this; one way is by pretending to be a switch that has a trunk established and thereby gaining all the information about the VLANs and the communication channels between switches. Another way is by using "double tags" to avoid security measures. VLAN hopping is almost never done because modern switches are all hardened against this attack.

 Exam Tip

To pass the Network+ N10-007 exam, understand a compromised system is any system that has been adversely impacted (intentionally or unintentionally) by an untrusted source. The compromise can relate to confidentiality, integrity, or availability.

Man-in-the-Middle

A man-in-the-middle places himself/herself between the two physical or logical communicating parties. The two communicating parties still assume that their communication is direct to each other, but actually it is not. The man-in-the-middle attacker sits between them and listens to the communication while learning new information, or the attacker may begin to change the communication between the parties to confuse or interrupt the communication. In any case, man-in-the-middle attacks are harmful to an organization. So, most organizations adopt methods including strong authentication and the latest protocols such as L2TP/IPsec with tunnel endpoint authentication.

Exploits vs. Vulnerabilities

Generally, vulnerabilities are some kind of weakness found in software systems, while exploits are attacks that take advantage of vulnerabilities.

Vulnerabilities are essentially weak points in software code that could sneak in during an update or when creating the base of the software code. Attackers or malicious users search for vulnerabilities by employing automation scans and tools that constantly search the web for weak points to exploit.

Vulnerabilities are open doors that exploits could use to access a target system. Simply put, an exploit needs a vulnerability to succeed. This means that without vulnerabilities, there would not be exploits. Exploits depend on oversights and mistakes, such as unpatched servers and out-of-date software, to achieve their objectives.

Network Hardening Techniques

Network-hardening techniques relate to using all new software, protocol, and practice to protect and secure the network. The network hardening techniques that will be considered in this section include changing default credentials, avoiding common passwords, upgrading firmware, patching and updating, file hashing, disabling unnecessary services, using secure protocols, generating new keys and disabling unused ports.

Changing Default Credentials

Changing default credentials should be the first line of defense in hardening a new device. Network devices come with default credentials, the username and password that enables users to log into the device for configuration. Every configurable device, like a switch or router, has a default password and default settings, all of which can create an unintended insider threat if not addressed. When any system takes into account, it best to change the default accounts and passwords.

Avoiding Common Passwords

Creating passwords by using the name of a country, a pet, a number, or a simple word for a password certainly makes the password easier to memorize. It also makes the passwords easier to be guessed or cracked by hackers.

Upgrading Firmware

While keeping operating system and application patches up-to-date requires most of the attention, there are many devices on the network that may require firmware updates periodically. Managed devices, like routers and switches, require good and basic maintenance. Many managed devices support firmware updates over the Internet.

Firmware updates are less common than software updates and usually are not as automated. In general, firmware patching is a manual process and is done in response to a

known issue. Remember that firmware updates are inherently risky because in many cases, it is difficult to recover from a bad patch. With firmware, it would be a good idea to record each upgrade and keep a separate copy for each patch in case a downgrade/rollback is needed.

Patching and Updates

All programs, including productivity software, antivirus software, and especially the operating system, release patches and updates periodically. It is developed to address potential security weaknesses. Administrators must be attentive for these patches and install them when they are released. Pay particular attention to unpatched/legacy systems and keep them as secure as possible.

File Hashing

A hash function can be used to convert digital data of any size into a fixed and much smaller sized data string. If the larger data is changed even in the slightest way, the resulting smaller data will change largely. It allows a system to quickly determine if the data sent through a network is the same as the data received, without having to examine the entire data stream or document. The two main hashing algorithms used in today's networks are MD5 and SHA.

Message Digest 5

Message Digest 5 (MD5) is a hashing algorithm that is still very commonly used, while some experts say that it has broken the processing power that hackers have today. It uses a 512-bit block and creates a 128-bit hash value that is typically expressed as a 32-digit hexadecimal number. It is often used to verify the integrity of data sent over network systems.

String	MD5
IPSpecialist...	a535590bec93526944bd4b94822a7625
IPspecialist...	997bd71ad0158de71f6e97a57261b9a7

Table 4-01: Comparing MD5 Values

Secure Hashing Algorithm (SHA)

Secure Hash Algorithm (SHA) belongs to cryptographic hash functions published by the National Institute of Standards and Technology. It currently has block sizes of 256 bits and 512 bits. The advanced versions of SHA (SHA-2 and SHA-3) are usually considered to be much more secure than MD5.

Syntax: **The password is 12345**

SHA-1:

567c552b6b559eb6373ce55a43326ba3db92dcbf

SHA-256:
5da923a6598f034d91f375f73143b2b2f58be8a1c9417886d5966968b7f79674

SHA-384:
929f4c12885cb73d05b90dc825f70c2de64ea721e15587deb34309991f6d57114500465243ba 08a554f8fe7c8dbbca04

SHA-512:
1d967a52ceb738316e85d94439dbb112dbcb8b7277885b76c849a80905ab370dc11d2b84dc c88d61393117de483a950ee253fba0d26b5b168744b94af2958145

Generating New Keys

Devices can use keys, which are long, randomly generated character streams, as input to encryption algorithms when encrypting data either in transit or at rest. At specified intervals, these keys must be renewed. While it is possible to renew the use of the same key, generating a new key or key pair is preferred. The longer a key is in use, the more likely the key will be compromised. Generating new keys at renewal time enhances security.

Disabling Unused Ports and Services

Disable the network services that are no longer in use for security concerns. There are two reasons to disable unnecessary services, one is that many operating systems use services to listen on open TCP or UDP ports then unintentionally leave the systems open to attacks. The other reason is that attackers often use services as a tool for the use and propagation of malware. Therefore, users should prevent this by disabling TCP/UDP ports and legacy services such as NetBIOS, Telnet, and any other unsecure protocols or services.

Using Secure Protocols

When you have disabled the unsecure protocols, then you should use the secure protocols. For example, use SSH instead of Telnet, use SNMPv3 instead of earlier versions, use SFTP instead of FTP, use HTTPS, SSL/TLS, rather than HTTP, and use IPsec whenever possible.

SSH

Secure Shell (SSH) has replaced an unsecure protocol Telnet. SSH involves SSH servers that use public key infrastructure (PKI) in the form of an RSA key. When a client tries to log into an SSH server, the server sends its public key to the client first then the client receives this key. It creates a session ID and encrypts it using the public key, and sends it back to the server. The server decrypts this session key ID and uses it to forward all data. It is secure therefore, only the client and the server knows this session ID.

SNMPv3

SNMPv3 adds additional security features with support for encryption and strong authentication. It also provides features for managing and controlling a large number of devices efficiently.

SSL

Secure Sockets Layer (SSL) requires a server with a certificate. When a client requests access to an SSL-secured server, the server sends a copy of the certificate to the client. The SSL client checks this certificate, and if the certificate works out, the server is authenticated. The client then negotiates a symmetric-key cipher for use in the session.

TLS

TLS is an updated version of Secure Sockets Layer protocol; it is more robust and flexible than SSL. TLS works with all TCP application and provides secure communications over the internet for such things as email, internet faxing, and other data transfers, securing Voice over IP (VoIP) and Virtual Private Networks (VPNs). The TLS Handshake Protocol allows servers and clients to authenticate each other and to negotiate an encryption algorithm and cryptographic keys before data is exchanged. Every web browser today uses TLS for HTTPS-secured.

SFTP

The SSH File Transfer Protocol (SFTP), also known as the Secure File Transfer Protocol, enables secure file transfer capabilities between networked hosts. Unlike the Secure Copy Protocol (SCP), SFTP provides additional functionalities such as remote file system management, allowing applications to continue interrupted file transfers, list the contents of remote directories, and delete remote files.

HTTPS

Hyper Text Transfer Protocol Secure (HTTPS) is the secure version of HTTP, the protocol over which data is sent between the browser and the connected website. The 'S' at the end of HTTPS stands for 'Secure'. It means all communications between the browser and the website are encrypted and secured. Web browsers such as Internet Explorer, Firefox, and

Chrome, YouTube, Facebook also display a padlock icon in the address bar to indicate that an HTTPS connection is in influence visually.

Figure 4-03: HTTPS

IPSec

The IP Security (IPsec) design comprises a suite of protocols developed to ensure the reliability, confidentiality, flexibility, and authentication of data communications over an IP network. IPsec may be used in three different security domains: virtual private networks, application-level security and routing security. Nowadays, IPsec is predominately used in VPNs. When used in application-level security or routing security, IPsec must be tied to other security measures to provide a complete solution.

IPsec works in two different modes: Transport mode and Tunnel mode. In Transport mode, only the actual payload of the IP packet is encrypted, the destination and source IP addresses and other IP header information are still readable. In Tunnel mode, the entire IP packet is encrypted and then placed into an IPsec endpoint, where it is encapsulated inside another IP packet. By default, IPv6 will use the IPsec Transport mode.

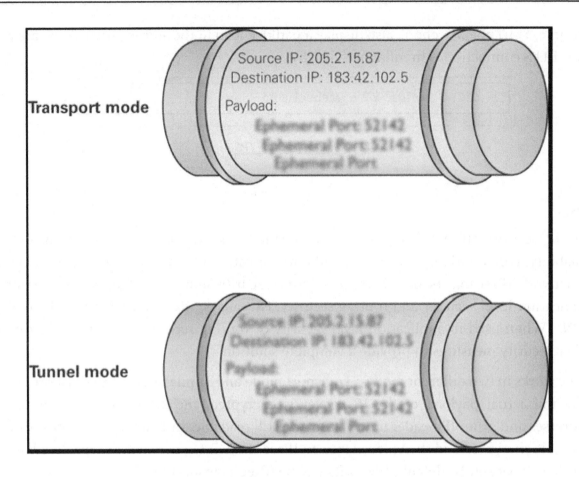

Figure 4-04: IPSec's Two Modes

Web/Content Filtering

Web/content filters are proposed to offer or block access to specific types of content on web servers used within the network and to reach the internet. The goal is to allow access to the content that is beneficial for the user, but at the same time, block access to objectionable content. This type of filter may be used on browsers, emails, client computers, search engines, network components, or a combination of any or all of these methods.

Port Filtering

A port filtering access list does not read the whole content of the message but only reads the header of the packets being sent. The header of the packets contains information such as the source and destination address of the packet and the ports that will be used. The list is generally made to deny all access except for the ports that have been explicitly allowed.

IP Filtering

IP filtering creates access lists that allow or deny a source address or range of source addresses to a destination IP address or range of IP addresses. This type of filtering may be

affected if a source address has been transformed by Network Address Translation (NAT) or Port Address Translation (PAT).

Common Mitigation Techniques

The word mitigation defines the act of reducing the severity or seriousness of the impact of something on a situation. IT Threat mitigation is therefore defined as the addressing actions, prevention techniques or remedies implement to combat or reduce IT threats on a computer, server or network. 'IT threats' is a very broad term that holds physical, software, and hardware threats that any IT system may encounter.

Signature Management

Digital signatures are the computerized equivalent of a sealed envelope and are intended to ensure that a file has not been altered in transit. Any file with a digital signature is used to verify not only the publishers of the content or file, but also to verify the content integrity at the time of download. On the network, PKI enables users to issue certificates to internal developers/contractors and allows any employee to verify the origin and integrity of downloaded applications.

Device Hardening

Device hardening is a technique that applies not only in routers or switches but also applies on all network devices including laptops, desktops and mobile devices. One of the current goals of operation security is to ensure that all systems have been hardened to the extent that is possible and still provide functionality. The hardening can be achieved both on a physical and logical basis.

From a logical perspective:

- Remove unnecessary applications
- Disable unnecessary services
- Block unrequired ports
- Tightly control the connection of external storage devices and media if it is allowed at all

Change Native VLAN

On switches, the native VLAN is the only VLAN that is not tagged in a trunk. This means that native VLAN frames are transmitted unchanged. By default, the native VLAN is port 1, and that default port represents a weakness that an attacker can take advantage of. To provide security, take some steps like changing the native VLAN to another port. The commands used to configure VLAN are dependent on the vendor and model of the port but can be easily found online.

Switch Port Protection

The switch port protection feature is a key implementation of the network switch security. It provides the ability to limit what addresses will be allowed to send traffic on individual switch ports within the switched network. Switch port security starts with understanding potential vulnerabilities and then addressing them through correct configuration. These addresses may include Spanning tree, flood guard, BPDU guard, root guard, and DHCP snooping.

 Exam Tip

To pass the Network+ N10-007 exam, understand the methods to securing switches, disabling unused ports, and using common-sense solutions can go far in improving network security.

Spanning Tree

Spanning tree is used to ensure that only one active path exists between two nodes at one time on the network. If a network has more than one active path, users can block all the redundant paths by enabling spanning tree. STP prevents network switching loops. STP has two main types; the original spanning tree 802.1d and the improved rapid spanning tree 802.1w. The leading advantage of 802.1w is much faster convergence on link failure. It is accomplished by the protocol automatically, determining the designated ports that will be used as well as the backups and alternates that might be used in case of a link failure.

Flood Guard

Switches can undergo a DoS attacks, flood guard are used to identify malicious traffic and take actions to prevent switches to stop. Considering DoS and DDoS attack, a flood guard is used as protection for a switch and can be purchased as a standalone device.

BPDU Guard

Bridge Protocol Data Unit (BPDU) guard prevents looping on a switch. It protects the spanning tree domain from external influence by altering a non-trunking port into an error state when a BPDU is received on that port. BPDUs are data messages that are exchanged across the switches via spanning tree protocol topology. These data packets contain information on ports, addresses, priorities, and costs and ensure that the data reaches the intended user; the guard shuts down interfaces that receive BPDUs instead of putting them into the spanning tree blocking state where they could generate looping.

Root Guard

Root guards are like BPDU guards in a way that they are used to prevent malicious exploitation of BPDU packets. The difference is that a root guard is used to prevent another switch from becoming the BPDU superior. Root guards are needed when we connect a network that we manage to a one that we do not manage.

DHCP Snooping

DHCP snooping is a method of controlling IP address assignments to prevent the possibility of attacks related to ARP spoofing. It uses a series of switches and ensures that only specific hosts with specific MAC addresses will receive specific IP addresses. It can consequently ensure that the recorded MAC address associated with an IP address will not approach the network. Furthermore, it can ensure than only authorized DHCP servers are added to the network.

Network Segmentation

Security is not the only reason for network segmentation. We also reduce the network congestion and limit network problems through segmentation. Network segmentation enhances the network performance. It is important to regulate network compliances with standards, laws, or best practices. We also segment network for easier troubleshooting.

DMZ

Generally, three zones are related with firewalls: Internal, External, and Demilitarized (DMZ). The internal zone is the zone inside of all firewalls, and it is considered to be the protected area where most critical servers, such as domain controllers that control sensitive information, are placed. The external zone is the area outside the firewall that represents the network against inside protection such as the internet. The DMZ is placed where the network has more than one firewall. It is a zone that is between two firewalls. It is created using a device that has at least three network connections, sometimes referred to as a three-pronged firewall. In DMZ, place the servers that are used by hosts on both the internal network and the external network that may include web, VPN, and FTP servers.

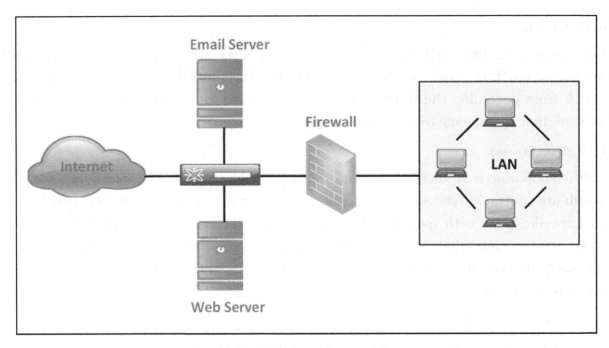

Figure 4-05: DMZ using One Firewall

VLAN

Switches and routers have physical interfaces, commonly known as a physical port; these ports can be configured in a variety of ways, depending upon the topology, design, type of encapsulation, duplex, and speed of the link.

VLANs on switches allow users to create network segmentation by creating multiple virtual subnets while maintaining a flexible network that is easy to modify when required. Alternatively, an improper VLAN assignment on a port will effectively place clients in a subnet that will not be controlled by the administrator. It is not only a connectivity issue, but it could also create security issues. While assigning a VLAN, it should be done with great care as to know which client computer is connected to which VLAN interface.

<u>Lab: Virtual Local Area Network (VLAN)</u>

Case Study: Configure a switch using Virtual Local Area Network (VLAN).

Topology Diagram:

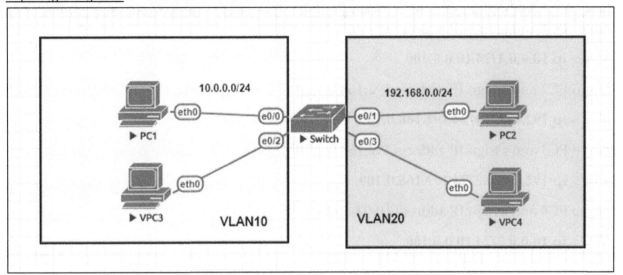

Figure 4-06: VLAN Topology

Configuration:

Switch
Switch>
Switch>en
Switch#config t
Enter configuration commands, one per line. End with CNTL/Z.
Switch(config)#vlan 10
Switch(config-vlan)#exit
Switch(config)#vlan 20
Switch(config-vlan)#exit
Switch(config)#int range ethernet 0/0, ethernet 0/2
Switch(config-if-range)#switchport mode access
Switch(config-if-range)#switchport access vlan 10
Switch(config-if-range)#ex
Switch(config)#int range ethernet 0/1 , ethernet 0/3
Switch(config-if-range)#switchport mode access
Switch(config-if-range)#switchport access vlan 20
Switch(config-if-range)#ex
Switch(config)#

VPC
Go to PC1 and assign IP address 10.0.0.1/24
VPC> **ip 10.0.0.1/24 10.0.0.100**
Go to PC2 and assign IP address 192.168.0.1/24
VPC> **ip 192.168.0.1/24 192.168.0.100**
Go to PC3 and assign IP address 192.168.0.2/24
VPC> **ip 192.168.0.2/24 192.168.0.100**
Go to PC4 and assign IP address 10.0.0.2/24
VPC> **ip 10.0.0.2/24 10.0.0.100**

Verification:

Switch#**show VLAN brief**

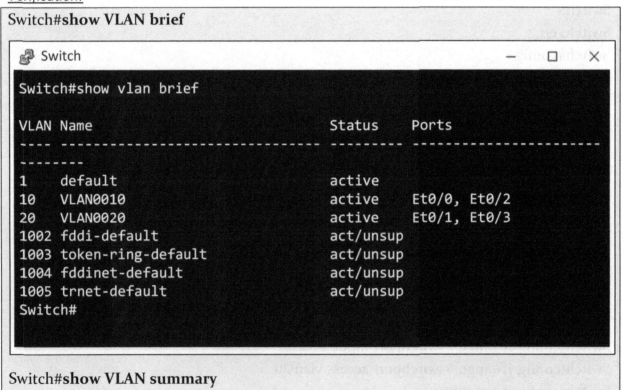

Switch#**show VLAN summary**

```
Switch                                                      —    □    ×

Switch#show vlan
*May 15 22:22:57.155: %SYS-5-CONFIG_I: Configured from console by
console
Switch#show vlan summary
Number of existing VLANs              : 7
 Number of existing VTP VLANs         : 7
 Number of existing extended VLANS    : 0

Switch#
```

Ping PC3 from PC1 (Same VLAN).

VPC> **ping 10.0.0.2**

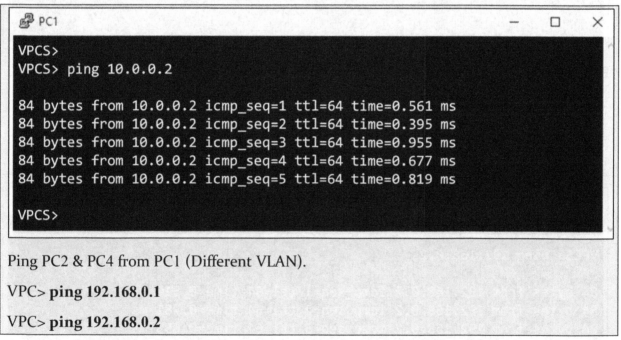

```
PC1                                                        —    □    ×

VPCS>
VPCS> ping 10.0.0.2

84 bytes from 10.0.0.2 icmp_seq=1 ttl=64 time=0.561 ms
84 bytes from 10.0.0.2 icmp_seq=2 ttl=64 time=0.395 ms
84 bytes from 10.0.0.2 icmp_seq=3 ttl=64 time=0.955 ms
84 bytes from 10.0.0.2 icmp_seq=4 ttl=64 time=0.677 ms
84 bytes from 10.0.0.2 icmp_seq=5 ttl=64 time=0.819 ms

VPCS>
```

Ping PC2 & PC4 from PC1 (Different VLAN).

VPC> **ping 192.168.0.1**

VPC> **ping 192.168.0.2**

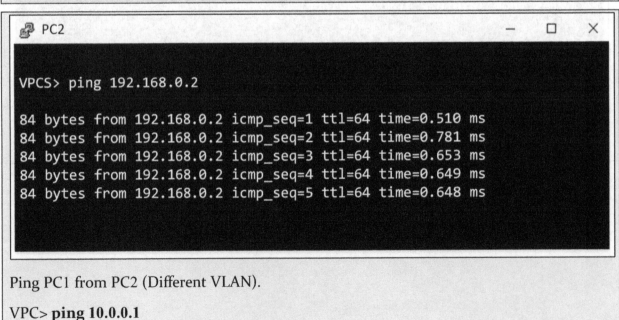

```
PC1                                                          —    □    ✕

VPCS> ping 192.168.0.1

192.168.0.1 icmp_seq=1 timeout
192.168.0.1 icmp_seq=2 timeout
192.168.0.1 icmp_seq=3 timeout
192.168.0.1 icmp_seq=4 timeout
192.168.0.1 icmp_seq=5 timeout

VPCS> ping 192.168.0.2

192.168.0.2 icmp_seq=1 timeout
192.168.0.2 icmp_seq=2 timeout
192.168.0.2 icmp_seq=3 timeout
192.168.0.2 icmp_seq=4 timeout
192.168.0.2 icmp_seq=5 timeout

VPCS>
```

Ping PC4 from PC2 (Same VLAN).

VPC> **ping 192.168.0.2**

```
PC2                                                          —    □    ✕

VPCS> ping 192.168.0.2

84 bytes from 192.168.0.2 icmp_seq=1 ttl=64 time=0.510 ms
84 bytes from 192.168.0.2 icmp_seq=2 ttl=64 time=0.781 ms
84 bytes from 192.168.0.2 icmp_seq=3 ttl=64 time=0.653 ms
84 bytes from 192.168.0.2 icmp_seq=4 ttl=64 time=0.649 ms
84 bytes from 192.168.0.2 icmp_seq=5 ttl=64 time=0.648 ms
```

Ping PC1 from PC2 (Different VLAN).

VPC> **ping 10.0.0.1**

Privileged User Account

The PoLP (Principle of Least Privilege) should always be observed when assigning or restricting user accounts. Do your best to ensure that the user can function at the level of their job description without exceeding it.

File Integrity Monitoring

Integrity is the process to ensure that the data received is same as the one originally sent. Integrity is designed to eliminate the situations where someone is tampering with your data. However, file integrity monitoring is performed as the concept of file hashing which was discussed earlier but with a software program. File integrity monitoring observes changed settings or access controls, attributes and sizes, and, of course, the hashes of files.

Role Separation

Role separation also known as separation of duties, requires one user to perform a specific task, and another one to perform a related task. This reduces the possibility that scam or error will occur, by implementing an equalized system between different users.

Restricting Access via ACLs

Firewalls generally contain Access Control Lists (ACLs) that allow or deny packets based on specified criteria such as IP addresses, ports, or data. The firewall generally processes from top to bottom when the traffic meets the criteria then the related action of authority or deny is applied. Usually, there is an implicit deny statement at the end of the firewall ACL that will deny any packets that have not been allowed before they reached that point. Sometimes, this statement is not implicit but is listed as the default statement at the end of the list.

Honeypot/Honeynet

Honeypots are security devices used as a decoy to act as a valuable server target to an attacker. When they are monitored and are inaccessible from any truly sensitive computer data, they also appear to be vulnerable to attack and are quite undefended. The idea is to get the attacker to take the lure, making them waste their time in the honeypot, while keeping the network's real data safe, and then gathering information about the attacker and giving it to proper authorities.

Two or more honeypots on the same network, make a honeynet. It is used in a large organization where a single honeypot server will not be sufficient. The honeynet simulates a production network but is deeply monitored and isolated from the true production network.

Penetration Testing

Penetration testing involves attacking the system or inviting someone else to attack it. The purpose of doing this is to determine the point of weaknesses. The best result of a penetration test would be that no weaknesses exist; although, any result can be turned into a positive one because the penetration test is performed in a controlled environment to expose a vulnerability that can be mitigated before it is exploited by an attacker. Penetration testing can be done by a skillful operator who understands the target and knows potential vulnerabilities, it can also be done by the number of tools like Aircrack-ng and Metasploit. Aircrack-ng is an open source tool for pentesting and pretty much every aspect of wireless networks. Metasploit, another unique open source tool, enables the pentester to use a massive library of attacks as well as tweak those attacks for unique penetrations.

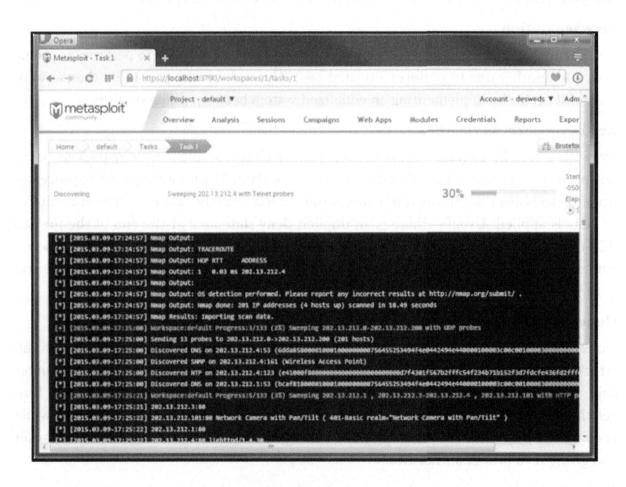

Figure 4-07: Metasploit Output

Mind Map of Network Security

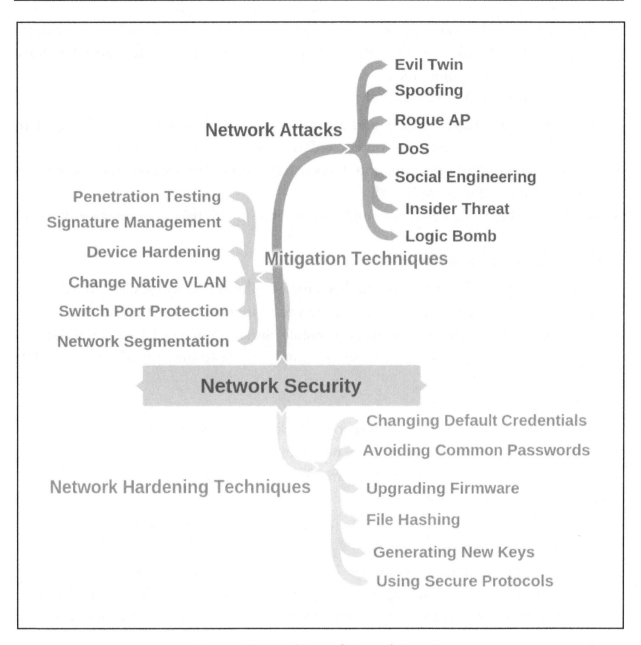

Figure 4-08: Mind Map of Network Security

Summary

Physical Security Devices

- With an understanding of the secure protocols, encryption algorithms, and access lists, it is also important to have a general sense of physical security for servers and network components

- Many types of physical components improve physical security, it includes mantraps, network closets, video monitoring, door access controls, proximity reader/key fobs, biometrics, keypad/cipher locks

Authentication and Access Control

- Authentication, Authorization, and Accounting (AAA) is a framework designed to control access to computing resources, enforce policies, and audit usage
- Authentication, Authorization, and Accounting (AAA) allows a network to possess a single database of user credentials
- RADIUS and TACACS+ are most commonly used protocols to communicate with a AAA server

Securing Basic Wireless Network

- WPA with TKIP-RC4 encryption has been replaced by WPA2 with CCMP-AES
- WPA and WPA2 can be configured to use a pre-shared key or RADIUS server
- Geo-fencing is the process of using a mobile device's built-in GPS capabilities and mobile networking capabilities to set geographical constraints on where the mobile device can be used

Common Network Attacks

- A network threat is any form of potential attack against your network
- A vulnerability is a weakness that can be exploited
- Reflective, amplified, and distributed are three types of DoS attacks

Network Hardening Techniques

- Network-hardening techniques relate to using all new software, protocol, and practice to protect and secure the network
- The network hardening techniques include changing default credentials, avoiding common passwords, upgrading firmware, patching and updating, file hashing, disabling unnecessary services, using secure protocols, generating new keys and disabling unused ports

Common Mitigation Techniques

- IT Threat mitigation is therefore defined as the addressing actions, prevention techniques or remedies implement to combat or reduce IT threats on a computer, server or network
- 'IT threats' is a very broad term that holds physical, software, and hardware threats that any IT system may encounter

Practice Questions

1. Which scanning tool do IT administrators use as an electron microscope?
   A. Interface Monitoring Tools
   B. Port Scanner
   C. Network/Packet Analyzer
   D. Top Talkers/Listeners

2. NetFlow is an example of _____.
   A. Port Scanner
   B. Network/Packet Analyzer
   C. Interface Monitoring Tools
   D. Packet Flow Monitoring

3. Which of the following is a security device that is actually a decoy?
   A. Honeynet
   B. IDS/IPS
   C. SIEM
   D. Honeypot

4. What is the most common packet sniffer in use today?
   A. NetFlow
   B. Nmap
   C. Wireshark
   D. Netstat

5. Which switching protocol can prevent switching loops in a network?
   A. STP
   B. VTP
   C. RSTP
   D. Tunneling Protocol

6. Which of the following is used for Penetration Testing?
   A. Metasploit
   B. Zenmap
   C. MBSA
   D. Nessus

7. In which attack, the attacker floods a network with ping packets sent to all target addresses?
   A. DoS
   B. DDoS
   C. Smurfing
   D. Friendly DoS

8. A Permanent DoS (PDoS) is somehow referred to as a _____ attack.
   A. Man-in-the-Middle
   B. Malware
   C. Spoofing
   D. Physical

9. Which one of these attacks does not depend on wireless technologies?
   A. Rogue AP
   B. Evil Twin
   C. ARP Cache Poisoning
   D. Bluejacking

10. Which of the following attack does not affect the technology?
    A. WarDriving
    B. Social Engineering
    C. DDoS
    D. DoS

11. Which of the following is not an unsecure protocol?
    A. FLIP
    B. Telnet
    C. HTTP
    D. SSH

12. Which method can prevent attacks related to ARP spoofing?
    A. DHCP Snooping
    B. ARP Cache Poisoning
    C. Smurfing
    D. None of the above

13. Which of the following is not an attack but is instead a method of securing network?

A. Man-in-the-Middle

B. Malware

C. ARP Inspection

D. Social Engineering

14. Which type of filtering may be affected if a source address has been transformed by Network Address Translation (NAT) or Port Address Translation (PAT)?

A. Port Filtering

B. IP Filtering

C. Web Filtering

D. MAC Address Filtering

15. What is the function of a DMZ?

A. To separate a security zone for an IPS and IDS server

B. To create a security zone for VPN terminations

C. To create a security zone that allows public traffic but is isolated from the private inside network

D. To create a security zone that allows private traffic but is isolated from the public network

16. Which method acts on behalf of the whole network to completely separate packets from internal hosts and external hosts?

A. Proxies

B. IDSs

C. IPSs

D. ACLs

17. Which of the following statements regarding firewalls is true?

A. Both host-based and network-based firewalls are implemented in hardware

B. A host-based firewall is implemented in software, whereas a network-based firewall is implemented in hardware

C. A host-based firewall is implemented in hardware, whereas a network-based firewall is implemented in software

D. Both host-based and network-based firewalls are implemented in software

18. Which firewall keeps track the major attributes of each connection?

A. Hardware

B. Software

C. Stateful

D. Stateless

19. Which system uses two doors authentication process?
    A. Mantraps
    B. Network Closets
    C. Proximity Readers
    D. Door Access Controls

20. If Single Point of Failure (SPOF) occurs, the whole system will _____.
    A. Restart
    B. Start
    C. Reboot
    D. Stop

Chapter 05: Network Troubleshooting & Tools

Technology Brief

The methodology of network troubleshooting evaluates the performance of a network, i.e., how long it continues to work. It also determines the different causes of problems. These problems can be distinguished by troubleshooting methods, there are a lot of troubleshooting methodologies in networking. This section will describe the basic troubleshooting methodologies.

Identify the Problem

Let's walk through a typical scenario that might occur on your network and see how using a troubleshooting methodology will help you get to the root of the problem faster. You will see how having some plan is much better than having no plan at all in this scenario.

- Gather information
- Duplicate the problem, if possible
- Question users
- Identify symptoms
- Determine if anything has changed
- Approach multiple problems individually

Exam Tip

Candidate should expect questions asking to identify the troubleshooting steps in exact order.

Establishing a Theory of Probable Cause

Once you have diagnosed the problem after gathering information about the issue, figure out a possible cause, which results in this problem. You should have a theory of probable causes. This theory may not be a fact, but later, you can establish a revised theory.

Top-to-Bottom / Bottom-to-Top OSI Model

Top-to-Bottom or Bottom-to-Top OSI layered Approach helps to establish a theory of probable causes by figuring out layers of OSI model by either a Top-to-Bottom or a Bottom-to-Top approach.

#	OSI Layer	Theory
7	Application Layer	Problem with the API results in unavailability of services to end users
6	Presentation Layer	Incorrect encryption algorithm
5	Session Layer	Authentication failure, issue with establishing a session, etc.
4	Transport Layer	Issues related to transport protocols such as heavy traffic flow, causing a delay in receiving acknowledgment packets
3	Network Layer	Incorrect IP address/subnet of the machine, missing routes, etc.
2	Data-Link Layer	The MAC address of the machine might be blacklisted, VLAN assignment issue or another layer 2 issues might be a probable cause
1	Physical Layer	A disconnected/bad cable, bad connector, or dead NIC can make for a bad causes

Table 5-01: Establishing Theory with OSI Layers

Sometimes, starting layer approach from layer 1 is found helpful such as a scenario where equipment and devices are newly deployed. However, you can use both approaches.

Divide and Conquer

Another approach is the Divide and Conquer approach; after gathering enough information about the problem, you will be focused on an appropriate OSI layer from where the issue arose. You can proceed to test the probable causes of that particular OSI layer. If you find your theory to be correct, further troubleshooting steps can be followed. If the theory does not seem to fit the issue, you can proceed to upper or lower layer.

Test the Theory to Determine the Cause

In the third phase, you have to evaluate the theory to diagnose the root cause of the problem. To understand this phase, consider a scenario where a printer is connected to the local network and an issue that no one is able access this printer arises. According to step 1, "Identify the Problem", you should explore the issue and gather information like troubleshooting network connectivity of users to the printer. Theory of probable cause could be disconnected or bad cabling. Now, testing the theory phase includes testing of network cables, connectors, ensuring whether the printer is powered on or not. If the

printer is not powered on, or cable is disconnected, you can proceed to the next step. If you find everything fine with layer 1, you can proceed to test layer 2 and so on.

Establishing an Action Plan

Once you found a possible reason for the problem, you can then establish an action plan to resolve the issue. For example, installation of new Ethernet cables, installation of new power cables, or re-installation of connectors could be an action plan to resolve the issue.

Implementation of Solutions

Implementation of solution phase is the action phase where several action plans can be enforced to eliminate the problem. Upon successful implementation, the issue must be resolved.

Verification of Functionality and Implementation of Preventative Measures

Verification of functionality is a phase where the resolution of an issue is verified by testing the process. For example, sending commands to print a test page from the user's machine will help to verify the functionality. Implementation of preventative measures could be preparing a policy for maintenance of cables and connectors, giving responsibility to ensure the powering of the devices, etc.

Document Findings and Outcomes

Documentation of all findings and outcomes helps to report the issue to higher administration. These documentations could be used for the legal purpose if you find any unauthorized intrusion to your devices. Furthermore, these documentations could also be used in future when a similar issue is reported.

Use Appropriate Tool

While working through the process of troubleshooting, we need some specific tools. These tools may be the software and hardware tools that provide information about the network and enact repairs. The knowledge about when and how to make use of these tools is a learning phase and we will be going through this phase in this section.

Hardware Tools

Hardware tools can be used in troubleshooting scenarios to help users eliminate or reduce the possible causes of certain problems related to hardware devices. Some of the hardware troubleshooting tools are described below.

> **Exam Tip**
>
> Read this section carefully! The CompTIA Network+ exam is filled with repair scenarios, and you must know what every tool does and when to use it.

Crimper

The cable crimper and stripper attach an RJ-45 connector to the end of a cable. The eight wires inside the cable strip about an inch of the outer cable insulation and then press down hard on the right place of the RJ-45, to close the connector around the cable and keep all of the wires strapped into place, so that the end of the cable sheath is safely tucked inside the connector as well. This entire process is accomplished by cable crimpers and strippers.

Cable Tester

A cable tester is a device that is used to test the strength and connectivity of a particular type of cable or other wired assemblies. There are some different types of cable testers, each able to test a specific type of cable or wire. A cable tester can test whether a cable or wire is set up properly, connected correctly, and if the communication strength between the source and destination is adequate for transmitting data.

Punch Down Tool

A punch down tool is a hand tool used to connect network wires to a patch panel. The process of properly punching down a wire, requires some force. If it is done without any special tool, it probably breaks the wire or does not connect properly. So, a punch down tool will help in connecting the wire in the right place.

OTDR

An Optical Time Domain Reflectometer (OTDR) is a more sophisticated device than a TDR. OTDR performs the same function as TDR, but it deals with light in fiber-optic cables. An OTDR tests the cables within several kilometers but TDR tests the copper cables shorter than 100 meters. For this reason, OTDR has become a vital tool in today's networking while dealing with long distances fiber-optic cable flows.

Light Meter

The light meter measures the amount of light. In computer networks, it is used to measure the strength of fiber-optic cables. The light meter system uses a high-powered source of light at one end of a run and a calibrated detector at the other end. This measures the amount of light that reaches the detector.

Toner Probe/ Tone Generator

Toner probe is used to test the connectivity of wires that run through walls and other obstructions. This tool works in a pair of devices, one device produces a signal or tone on one end, and another device determines if that signal can still be heard on the other end. The device that produces the signal is called the tone generator. The other device that locates the generated signal is called the tone locator. These devices not only verify

connectivity, but they also trace the wire connections from the wall outlet to the patch panel.

Loopback Adapter

A hardware loopback adapter is inserted into the NIC's port to analyze the transmitting and receiving capabilities of a NIC.

Multimeter

A multimeter is a device that provides a digital readout of numerous tests including continuity, resistance, voltage, current, and so on. Simply set the multi-meter for what you want to measure. Some troubleshooting might require taking two measurements, one is having good connectivity and the other one is what you are troubleshooting, and then comparing the two measurements. For example; in case of resistance, a good cable will have zero resistance (0 ohms) while the faulty or broken cable will show a higher-than-normal resistance—anything above a few ohms to infinity.

Spectrum Analyzer

A spectrum analyzer is any device that identifies and documents all existing wireless networks in the area. Spectrum analyzers are convenient tools that are useful for diagnosing wireless network issues in the 2.4-GHz and 5.0-GHz ranges, and are also great tool for conducting site surveys.

Certifiers

Cable certifier certifies the cable after installation and ensures proper connectivity with their respective connectors. It certifies that the installed cables perform their tasks properly and are ready to provide the result as per their characteristics. Many cable certifiers are available for all cable types and even for wireless networks.

Line Testers

Line testers are relatively simple devices usually used to check the reliability of twisted pair cables. A line tester is used to check a twisted pair line to see whether it is good, dead, reverse wired, or if there is AC voltage on the line.

Looking Glass Sites

Looking glass sites are publicly available sites on which you can test your connectivity to the internet backbone routers. Looking glass sites are remote servers available with a browser that contains common collections of diagnostic tools such as ping and traceroute, with some Border Gateway Protocol (BGP) query tools. Most looking glass sites allow you to select where the diagnostic process will originate from a list of locations, as well as the target destination. You can use a site like www.us.ntt.net to make specific queries to specific backbone routers.

Software Tools

This scenario belongs to the network administrator of a company who troubleshoots the network issues. In this scenario, there are a great number of software tools and utilities to choose from that will assist them in troubleshooting connectivity issues. In fact, many troubleshooting utilities are built into the most common operating systems.

Network/Packet Analyzer

A packet analyzer is like an electron microscope for IT administrators as it inspects the network traffic. Network analyzers are also valuable tools for testing protocols, diagnosing network problems, identifying configuration issues, and resolving network bottlenecks. Finally, information security teams rely on these tools to discover network misuse, vulnerabilities, malware, and attack attempts.

There are many types of packet analyzers but the most commonly used is Wireshark. Wireshark is the world famous, and widely used network protocol analyzer. The figure on next page shows the operation of DHCP on Wireshark by searching DHCP offers and DHCP ACK packets.

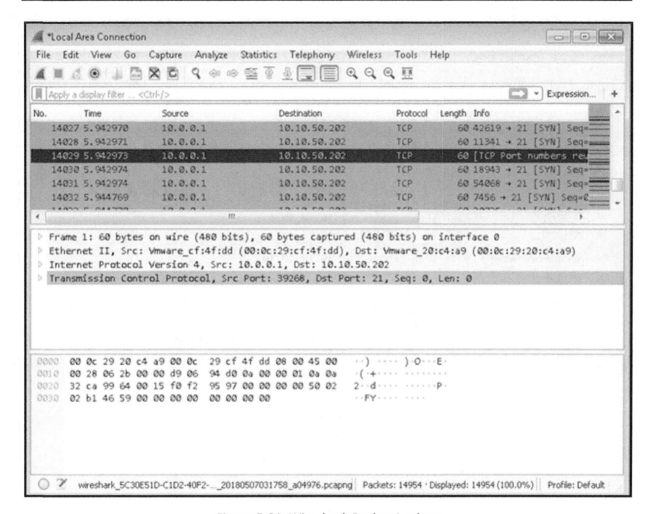

Figure 5-01: Wireshark Packet Analyzer

Port Scanner

A port scanner is a software application designed to examine a server or client for open ports. It is used as a weapon or as a useful tool depending upon the way it is handled. Port scanners are used to verify the security policies on a network. Without prior permission, nobody can use a port scanner on another organization's network. Common port scanners are Nmap, Pentest, and others.

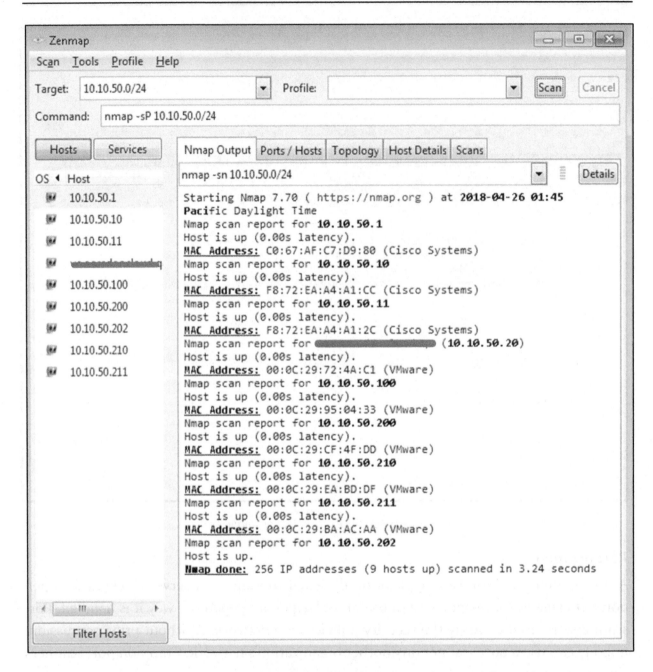

Figure 5-02: Nmap in Action

Protocol Analyzer

Protocol analyzers monitor the different protocols running at different layers on the network. A good protocol analyzer will provide Application, Session, Transport, Network, and Data Link layer information on every frame going through the network. A protocol analyzer tools come in both software and hardware versions. In its hardware interpretation, a protocol analyzer is a specified piece of hardware that is made to be carried around to

various areas of the network and get information about the traffic in that area. In software version, the best and most useful protocol analyzer is Wireshark.

A network protocol analyzer can perform the following functions:

- Helps troubleshoot hard-to-solve problems
- Helps you detect and identify malicious software (malware)
- Helps gather information such as baseline traffic patterns and network-utilization metrics
- Helps you identify unused protocols so that you can remove them from the network
- Provides a traffic generator for penetration testing
- Possibly even works with an IDS

WiFi Analyzer

A Wi-Fi analyzer is any device that looks for and documents all existing wireless networks in the area. Wireless analyzers are handy tools that are useful for diagnosing wireless network issues and conducting site surveys. If your wireless network is experiencing interference, a Wi-Fi analyzer can help you find the source of the interference. It is available in dedicated, hand-held wireless analyzer tools or you can run a site survey software on a laptop or mobile wireless device.

Bandwidth Speed Tester

A simple way to test your network speed is to use a speed test site, such as www.speedtest.net or www.speakeasy.net. These sites provide marketing services and attract people by providing a free speed test that gives the digital results on a meter. People should trust only the first test after they connect to the site because afterwards the cached information might tend to make your results look better than they actually are. These tests are helpful in troubleshooting the speed because they can be counted as reliable.

Interface Monitoring Tools

Interface monitoring tools are used to monitor the traffic flow across specific network interfaces. Using a common tool like PuTTY on a specific router interface, examine the traffic flow. For example, if you use PuTTY into a router, enter the following command:

"debug packet display interface Nic_0 port-80."

This would show you any HTTP (port 80) traffic that was on that interface.

Command Line Tools

Most of the utilities are based on the command line and are not obvious to the end user. For the network administrator, knowledge about these tools and their application regarding troubleshooting will help to set them apart from their peers.

ping/ping6

The ping utility generally is used in all operating systems to tests connections between two nodes. The ping utility uses Internet Control Message Protocol (ICMP) to send an ICMP Echo Request to determine whether the other node can receive the test packet and reply to it. A node that can be reached will respond, and the ping utility will report back successfully. Ping6 utility is used in IPv6 protocol.

```
C:\Users>ping /?

Usage: ping [-t] [-a] [-n count] [-l size] [-f] [-i TTL] [-v TOS]
            [-r count] [-s count] [[-j host-list] | [-k host-list]]
            [-w timeout] [-R] [-S srcaddr] [-c compartment] [-p]
            [-4] [-6] target_name

Options:
    -t              Ping the specified host until stopped.
                    To see statistics and continue - type Control-Break;
                    To stop - type Control-C.
    -a              Resolve addresses to hostnames.
    -n count        Number of echo requests to send.
    -l size         Send buffer size.
    -f              Set Don't Fragment flag in packet (IPv4-only).
    -i TTL          Time To Live.
    -v TOS          Type Of Service (IPv4-only. This setting has been deprecated
                    and has no effect on the type of service field in the IP
                    Header).
    -r count        Record route for count hops (IPv4-only).
    -s count        Timestamp for count hops (IPv4-only).
    -j host-list    Loose source route along host-list (IPv4-only).
    -k host-list    Strict source route along host-list (IPv4-only).
    -w timeout      Timeout in milliseconds to wait for each reply.
    -R              Use routing header to test reverse route also (IPv6-only).
                    Per RFC 5095 the use of this routing header has been
                    deprecated. Some systems may drop echo requests if
                    this header is used.
    -S srcaddr      Source address to use.
```

Figure 5-03: The Ping Tool

tracert/ traceroute

The tracert command traces the route between two hosts. Traceroute tool or tracert tool is a network utility that uses ICMP to create a list of routers through which a packet is transmitted. Using the traceroute tool, users can determine not only the path followed by

the router to reach the packet to the specified destination, but also give details of how long each packet will take to reach the destination.

You can initiate the tracert tool on a Microsoft client by typing tracert at the command prompt followed by a space and then the IP address or hostname of the computer to which you want to test connectivity. You can find a complete list of tracert commands by typing "tracert /?".

Fig 5-04 shows the connection between the windows client and Google.

```
C:\Users\User>tracert googl.com

Tracing route to googl.com [216.58.205.132]
over a maximum of 30 hops:

  1     1 ms    <1 ms    <1 ms   192.168.0.1
  2     *        *        *       Request timed out.
  3    10 ms     3 ms     2 ms   110.37.216.157
  4     3 ms     3 ms     3 ms   58.27.182.149
  5     5 ms     4 ms     7 ms   58.27.209.54
  6     2 ms     2 ms     5 ms   58.27.183.230
  7    18 ms    10 ms    23 ms   tw129-static213.tw1.com [119.63.129.213]
  8     5 ms    12 ms     5 ms   110.93.253.117
  9    53 ms    31 ms    28 ms   72.14.204.14
 10    20 ms    25 ms    27 ms   108.170.240.51
 11   118 ms   119 ms   120 ms   216.239.56.13
 12   119 ms   116 ms   120 ms   108.170.245.81
 13   119 ms   115 ms   122 ms   216.239.42.13
 14   126 ms   126 ms   183 ms   mil04s27-in-f132.1e100.net [216.58.205.132]

Trace complete.
```

Figure 5-04: The Tracert Tool

nslookup

The nslookup utility allows you to troubleshoot problems related to DNS. You can use nslookup to research information about a DNS server or to set a DNS configuration on the server. You can use nslookup in either non-interactive or interactive mode.

If you use the command in non-interactive mode, simply type nslookup in command prompt and press enter then type "?" to see the list of all commands that you want to execute and then type "exit" to close the session. Commands used in interactive mode are the same as those in non-interactive mode, except that you do not have to type nslookup before each command.

Figure 5-05 shows the output of nslookup in interactive mode.

```
C:\Users\User>nslookup
Default Server:  UnKnown
Address:  192.168.0.1

> server
Server:  UnKnown
Address:  192.168.0.1

*** UnKnown can't find server: Non-existent domain
> www.yahoo.com
Server:  UnKnown
Address:  192.168.0.1

Non-authoritative answer:
Name:     atsv2-fp.wg1.b.yahoo.com
Addresses:  2001:4998:44:41d::4
          2001:4998:c:1023::5
          2001:4998:44:41d::3
          2001:4998:c:1023::4
          98.137.246.7
          98.137.246.8
Aliases:  www.yahoo.com

> exit
```

Figure 5-05: The nslookup Tool in Interactive Mode

ipconfig and ifconfig

When troubleshooting a system connected to the network, the basic thing they will most likely want to find out is whether the system has an IP address. The following commands can be used to determine the IP settings on the system:

ipconfig: The ipconfig command is used in Windows to display the IP address information of the system. The following is a list of popular ipconfig commands:

- **ipconfig /all**   Displays all TCP/IP settings and the MAC address

- **ipconfig /displaydns**   Displays the DNS resolver cache

- **ipconfig /flushdns**   Clears out the DNS resolver cache

- **ipconfig /renew**   Releases and renews the IP address of an adapter

- **ipconfig /release**   Releases an IP address that was obtained automatically but does not renew an address

ifconfig: The ifconfig tool is used in Unix and Linux Operating Systems to configure interfaces and view information about configured interfaces. Remember that the syntax of the ifconfig tool is different from the syntax of ipconfig.

The following is a list of popular ifconfig commands:

- **ifconfig**   Displays the network card and IP settings
- **ifconfig eth0 up**   Enables the first Ethernet card
- **ifconfig eth0 down** Disables the Ethernet card

iptables

The iptables utility in Linux enabled command-line control over IPv4 tables governs what happens with an IPv4 packet when it encounters a firewall.

netstat

The netstat command is used in all operating systems, this enables a network administrator to examine network statistics about a system. These statistics include information such as the ports listening on the system and any connections that have been established. This is an output from the netstat command:

```
C:\Users\User>netstat

Active Connections

  Proto  Local Address          Foreign Address        State
  TCP    192.168.0.36:57098     xiva-daria:https       ESTABLISHED
  TCP    192.168.0.36:57112     13.94.24.143:https     ESTABLISHED
  TCP    192.168.0.36:57115     52.230.84.217:https    ESTABLISHED
  TCP    192.168.0.36:57116     sc-in-f188:5228        ESTABLISHED
  TCP    192.168.0.36:57133     fjr02s04-in-f3:https   ESTABLISHED
  TCP    192.168.0.36:57134     172.217.194.94:https   ESTABLISHED
  TCP    192.168.0.36:57136     151.101.9.132:https    ESTABLISHED
  TCP    192.168.0.36:57137     192.168.1.255:1688     SYN_SENT
```

```
C:\Users>netstat /a

Active Connections

  Proto  Local Address          Foreign Address        State
  TCP    0.0.0.0:135            IPSpecialist-18:0       LISTENING
  TCP    0.0.0.0:445            IPSpecialist-18:0       LISTENING
  TCP    0.0.0.0:2869           IPSpecialist-18:0       LISTENING
  TCP    0.0.0.0:5040           IPSpecialist-18:0       LISTENING
  TCP    0.0.0.0:7680           IPSpecialist-18:0       LISTENING
  TCP    0.0.0.0:49664          IPSpecialist-18:0       LISTENING
  TCP    0.0.0.0:49665          IPSpecialist-18:0       LISTENING
  TCP    0.0.0.0:49666          IPSpecialist-18:0       LISTENING
  TCP    0.0.0.0:49667          IPSpecialist-18:0       LISTENING
  TCP    0.0.0.0:49668          IPSpecialist-18:0       LISTENING
  TCP    0.0.0.0:49669          IPSpecialist-18:0       LISTENING
  TCP    0.0.0.0:59492          IPSpecialist-18:0       LISTENING
  TCP    127.0.0.1:10000        IPSpecialist-18:0       LISTENING
  TCP    127.0.0.1:49954        IPSpecialist-18:49955   ESTABLISHED
  TCP    127.0.0.1:49955        IPSpecialist-18:49954   ESTABLISHED
  TCP    127.0.0.1:49957        IPSpecialist-18:49958   ESTABLISHED
  TCP    127.0.0.1:49958        IPSpecialist-18:49957   ESTABLISHED
  TCP    127.0.0.1:49959        IPSpecialist-18:49960   ESTABLISHED
  TCP    127.0.0.1:49960        IPSpecialist-18:49959   ESTABLISHED
  TCP    127.0.0.1:49973        IPSpecialist-18:49974   ESTABLISHED
  TCP    127.0.0.1:49974        IPSpecialist-18:49973   ESTABLISHED
  TCP    127.0.0.1:50117        IPSpecialist-18:50118   ESTABLISHED
  TCP    127.0.0.1:50118        IPSpecialist-18:50117   ESTABLISHED
  TCP    127.0.0.1:50151        IPSpecialist-18:50152   ESTABLISHED
```

Figure 5-06: Common Netstat Tool

tcpdump

The tcpdump command is a Linux/UNIX based utility used to print the contents of network packets. It can read packets from a network interface card or from a previously created saved packet file and write packets to either standard output or a file.

pathping

Pathping is the combination of ping and tracert utility that performs the function of the connectivity test of ping with the path discovery of traceroute into one command. Pathping displays the connectivity statistics and the specific paths that follow the packets. The only disadvantage to pathping is that it can be slow to run.

```
C:\Users>pathping

Usage: pathping [-g host-list] [-h maximum_hops] [-i address] [-n]
                [-p period] [-q num_queries] [-w timeout]
                [-4] [-6] target_name

Options:
    -g host-list      Loose source route along host-list.
    -h maximum_hops   Maximum number of hops to search for target.
    -i address        Use the specified source address.
    -n                Do not resolve addresses to hostnames.
    -p period         Wait period milliseconds between pings.
    -q num_queries    Number of queries per hop.
    -w timeout        Wait timeout milliseconds for each reply.
    -4                Force using IPv4.
    -6                Force using IPv6.
```

Figure 5-07: pathping in Action

nmap

Another way to ping a host is by performing a ping using Nmap. Using the Windows or Linux command prompt, enter the following command:

nmap –sP –v *<target IP address>*

Upon successful response from the targeted host, if the command successfully finds a live host, it returns a message indicating that the IP address of the targeted host is up, along with the Media Access Control (MAC) address and the network card vendor.

Apart from ICMP echo request packets and ping sweep, Nmap also offers a quick scan. Enter the following command for a quick scan:

nmap –sP –PE –PA*<port numbers> <starting IP/ending IP>*
For example:
nmap –sP –PE –PA 2 1,23,80,3389 < 192. 168.0. 1-50>

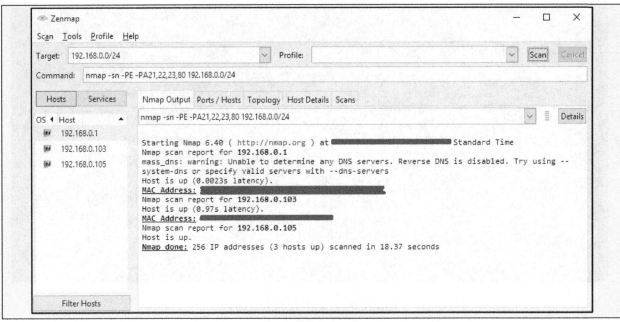

Figure 5-08: Nmap

Nmap, in a nutshell, offers host discovery, port discovery, service discovery, version information of an operating system, hardware (MAC) address information, service version detection, vulnerabilities, and exploit detection using the Nmap Scripting Engine (NSE).

Note
Nmap Scripting engine is the most powerful engine for network discovery, version detection, vulnerability detection, and backdoor detection.

route

The route utility is an often-used and very handy tool. With the route command, we can display and modify the routing table on Windows and Linux systems.

Figure 5-09 shows the output from a **route print** command on a Windows system.

```
C:\Users>route print
===========================================================================
Interface List
 18...ec b1 d7 99 6a 4b ......Intel(R) Ethernet Connection I218-LM
 17...80 19 34 f3 84 24 ......Microsoft Wi-Fi Direct Virtual Adapter
 16...82 19 34 f3 84 23 ......Microsoft Wi-Fi Direct Virtual Adapter #2
  9...80 19 34 f3 84 23 ......Intel(R) Dual Band Wireless-N 7260
  1...........................Software Loopback Interface 1
===========================================================================

IPv4 Route Table
===========================================================================
Active Routes:
Network Destination        Netmask          Gateway       Interface  Metric
          0.0.0.0          0.0.0.0      192.168.0.1    192.168.0.113     45
        127.0.0.0        255.0.0.0         On-link        127.0.0.1    331
        127.0.0.1  255.255.255.255         On-link        127.0.0.1    331
  127.255.255.255  255.255.255.255         On-link        127.0.0.1    331
      192.168.0.0    255.255.255.0         On-link    192.168.0.113    301
    192.168.0.113  255.255.255.255         On-link    192.168.0.113    301
    192.168.0.255  255.255.255.255         On-link    192.168.0.113    301
        224.0.0.0        240.0.0.0         On-link        127.0.0.1    331
        224.0.0.0        240.0.0.0         On-link    192.168.0.113    301
  255.255.255.255  255.255.255.255         On-link        127.0.0.1    331
  255.255.255.255  255.255.255.255         On-link    192.168.0.113    301
===========================================================================
Persistent Routes:
  None
```

Figure 5-09: The Output from a "route print" Command

arp

The arp utility usually found in all operating systems helps to diagnose the problems associated with the Address Resolution Protocol (ARP). ARP is a service that operates in the background and resolves IP addresses to MAC addresses so that packets can be delivered to their destination. As you may know, each computer keeps an arp cache of entries that have been recently resolved probably within the past 10 minutes. Primarily, the computer checks the arp cache then, if the entry is not in the cache, arp will be used to broadcast into the local network and request that the computer with a specific IP address responds with its MAC address so that the packet can be addressed and delivered.

```
C:\Users>arp -a

Interface: 192.168.0.113 --- 0x9
  Internet Address        Physical Address        Type
  192.168.0.1             b0-be-76-17-d9-76        dynamic
  192.168.0.255           ff-ff-ff-ff-ff-ff        static
  224.0.0.22              01-00-5e-00-00-16        static
  224.0.0.251             01-00-5e-00-00-fb        static
  224.0.0.252             01-00-5e-00-00-fc        static
  239.255.255.250         01-00-5e-7f-ff-fa        static
  255.255.255.255         ff-ff-ff-ff-ff-ff        static
```

Figure 5-10: The arp Tool

dig

dig is used on a Linux, UNIX, or Mac OS to perform manual DNS lookups. dig performs the same basic task as nslookup, but with one major difference; The dig command does not have an interactive mode and instead uses only command-line switches to modify results. Like nslookup, dig can be used to perform simple name resolution requests.

nbtstat

The nbtstat (NetBIOS over TCP/IP statistics) is a utility that displays protocol statistics and current TCP/IP connections using NBT (NetBIOS over TCP/IP), which allows the user to troubleshoot NetBIOS name resolution issues. Normally, name resolution is made when NetBIOS over TCP/IP is functioning correctly. It does this through local cache lookup, WINS or DNS server query or Hosts lookup.

```
C:\Users>nbtstat

Displays protocol statistics and current TCP/IP connections using NBT
(NetBIOS over TCP/IP).

NBTSTAT [ [-a RemoteName] [-A IP address] [-c] [-n]
        [-r] [-R] [-RR] [-s] [-S] [interval] ]

  -a   (adapter status) Lists the remote machine's name table given its name
  -A   (Adapter status) Lists the remote machine's name table given its
                        IP address.
  -c   (cache)          Lists NBT's cache of remote [machine] names and their IP addresses
  -n   (names)          Lists local NetBIOS names.
  -r   (resolved)       Lists names resolved by broadcast and via WINS
  -R   (Reload)         Purges and reloads the remote cache name table
  -S   (Sessions)       Lists sessions table with the destination IP addresses
  -s   (sessions)       Lists sessions table converting destination IP
                        addresses to computer NETBIOS names.
  -RR  (ReleaseRefresh) Sends Name Release packets to WINS and then, starts Refresh

  RemoteName   Remote host machine name.
  IP address   Dotted decimal representation of the IP address.
  interval     Redisplays selected statistics, pausing interval seconds
               between each display. Press Ctrl+C to stop redisplaying
               statistics.
```

Figure 5-11: The nbtstat Tool

Here are some nbtstat options with their functions:

nbtstat –n Displays name registered locally by the system

nbtstat –c Displays the NetBIOS name cache entries

nbtstat –a Displays the names registered by a remote system

Exam Tip

Although we have commonly used the Windows tracert command to provide sample output, the output from traceroute on a UNIX, Linux, or Mac OS is extremely similar.

Mind Map of Network Troubleshooting Tools

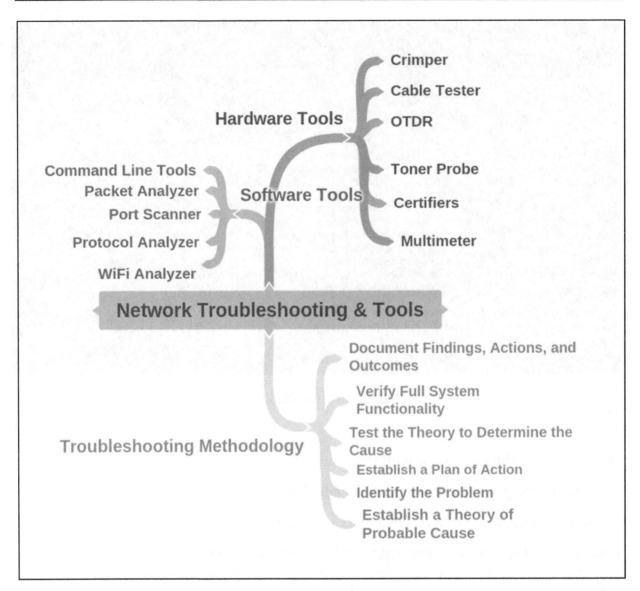

Figure 5-12: Mind Map of Network Troubleshooting Tools

Troubleshooting Wired Connectivity and Performance Issues

Wired connectivity and performance issues can be caused by a wide variety of objects, including configuration, hardware, software, and interference.

Attenuation/Db loss

Attenuation is a loss of signal strength. It is calculated in decibels (dB). During any transmission, if attenuation factor rises, transmissions increase. Several factors such as noise, surroundings, and distance causes attenuation. To overcome attenuation, several repeaters are installed to boost the signal.

Latency

Latency metric is similar to delay metric that defines the amount of time taken by the data packets to travel from a source to destination. The difference is that delay is only a routing metric, whereas latency also deals beyond routing such as in hard drive or memory.

Jitter

Jitter is formed when certain amount of latency is expected between connections, when the latency and response rate starts to vary, and becomes inconsistent. Usually, this is noticeable in streaming applications and can be directly affected by the bandwidth. Jitter is one of the biggest problems with VoIP.

Crosstalk

Crosstalk is a scenario where signals are interfering with each other. Consider two copper wires installed close to each other. Signals passing through one cable may interfere with the signal transmission of another cable. There are two types of crosstalk:

1. Near-End Crosstalk (NEXT)
2. Far-End Crosstalk (FEXT)

Near-End Crosstalk (NEXT)

Near-End Crosstalk (NEXT) is an undesired condition of cabling when interference is observed in communication due to adjacent pairs of the copper cable. Basically, NEXT is observed in adjacent pairs of twisted pair cables. NEXT is usually caused by crossed or crushed wire pairs.

Far-End Crosstalk (FEXT)

Far-End Crosstalk (FEXT) is coupling between transmitting pairs. As a result, outgoing signals are coupled back into a receiving signal.

EMI/RFI

Electromagnetic Interference (EMI) or Radio-Frequency Interference (RFI) is basically interference in a radio spectrum, which may degrade the performance of the signal. It is an interference in a signal by an external source, either by coupling, electromagnetic induction or by conductivity.

Shorts

Short is a scenario in which one or more pins of the cable are connected to the wrong pin. Using cable testers, you can easily check the connectivity of pins.

Opens

Opens are a faulty installation of a copper cable when one or more pins of the cable is unable to provide connectivity. Improper installation of a connector and faulty trimming of wires cause no connectivity across the pins.

Bad Wiring

Bad wiring is where the abnormal sequence of wiring scheme is used to install a connector of a copper cable. No connection will take place in result of bad wiring. After installation of a connector, you can check the connectivity using cable testers.

Incorrect Termination

Copper cables require appropriate wiring scheme on both ends of the cable. There are two standards for Ethernet cable: TIA-568A and TIA-568B. Straight-through cables must be ended with either TIA-568A on both ends or TIA-568B on both ends. Similarly, crossover cables should be ended with TIA-568A on one end, and TIA-568B at the other.

Straight-through Cable

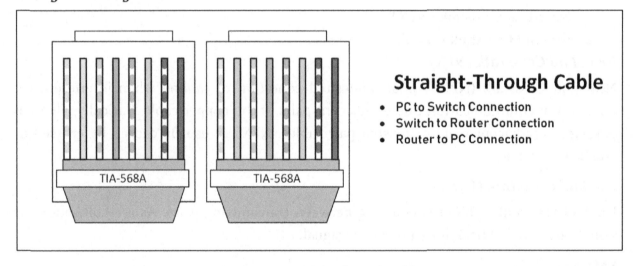

Figure 5-13: Straight-through Cable

Crossover

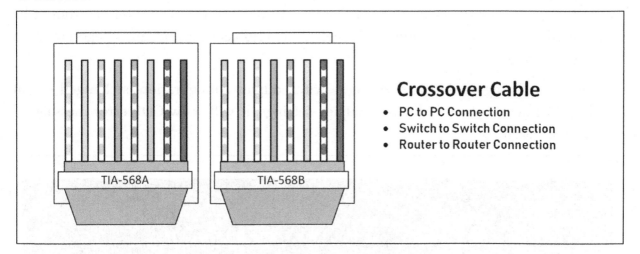

Figure 5-14: Crossover Cable

Bad Connector

Connectors of the Ethernet cable must be checked after installation. Any looseness or damage to the connector will affect the communication. Improper installation of the connector will result in the unavailability of the network.

Bad Port

Most probably, connectivity issue is generated by the port into which the cable is connected. On many devices, ports have LEDs that can alert users to a bad port. In most cases, a lack of any light whatsoever indicates an issue with the port. Loopback plugs can be used to test the functionality of a port. These devices send a signal out and then back in the port to test the port.

Transceiver Mismatch

Interfaces that function as sender and receiver are called transceivers. When a NIC is connected to a port, the two transceivers must have some same settings or otherwise issues will occur. These settings are duplex and speed setting. If the speed settings do not match, there will be no communication. If the duplex settings are incorrect, there may be functionality but the performance will be poor.

Tx/Rx Reverse

Old device NICs do not support Medium-Dependant Interface Crossover (MDIX). Auto MDIX is a feature that can automatically detect the cable type connected to the NIC to avoid reversing the Tx/Rx signals.

Speed and Duplex Mismatch

A different configuration of interfaces like speed and negotiation, connected with each other through a link, will cause Speed/Duplex Mismatch error. The interface should be configured with either the same parameters, or auto-sensing and auto-negotiation to prevent a mismatch.

As shown in the figure on the next page, switch duplex configuration is changed to full duplex. As a switch detects different duplex settings, it will show CDP error message of duplex mismatch.

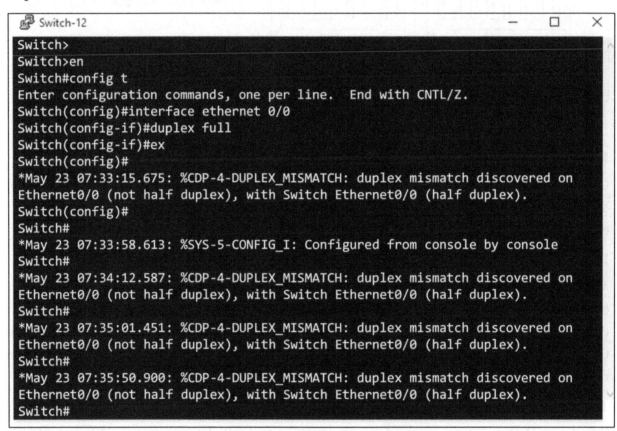

Figure 5-15: Duplex Mismatch Error

Damaged Cable

Sometimes, the cable could be damaged by the environmental factors from outside or sometimes, it could be the mishandling by an employee from inside. In any cases, the communication will stop.

Bent Pins

Many of the connectors we encounter have small pins on the end that must go into particular holes on the interface to which they plug. If these pins get bent, either they will not go into the correct hole or they will not plug in completely. When this occurs, the cable

either will not work at all or will not work properly. Taking care not to bend these fragile pins when working with such cable types will prevent this issue from occurring.

Split Pairs

A split pair is a faulty wiring scenario where wires of a twisted pair are twisted again with the wires of another pair. Wires of the same twisted pairs, are twisted to reduce or cancel interference. Hence, split pair condition creates interference.

Bottleneck

A network bottleneck refers to a discrete condition in which data flow is limited by network resources. There are four vital resources on any network or any devices on the network: processor, memory, disk subsystem, and a network subsystem. A serious weakness in any of the network resources can easily spread and affect the other resources. This will cause a network bottleneck.

VLAN Mismatch

As we know, VLANs provide Layer 2 segmentation. If a computer is in the same VLAN, it will communicate whether it is located next to the source computer or located anywhere on the network. To establish communication between different VLANs, we require Inter-VLAN routing.

Issues related to incorrect VLAN assignment, may result in unavailability of network resources, higher or limited security permissions, etc. To prevent incorrect assignment of VLANs, the network administrator must document the arrangement or division of VLANs. When any device is moved, making sure it is properly assigned to the correct VLAN.

Network Connection LED Status Indicators

When you are facing hardware failure, pay attention to the blinking lights that indicate the connectivity status of a network. LED status indicators, such as solid green represents connection, blinking green represents communication, amber represents possible connection issue, and other colors on various devices enable technicians to notice certain problems, and then take responsive action.

Troubleshooting Wireless Connectivity and Performance Issues

Wireless networks are pretty magical when they work right, but their nature of being wireless often makes them vexing things to troubleshoot when they do not. Let's consider a scenario in which you are in charge of the wireless connectivity for your network. There are many issues specific to wireless networks that can keep them from functioning properly.

Reflection

Reflection is caused due to bouncing off lights on objects, which causes multipath propagation of signals. This makes the signals vulnerable to interference and even fading. Furthermore, Wireless Access Points (WAPs) get overloaded when a signal sent by one device takes many different paths to get to the receiving point. These multiple signals are difficult for an 802.11 receiver to modulate. We should minimize reflection first by trying to reduce issues that might reflect a signal. Secondly, we use WAPs with multiple antennas in a process called multipath.

Refraction

Refraction involves the bending of light, and occurs when a signal goes through an object and, on the other side, follows a different angle. This is caused when light travels from one medium to another. This also causes multipath propagation and its resulting effects. Similar to addressing reflection, we minimize refraction first by trying to reduce issues that might refract a signal, and secondly by using WAPs with multiple antennas to achieve multipath.

Absorption

Absorption also involves a signal passing through an object like refraction, but in this case, some of the signal strength stays behind, and is absorbed. Now, when the signal continues to propagate, it will be much weaker. This can cause the greatest effect on wireless connectivity and performance. Again, we minimize absorption first by trying to reduce issues that might absorb a signal, and secondly by using multiple antennas.

Latency

Latency metric is similar to delay metric that defines the amount of time taken by the data packets to travel from a source to destination. The difference is that delay is only a routing metric whereas latency also deals with beyond routing such as in hard drive or memory.

Jitter

Jitter is formed when certain amount of latency is expected between connections, when the latency and response rates start to vary, and become inconsistent. Usually this is noticeable in streaming applications, and can be directly affected by the bandwidth. Jitter is one of the biggest problems with VoIP.

Attenuation

Attenuation is a loss of signal strength. It is calculated in decibels (dB). During any transmission, if attenuation factor rises, transmissions increase. Several factors such as noise, surroundings, and distance causes attenuation. To overcome attenuation, several repeaters are installed to boost the signal.

Incorrect Antenna Type

Many wireless installations ignore the type of antennas, and leave it on the WAPs to use their default antennas. In most cases, the omnidirectional antennas give the best support for WAPs and they are often used as a default antenna in many WAPs. In some cases, the default antenna type placed in WAPs are incorrect or not the omnidirectional antenna and needs to be replaced. Hence, if signal becomes faded or lost, do not forget to consider the antenna type for wireless setup.

Interference

One of the factors that can cause a signal loss is an interference. The interference is usually caused by radio frequency sources, RFI from non-Wi-Fi sources and RFI from Wi-Fi networks. Non-Wi-Fi sources of RFI include lighting and low-power RF devices such as Bluetooth, wireless phones, and microwaves that are close to wireless frequency can cause a signal bleed and inhibit or even prevent wireless communications.

On the other hand, environmental factors such as the distance between the client and WAP as well as the type of construction between them can also affect the power of the intended signal and therefore make any interference from other signals more prominent. To prevent the signal from interference, you should place a WAP in such a way that no other device in the area can cause interference. If the interference is on the client side, you can move the client away from the source of the interference.

Incorrect Antenna Placement

Antenna placement on WAPs is very important to avoid signal loss or dead spots. A dead spot is a place that should be covered by the network signal but where devices get no signal. Dead spots just happen in a wireless network due to environmental factors. When installing a network, you must look out for concrete walls, metal especially metal studs, and the use of special RF-blocking window film. To avoid these type of blocking, carefully plan the WAP placement and understand that even in the best-planned environment, it is not at all unusual to move WAPs based on the need to clear dead spots.

Optimal antenna placement varies according to the filled dead spots and security concerns. Use the site survey and the wireless analyzer tools to find dead spots, odd corners, and so on.

Overlapping Channels

Wireless networks operate at many different frequencies within a band of frequencies typically the 2.4 GHz or 5 GHz band. These frequencies are sometimes combined to provide greater bandwidth for the user. A combination of these frequencies that can be used by the

end user is referred to as a channel. To establish communication between the WAP and the clients, they both must be on the same channel. Most often, wireless networks use channel 1, 6, or 11 because the frequencies in those channels do not overlap each other. All channels except 1, 6, or 11 are overlapping and can cause interference and signal loss.

Standard	Frequency	Modulation	Speed
802.11a	5 GHz	OFDM	54 Mbps
802.11b	2.4 GHz	DSSs	11 Mbps
802.11g	2.4 GHz	OFDM , DSSS	54 Mbps
802.11n	2.4 , 5 GHz	OFDM	54 Mbps
802.16 (WiMAX)	10 - 66 GHz	OFDM	70-1000 Mbps
Bluetooth	2.4 GHz		1 – 3 Mbps

Table 5-02: Wireless Standards

Overcapacity

When wireless users complain that the network is slow (latency) or that they are losing their connection to applications during a session, it is usually a problem of capacity or distance. Remember, 802.11 is a shared medium, and as more users connect, all user throughput goes down. If this becomes a constant problem as opposed to the occasional issue where 20 members with laptops gather for a meeting every six months in a conference room, it may be the time to consider placing a second AP in the area. When doing this, you must place the second AP on a different non-overlapping channel from the first and make sure the second AP uses the same SSID as the first.

Distance Limitations

Wireless networking speed ranges from 2 Mbps to a theoretical limit of 1 Gbps for 802.11ac. The speed is affected by the distance between wireless nodes, interference from other wireless devices such as wireless phones, and other solid objects such as metal plumbing or air conditioning units.

Frequency Mismatch

Wireless networks operate at many different frequencies within a band of frequencies typically the 2.4 GHz or 5 GHz band. These frequencies are sometimes combined to provide greater bandwidth for the user. A combination of these frequencies that can be used by the end user is referred to as a channel. To establish communication between the WAP and the clients, they must be on the same channel. Most often, wireless networks use channel 1, 6, or 11 because the frequencies in those channels do not overlap each other.

Wrong SSID

It is easy to access the wrong SSID. Some 802.11 clients are notorious for moving their list of discovered SSIDs in such a way that you think you are clicking one SSID when you are actually (accidentally) clicking the wrong one. The only fix to this is to be attentive when logging onto a new SSID. Manually entering an SSID can obviously result in a typing error. Luckily, in these cases your typing error will not redirect you to another SSID. You will just get an error.

Wrong Passphrase

The passphrase must be entered correctly on the wireless client node or communication will fail. The wrong passphrase will not give access to users on a wireless network.

Security Type Mismatch

Wireless networks can use encryption to secure their communications and different encryption techniques are used for wireless networks, like Wired Equivalent Privacy (WEP) and Wi-Fi Protected Access 2 (WPA2) with Advanced Encryption Standard (AES). To enable the highest security feature, configure the wireless networks with the highest encryption protocol that both the WAP and the clients can support. Also, make sure the AP and its clients are configured with the same type of encryption.

Power Levels

While deploying a wireless network, it is important to consider that an access point should not be placed so far that it cannot cover the premises. For example, if you are in your office and you are facing trouble connecting with the access point, you have to come closer to the access point because of the lower power level. Similarly, an access point with higher power level will cover more area.

Signal-to-Noise Ratio

The Signal-to-Noise Ratio (SNR) compares the level of the Wi-Fi signal to the level of background noise. Sources of noise can include microwave ovens, cordless phones, Bluetooth devices, wireless video cameras, wireless game controllers, fluorescent lights, and more. A ratio of 10-15dB is the accepted minimum to establish an unreliable connection; 16-24dB (decibels) is usually considered poor; 25-40dB is good, and a ratio of 41dB or higher is considered excellent.

Troubleshooting Common Network Issues

Certain scenarios can be indicative of network service issues. There could be DNS issues, DHCP issues, default gateway issues, certificate issues, firewall issues, hardware issues, and more. These logical issues can cause an abundance of network problems. Most of these happen due to the device being improperly configured.

Names not Resolving

When a DNS is misconfigured, DNS queries will not resolve it. The user can ping the destination by its IP address but not by its name. Misconfigured DNS settings on a client will stop name resolution, and network may appear to be down.

Incorrect IP configuration/default gateway

Incorrect IP configuration or wrong gateway configuration will result in the unavailability of the network. Most common problems are using static IP configuration in a dynamic host configuration environment and using incorrect static IP, subnet or gateway configuration.

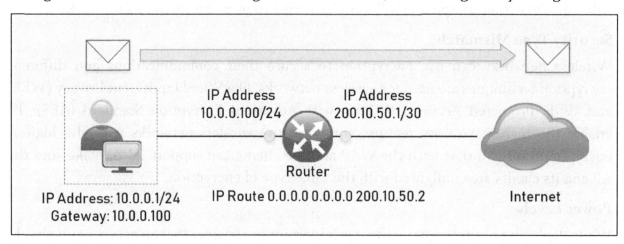

Figure 5-16: Default Routing

The figure above shows a small network connected to the internet with the correct configuration. Now, consider the same scenario where a host user is configured with an incorrect IP address. This incorrect configuration prevents the user from accessing the network to which it is physically connected.

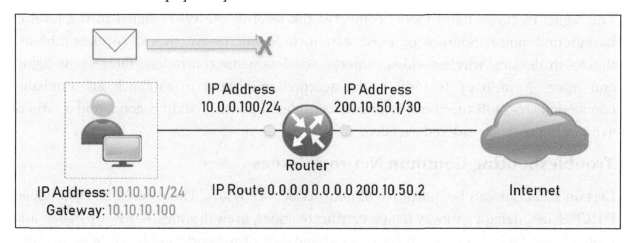

Figure 5-17: Misconfigured Default Gateway

Similarly, wrong default gateway configuration will not route the traffic destined toward the internet. The user can send traffic to the router, but the router will not forward the traffic to correct next hop because of incorrect default gateway configuration.

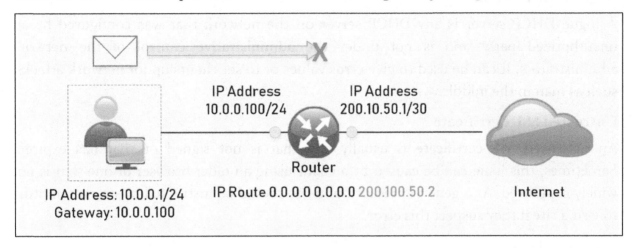

Figure 5-18: Misconfigured Route

Incorrect Netmask

When the subnet mask is incorrect, the router thinks the network is divided into segments other than how it is actually configured. As the purpose of the router is to route traffic, a wrong subnet mask here can cause it to try to route traffic to subnets that do not exist. The value of the subnet mask on the router must be same as the true configuration of the network.

Duplicate IP Addresses

In static IP addressing, there is a chance of assigning duplicate IP addresses. In a network, each network device must be configured with a unique IP address to be identified. If more than one devices have the same IP address, there will be a conflict of IP addresses.

Duplicate MAC Addresses

MAC addresses should never be duplicated in our environment. Each interface vendor is issued an Organizationally Unique Identifier (OUI), which will match all interfaces produced by that vendor, and then the vendor will be responsible for ensuring unique MAC addresses. Thus, duplicate MAC addresses usually indicate a MAC spoofing attack, in which some malicious individual changes their MAC address, which can be done quite easily in the properties of the NIC.

Expired IP Address

An expired IP address can lead a system not to connect. Normally, DHCP clients will renew existing leases before they expire, but this problem could manifest itself if the DHCP servers

go down and are unable to renew leases. Try resetting the NIC and consulting the DHCP servers.

Rogue DHCP Server

A rogue DHCP server is any DHCP server on the network that was configured by an unauthorized party and is not under the administrative control of the network administrators. It can be used to give error values or to set clients up for network attacks, such as man in the middle.

Untrusted SSL Certificate

An untrusted SSL certificate is usually one that is not signed or that has expired. Sometimes, this issue can be caused by a client using an older browser or one that is not widely supported. As a general precaution, users should be instructed to stop attempting to visit a site if they suspect this error.

Incorrect Time

Incorrect time on a network can be the most annoying thing because timestamps are important in the event of trying to commit an attack. Most network devices use Network Time Protocol (NTP) to keep the system time updated as defined by a designated server. Make sure that server has the correct time on it and is updated, patched, and secured.

Exhausted DHCP Scope

If the DHCP server's scope of IP addresses has been compromised, a simple ipconfig /renew will not mitigate. Users will get an error that directs to an exhausted DHCP scope. Assuming this is not caused by a DHCP starvation attack, the only fix is to make changes at the DHCP server.

Blocked TCP/UDP Ports

As a security perspective, only needed ports should be enabled and allowed on a network. Unfortunately, users do not know exactly which ports they need, and it is possible to inadvertently have some blocked TCP/UDP ports that they need to use. If users find their firewall is blocking a needed port, that port should be opened, made an exception, and allowed to be used.

Incorrect Firewall Settings

Incorrect firewall settings typically fall under the category of blocking ports that need to be opened or allowing ports that do not. From a security perspective, the following situation is the worse because every open port represents a door that an intruder could use to access the system or at least a vulnerability. Be sure to know which ports to keep opened, and close any that are not needed.

Incorrect ACL Settings

Access Control Lists (ACLs) are used to control which traffic types can enter and exit ports on the router. When mistakes are made either in the configurations of the ACLs or in their application, many devices may be affected. The creation and application of these tools should only be done by those who have been experienced in their syntax and in the logic ACLs used in their operation.

Unresponsive Service

When a service does not respond, it could be due to overload, being down, or bad configuration. The first order of business is to determine which of these three the situation is and then decide what we need to do to fix it. If the server/service is overloaded, look for a way to increase the capacity or balance the load. If the server/service is down, investigate why and what needs to be done to restore it again. If the server/service is misconfigured, make the necessary changes to configure it properly.

Hardware Failure

A hardware failure can certainly make a network device unresponsive. When we are facing hardware failure, pay attention to the blinking lights that indicates the connectivity status of a network. LED status indicators, such as solid green represents connection, blinking green represents communication, amber represents possible connection issue, and other colors on many devices enable technicians to notice certain problems, and then take responsive action.

Mind Map of Network Troubleshooting

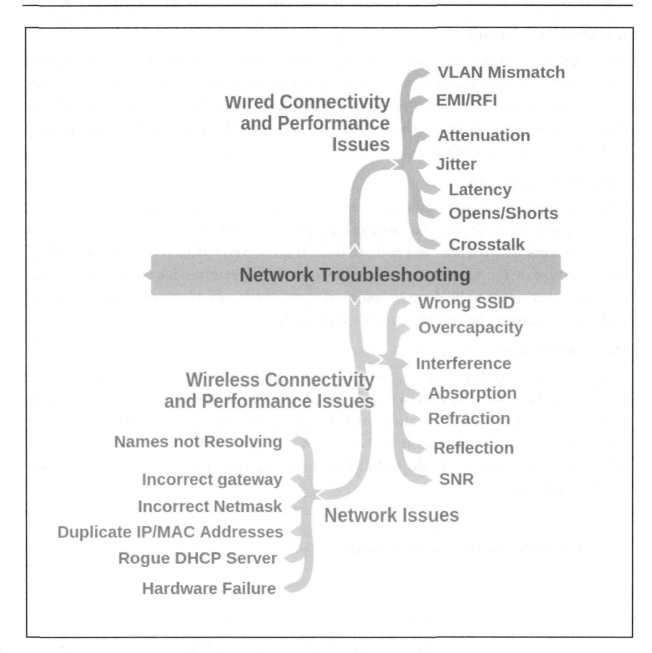

Figure 5-19: Mind Map of Network Troubleshooting

Summary

Network Troubleshooting Methodology

- There is no reference guide to troubleshooting every possible network problem because such a guide would be obsolete the moment it is created
- A basic troubleshooting model may include the following steps:
  1. Identify the problem.
  2. Establish a theory of probable cause.

3. Test the theory to determine cause.
4. Establish a plan of action to resolve the problem and identify potential effects.
5. Implement the solution or escalate as necessary.
6. Verify full system functionality and, if applicable, implement preventative measures.
7. Document findings, actions, and outcomes.

Use Appropriate Tool

- While working through the process of troubleshooting, we need some specific tools
- These tools may be the software and hardware tools that provide information about the network and enact repairs
- Typical built-in command-line utilities used for troubleshooting include ping, tracert/traceroute, nslookup, dig, ipconfig, ifconfig, iptables, netstat, pathping, route, and arp

Troubleshooting Wired Connectivity and Performance Issues

- Wired connectivity and performance issues can be caused by a wide variety of objects, including configuration, hardware, software, and interference
- Attenuation is the weakening of a signal as it travels long distances
- Network connection LED status indicators can give you a quick glance as to what's going right and what's going wrong on your network

Troubleshooting Wireless Connectivity and Performance Issues

- Wireless networks are pretty magical when they work right, but their nature of being wireless often makes them vexing things to troubleshoot when they do not
- The concepts of latency, jitter, and attenuation apply to wireless connectivity in the same way they relate to wired connectivity
- Entering the wrong SSID, wrong passphrase, or wrong encryption key will cause a wireless network connection to fail

Troubleshooting Common Network Issues

- Certain scenarios can be indicative of network service issues
- There could be DNS issues, DHCP issues, default gateway issues, certificate issues, firewall issues, hardware issues, and more
- These logical issues can cause an abundance of network problems. Most of these happen due to a device being improperly configured

Practice Questions

1. What is the purpose of the "ipconfig" command?
   A. It displays IP addresses information
   B. It displays interface configuration
   C. It is used to configure an interface
   D. It is used to assign an IP address

2. To which operating system does "ifconfig" command belong?
   A. Windows
   B. Linux
   C. MAC
   D. Android

3. To which operating system does "ipconfig" command belongs?
   A. Windows
   B. Linux
   C. MAC
   D. Android

4. Which of the following command can be used to examine active connections' information?
   A. Netstat
   B. Nslookup
   C. Ping
   D. Nbstat

5. "tracerout" command is used in _____.
   A. Windows NT-based OS
   B. Unix OS
   C. MacOS
   D. None of the above

6. "tracert" command is used in _____.
   A. Windows NT-based OS
   B. Unix OS
   C. MacOS
   D. None of the above

7. The command "nbtstat -a" displays the list of _____.
   A. NBT's cache of remote [machine] names and their IP addresses
   B. Remote machine's name table given its IP address
   C. Local NetBIOS names
   D. Remote machine's name table given its name

8. Most Appropriate command to troubleshoot DNS related issues is _____.
   A. Ping
   B. Nslookup
   C. Traceroute
   D. ARP

9. Which tool is used to test the connectivity of wires that run through walls and other obstructions?
   A. Speed Test Sites
   B. Cable Tester
   C. Toner Probe
   D. Looking Glass Sites

10. Which of the following cable issues is caused by signal bleed from wires running next to each other in a cable?
    E. Short
    F. Open
    G. Crosstalk
    H. EMI

11. Which handy tool is used to connect network wires to a patch panel?
    A. Cable Crimpers
    B. Wire Strippers
    C. Punch Down
    D. Snips

12. The command "nbtstat -n" displays the list of _____.
    A. NBT's cache of remote [machine] names and their IP addresses
    B. Remote machine's name table given its IP address
    C. Local NetBIOS names
    D. Remote machine's name table given its name

13. Which of the following are characteristics of RADIUS? (Choose 2)
    A. It is TCP based
    B. It is UDP based
    C. It encrypts an entire authentication packet
    D. It only encrypts the password in an authentication packet

14. What is the purpose of packet sniffers?
    A. It is used for discarding frames
    B. It is used for sending transmissions from one port to another port
    C. It is used for looking inside every packet on a network segment
    D. It is used for stopping malicious behavior on the network

15. You need to trace cables in multiple-pair wiring. What tool will you use?
    A. Toner Probe
    B. IDS
    C. Cable Tester
    D. Line Testers

16. Which of the following tools can test a port on a device?
    A. Cable Certifier
    B. Loopback Plug
    C. Line Testers
    D. Toner Probe

17. Which device would be used to measure voltage?
    A. Multimeter
    B. OTDR
    C. Line Testers
    D. Toner Probe

18. Which tool would you use if you want to find a break in a fiber-optic connection and test the fiber connectivity on the network?
    A. Multimeter
    B. OTDR
    C. Line Testers
    D. Toner Probe

19. Which of the following are not steps stated in the Network+ troubleshooting model?
    A. Reboot the servers
    B. Identify the problem
    C. Test the theory to determine the cause
    D. Implement the solution or escalate as necessary
    E. Document findings, actions, and outcomes

20. When wireless users complain that they are losing their connection to applications during a session, what is the source of the problem?
    A. Incorrect SSID
    B. Latency
    C. Incorrect Encryption
    D. MAC Address Filter

Answers:

Chapter 01: Networking Concept

1. **A. & D.** (Easier Administration & Assigning IP Addresses to Hosts)
   Explanation: DHCP servers assign IP addresses to hosts. Thus, DHCP allows easier administration by providing IP information to each host automatically.

2. **B.** (Translates human name to IP address)
   Explanation: DNS translates human names to IP addresses for routing your packet through the internet. Hosts can receive the IP address of this DNS server and then resolve hostnames to IP addresses.

3. **B.** (NAT Translation)
   Explanation: Network Address Translation (NAT) server is used for the mapping of IP addresses, and it translates the private addresses inside the network into authorized addresses before packets are delivered to another network.

4. **C.** (RJ-45)
   Explanation: RJ-45 provides communication and control factor in network devices.

5. **A. & B. & D.** (ST & SC & LC)
   Explanation: The three fiber optic connectors are ST, SC and LC. Bayonet Neill–Concelman (BNC) connector is used to connect coaxial cables.

6. **B.** (Star)
   Explanation: A star topology is the most common topology in use today. It consists of a group of computers connected to a central point such as hubs or switches.

7. **C.** (Bluetooth)
   Explanation: Bluetooth is designed for short-range connectivity for mobile personal devices. Operational frequency of Bluetooth is 2.45 GHz and coverage area is less than 1 meter.

8. **B. & D.** (An IPv4 address is 32 bits long, represented in decimal & An IPv6 address is 128 bits long, represented in hexadecimal)
   Explanation: IPv4 addresses are 32 bits long and are represented in decimal format. IPv6 addresses are 128 bits long and represented in hexadecimal format.

9. **C.** (EIGRP)

   Explanation: Enhanced Interior Gateway Routing Protocol (EIGRP) belongs to hybrid routing protocols and Cisco proprietary protocol.

10. **C.** (SNMPv2c)

    Explanation: SNMPv2c supports plaintext authentication with MD5 or SHA with no encryption.

11. **C.** (Run)

    Explanation: Run is not included in SNMP utility.

12. **A.** (STP)

    Explanation: STP prevents network switching loops in a network.

13. **B.** (Twisted-pair Cable)

    Explanation: PoE (802.3af) and PoE+ (802.3at) technologies describe a system for transmitting electrical power along with data to remote devices over a twisted-pair cable in an Ethernet network.

14. **D.** (The amount of usable bits transferred in a given period of time)

    Explanation: Goodput measures the number of useful bits per unit of time sent by the network from source to destination.

15. **B. & C.** (5.0 GHz & 2.4 GHz)

    Explanation: Wireless networks use many different frequencies within a band of frequencies, typically the 2.4 GHz and 5.0 GHz bands.

16. **B.** (Logical Link Control)

    Explanation: The LLC sublayer serves as the midway between the physical link and all higher layer protocols. It ensures that protocols like IP can function irrespective of what type of physical technology is being used. Additionally, the LLC sublayer can perform flow-control and error-checking.

17. **D.** (IP)

    Explanation: Internet Protocol (IP) belongs to Layer 3 (Network Layer).

18. **A.** (TCP)

Explanation: TCP functions by opening connections to a remote computer. This is called connection-oriented communication. TCP maintains status information regarding the connections it makes and is therefore a reliable protocol.

19. **C.** (Multiplexing)

Explanation: Multiplexing is the process in which multiple Data Streams, coming from different sources, are combined and transmitted over a Single Data Channel. In networking, the two basic forms of multiplexing are Time Division Multiplexing (TDM) and Frequency Division Multiplexing (FDM).

20. **C. & D.** (802.11g & 802.11b)

Explanation: The wireless standards of 802.11b and 802.11g use only the 2.4 GHz frequency band.

21. **B.** (Transport Layer)

Explanation: The Transport Layer (Layer-4) is responsible for the reliable transfer of data, by ensuring that data arrives at its destination error-free and in order.

22. **C.** (Application Layer)

Explanation: The Application Layer protocol includes FTP, HTTP, Telnet, SNMP and others.

23. **A.** (Layer 6)

Explanation: The Presentation Layer (Layer-6) controls the formatting and syntax of user data for the application layer.

24. **D.** (Protocol Data Units)

Explanation: In encapsulation, Protocol Data Units (PDUs) is the process is of adding headers.

25. **D.** (Error Checking)

Explanation: While the error checking is also performed by ICMP, the most popular function is ping utility that helps in troubleshooting.

26. **B.** (Low Overhead)

Explanation: UDP is quite demanding for low overhead, it has 4 fields.

27. **C.** (11)

Explanation: TCP header has 11 fields.

28. **D.** (443)

> **Explanation:** HTTPS uses port 443 by default.

Chapter 02: Infrastructure

1. **C.** (ST)
   Explanation: ST connectors are associated with fiber-optic cables.

2. **C.** (6a)
   Explanation: Cat 6a is the latest standard approved by TIA/EIA.

3. **B.** (Switch to switch)
   Explanation: Crossover cables are used to connect similar devices together.

4. **B.** (Destination IP Address)
   Explanation: Routers match the destination IP address to a network in their routing table.

5. **C.** (Both an IDS and an IPS)
   Explanation: Intrusion detection systems and intrusion prevention systems both have capabilities to inform firewalls of intrusions.

6. **C.** (Auditing)
   Explanation: Auditing during an important task is not part of the AAA model of security.

7. **B.** (Type-2)
   Explanation: A hypervisor that runs on top of a host operating system is a Type-2 hypervisor.

8. **B.** (Layers 2 and 3)
   Explanation: Multiprotocol Label Switching labels sit between the Ethernet frame at Layer 2 and the IP packet at Layer 3.

9. **A. & C.** (PVC & SVC)
   Explanation: ATM uses two types of circuit switching: PVC and SVC. VCD and PCV are not the names of switching methods.

10. **B.** (Virtual-Circuit Packet Switching)
    Explanation: When virtual-circuit switching is used, a logical connection is established between the source and the destination device.

11. **C. (Coaxial)**

Explanation: F-type connectors are used with coaxial cables. They are not used with fiber-optic, Unshielded Twisted-Pair (UTP), or Shielded Twisted-Pair (STP) cabling.

12. **A. (ST)**

Explanation: ST fiber connectors use a twist-type connection method. SC connectors use a push-type connection method. The other choices are not valid fiber connectors.

13. **B. (Switch)**

Explanation: Switches automatically segment the network and dramatically decrease the traffic in the segments that are less used.

14. **C. (Layer 2 and Layer 3)**

Explanation: A multilayer switch can perform its function on both layer 2 and layer 3.

15. **D. (Firewall)**

Explanation: Firewalls filter the flow of traffic; it can either be inbound traffic or outbound traffic of a network.

16. **D. (Frame Relay)**

Explanation: Frame relay is a powerful WAN technology that operates at physical and data link layer of the OSI model and it was designed to use over Integrated Service Digital Network (ISDN) interfaces.

17. **C. (Routing Metrics)**

Explanation: Routers use routing metrics to make routing decisions.

18. **B. (VoIP)**

Explanation: Voice over Internet Protocol (VoIP) is the transmission of voice and multimedia content over IP networks.

19. **C. (Either A or B)**

Explanation: There are two standards for Ethernet cable TIA-568A and TIA-568B. Straight through cables must be ended with either TIA-568A on both ends or TIA-

568B on both ends. Similarly, crossover cables should be ended with TIA-568A on one end while TIA-568B at the other end.

20. **C. (Crosstalk)**

Explanation: Crosstalk is signal bleed caused by two wires running next to each other inside a cable.

Chapter 03: Network Operations

1. **B.** (Physical diagram)

Explanation: A physical diagram represents how a network looks, while a logical diagram represents how the traffic flows on the network.

2. **A.** (NIC Teaming)

Explanation: NIC teaming, also known by other terms like port aggregation, combines multiple physical interfaces on a router or switch into one logical interface.

3. **A.** (Hot Site)

Explanation: A hot site has equipment, data, and links ready to go.

4. **A.** (UPS)

Explanation: A UPS (Uninterruptible Power Supply) is only a temporary provision of power, to enable servers to properly shut down. A power generator is required for extended power.

5. **D.** (FTPS)

Explanation: FTPS is FTP using SSL/TLS, and is not used for VPNs.

6. **D.** (HTTP)

Explanation: HTTP is primarily used to deliver web pages and content to browsers, not for uploading and downloading files.

7. **A.** (Longer is better)

Explanation: One of the best ways to strengthen your password, is to make it longer, preventing a brute-force attack.

8. **B.** (AUP)

Explanation: The Acceptable Use Policy (AUP) clearly differentiates between right and wrong in terms of using a company's resources.

9. **C.** (Packet Analyzer)

Explanation: A packet analyzer is like an electron microscope for IT administrators as it inspects the network traffic.

10. **B.** (On-boarding)

Explanation: On-boarding is where administrators allow users' devices to connect.

11. **C.** (Port Bonding)

Explanation: LACP, in CompTIA term, is referred to as Port Bonding.

12. **C.** (Disaster Recovery)

Explanation: Key metrics related to Disaster Recovery (DR) concept include Recovery Point Objective (RPO) and Recovery Time Objective (RTO).

13. **C.** (Service Level Agreement)

Explanation: A Service-Level Agreement (SLA) is the part of a service contract between a service provider and the customer that fully defines what services are expected and how they are to be accomplished. It might include a contracted delivery time for initial services and then an expectation of Mean Time Between Failures (MTBF) and Mean Time to Repair (MTTR) when a failure occurs.

14. **B.** (Cable Trays)

Explanation: Cable trays are metal trays used to organize the cabling neatly and keep it away from the heating areas.

15. **A. & C.** (Full & Incremental)

Explanation: The archive bit is reset after a full backup and an incremental backup.

16. **C.** (Cold Site)

Explanation: A cold site provides an alternative location but typically nothing more. A cold site often requires the delivery of computer equipment and other services.

17. **B.** (Warm Site)

Explanation: Warm sites have the equipment needed to bring the network to an operational state but require configuration and potential database updates.

18. **B. & C.** (Vulnerability Scanners & Penetration Testers)

Explanation: Vulnerability scanning and penetration testing should be used to find the weaknesses in systems before others do.

19. **C.** (Turned on)

Explanation: By default, the automatic update feature is usually turned on.

20. **A.** (NDA)

Explanation: A Non-Disclosure Agreement (NDA) protects the privacy of a network, as those who sign the NDA agree to keep everything confidential.

Chapter 04: Network Security

1. **C.** (Network/Packet Analyzer)
   Explanation: A packet analyzer is like an electron microscope for IT administrators as it inspects the network traffic.

2. **D.** (Packet Flow Monitoring)
   Explanation: The most prevalent packet flow monitoring tool is NetFlow. It consists of flow caching, a flow collector, and a data analyzer.

3. **D.** (Honeypots)

Explanation: Honeypots are security devices used as a decoy to act as a valuable server target to an attacker.

4. **C.** (Wireshark)
   Explanation: Wireshark is the most famous packet sniffer.

5. **A.** (STP)
   Explanation: STP prevents network switching loops in network.

6. **A.** (Metasploit)
   Explanation: Metasploit is an open-source tool used for penetration testing.

7. **C.** (Smurfing)
   Explanation: In smurfing, the attacker floods a network with ping packets sent to all target addresses.

8. **D.** (Physical)
   Explanation: Physical attack is another name of Permanent DoS (PDoS)

9. **C.** (ARP Cache Poisoning)
   Explanation: Both wired and wireless clients can be victims of ARP cache poisoning. The other three attack types are specific to wireless clients.

10. **B.** (Social Engineering)
    Explanation: Social Engineering in Information Security refers to the technique of psychological manipulation.

11. **D.** (SSH)
    Explanation: Secure Shell Protocol (SSH) is secure protocol and it has replaced unsecure protocol Telnet.

12. **A.** (DHCP Snooping)
    Explanation: DHCP snooping is a method of controlling IP address assignment to prevent the possibility of attacks related to ARP spoofing.

13. **C.** (ARP Inspection)
    Explanation: ARP inspection is a method of securing your network by assuring that only authorized traffic is allowed on it.

14. **A.** (Port Filtering)

    Explanation: Port filtering may be affected if a source address has been transformed by Network Address Translation (NAT) or Port Address Translation (PAT).

15. **C.** (To create a security zone that allows public traffic but is isolated from the private inside network)

    Explanation: A DMZ can be set up in many different ways, but the best explanation is that the DMZ is used to separate and secure your inside network from the internet while still allowing hosts on the internet to access your servers.

16. **A.** (Proxies)

    Explanation: Proxies act on behalf of the whole network to completely separate packets from internal hosts and external hosts.

17. **B.** (A host-based firewall is implemented in software, whereas a network-based firewall is implemented in hardware)

    Explanation: Host-based firewalls are of the software variety, whereas network-based firewalls are implemented through hardware.

18. **C.** (Stateful)

    Explanation: Stateful firewalls can hold in memory the major attributes of each connection.

19. **A.** (Mantraps)

    Explanation: A mantrap typically consists of a two-door system that requires authentication to open each door.

20. **D.** (Stop)

    Explanation: A Single Point of Failure, also known as SPOF is any component of a system that causes the whole system to stop working if it fails.

Chapter 05: Network Troubleshooting & Tools

1. **A.** (It displays IP addresses information)
   Explanation: The ipconfig command is used in Windows to display the IP address information of the system.

2. **B.** (Linux)
   Explanation: The ifconfig tool is used in Unix and Linux Operating Systems to configure interfaces and view information about configured interfaces.

3. **A.** (Windows)
   Explanation: The ipconfig command is used in Windows to display the IP address information of the system.

4. **A.** (Netstat)
   Explanation: Netstat command is used to examine network statistics about a system. These statistics include information such as the ports listening on the system and any connections that have been established.

5. **B.** (Unix OS)
   Explanation: The command is available in Unix OS as 'traceroute', while it is available as 'tracert' in Windows NT-based OS.

6. **A.** (Windows NT based OS)
   Explanation: The command is available in Unix OS as 'traceroute', while it is available as 'tracert' in Windows NT-based OS.

7. **D.** (Remote machine's name table given its name)
   Explanation:
   nbtstat -a lists the remote machine's name table given its name.
   nbtstat -A lists the remote machine's name table given its IP address.
   nbtstat -c lists NBT's cache of remote [machine] names and their IP addresses.
   nbtstat -n lists local NetBIOS names.

8. **B.** (Nslookup)
   Explanation: The nslookup utility allows you to troubleshoot problems related to DNS. You can use nslookup to research information about a DNS server or to set a

DNS configuration on the server. You can use nslookup in either non-interactive or interactive mode.

9. **C.** (Toner Probe)

   Explanation: Toner probe is used to test the connectivity of wires that run through walls and other obstructions.

10. **C.** (Crosstalk)

    Explanation: Crosstalk is a signal bleed caused by two wires running next to each other inside a cable.

11. **C.** (Punch Down)

    Explanation: Punch down tool is a hand tool used to connect network wires to a patch panel.

12. **C.** (Local NetBIOS names)

    Explanation:
    nbtstat -a lists the remote machine's name table given its name.
    nbtstat -A lists the remote machine's name table given its IP address.
    nbtstat -c lists NBT's cache of remote [machine] names and their IP addresses.
    nbtstat -n lists local NetBIOS names.

13. **B. & D.** (It is UDP based) & (It only encrypts the password in an authentication packet)

    Explanation: RADIUS uses UDP and does not encrypt the entire packet.

14. **C.** (It is used for looking inside every packet on a network segment)

    Explanation: The basic purpose of packet sniffers or network analyzers is to collect and analyze each individual packet that is captured on a specific network segment to determine whether problems are happening.

15. **A.** (Toner Probe)

    Explanation: A toner probe sends a signal down a pair of wires so that the wires can be traced. Typically, a butt set is used to find this signal, but toner probe is the best answer to this question.

16. **B.** (Loopback Plug)

> **Explanation:** A loopback test is a diagnostic procedure in which a signal is transmitted and returned to the sending device after passing through all or a portion of a network or circuit. A loopback plug makes this test possible.
>
> 17. **A.** (Multimeter)
> **Explanation:** A multimeter, or a Volt/Ohm Meter (VOM), is used to measure voltage, current, and resistance.
>
> 18. **B.** (OTDR)
> **Explanation:** An Optical Time-Domain Reflectometer (OTDR) is an optoelectronic instrument used to give you the skinny on optical fibers. It performs putting out a series of optical pulses into the specific fiber to test and inform the breaks in that fiber.
>
> 19. **A.** (Reboot the servers)
> **Explanation:** Rebooting servers and routers are not part of the troubleshooting model.
>
> 20. **B.** (Latency)
> **Explanation:** When wireless users complain that the network is slow (latency) or that they are losing their connection to applications during a session, it is usually latency arising from a capacity issue.

Acronyms:

AAA	Authentication Authorization and Accounting
AAAA	Authentication, Authorization, Accounting and Auditing
ACL	Access Control List
ADSL	Asymmetric Digital Subscriber Line
AES	Advanced Encryption Standard
AH	Authentication Header
AP	Access Point
APC	Angle Polished Connector
APIPA	Automatic Private Internet Protocol Addressing
APT	Advanced Persistent Tool
ARIN	American Registry for Internet Numbers
ARP	Address Resolution Protocol
AS	Autonomous System
ASIC	Application Specific Integrated Circuit
ASP	Application Service Provider
ATM	Asynchronous Transfer Mode
AUP	Acceptable Use Policy
BCP	Business Continuity Plan
BERT	Bit-Error Rate Test
BGP	Border Gateway Protocol
BLE	Bluetooth Low Energy
BNC	British Naval Connector/Bayonet Niel-Concelman
BootP	Boot Protocol/Bootstrap Protocol
BPDU	Bridge Protocol Data Unit
BRI	Basic Rate Interface
BSSID	Basic Service Set Identifier

BYOD	Bring Your Own Device
CaaS	Communication as a Service
CAM	Content Addressable Memory
CAN	Campus Area Network
CARP	Common Address Redundancy Protocol
CASB	Cloud Access Security Broker
CAT	Category
CCTV	Closed Circuit TV
CDMA	Code Division Multiple Access
CSMA/CD	Carrier Sense Multiple Access/Collision Detection
CHAP	Challenge Handshake Authentication Protocol
CIDR	Classless Inter-Domain Routing
CNAME	Canonical Name CoS Class of Service
CPU	Central Processing Unit
CRAM-MD5	Challenge-Response Authentication Mechanism–Message Digest 5
CRC	Cyclic Redundancy Checking
CSMA/CA	Carrier Sense Multiple Access/Collision Avoidance
CSU	Channel Service Unit
CVW	Collaborative Virtual Workspace
CWDM	Course Wave Division Multiplexing
DaaS	Desktop as a Service
dB	Decibel
DCS	Distributed Computer System
DDoS	Distributed Denial of Service
DHCP	Dynamic Host Configuration Protocol
DLC	Data Link Control
DLP	Data Loss Prevention
DLR	Device Level Ring

DMZ	Demilitarized Zone
DNAT	Destination Network Address Translation
DNS	Domain Name Service/Domain Name Server/Domain Name System
DOCSIS	Data-Over-Cable Service Interface Specification
DoS	Denial of Service
DR	Designated Router
DSCP	Differentiated Services Code Point
DSL	Digital Subscriber Line
DSSS	Direct Sequence Spread Spectrum
DSU	Data Service Unit
DWDM	Dense Wavelength Division Multiplexing
E1	E-Carrier Level 1
EAP	Extensible Authentication Protocol
EDNS	Extension Mechanisms for DNS
EGP	Exterior Gateway Protocol
EIA/TIA Association	Electronic Industries Alliance/ Telecommunication Industries
EMI	Electromagnetic Interference
ESD	Electrostatic Discharge
ESP	Encapsulated Security Payload
ESSID	Extended Service Set Identifier
EUI	Extended Unique Identifier
FC	Fibre Channel
FCoE	Fibre Channel over Ethernet
FCS	Frame Check Sequence
FDM	Frequency Division Multiplexing
FHSS	Frequency Hopping Spread Spectrum
FM	Frequency Modulation

FQDN	Fully Qualified Domain Name
FTP	File Transfer Protocol
FTPS	File Transfer Protocol Security
GBIC	Gigabit Interface Converter
Gbps	Gigabits per second
GLBP	Gateway Load Balancing Protocol
GPG	GNU Privacy Guard
GRE	Generic Routing Encapsulation
GSM	Global System for Mobile Communications
HA	High Availability
HDLC	High-Level Data Link Control
HDMI	High-Definition Multimedia Interface
HIDS	Host Intrusion Detection System
HIPS	Host Intrusion Prevention System
HSPA	High-Speed Packet Access
HSRP	Hot Standby Router Protocol
HT	High Throughput
HTTP	Hypertext Transfer Protocol
HTTPS	Hypertext Transfer Protocol Secure
HVAC	Heating, Ventilation and Air Conditioning
Hz	Hertz
IaaS	Infrastructure as a Service
IANA	Internet Assigned Numbers Authority
ICA	Independent Computer Architecture
ICANN	Internet Corporation for Assigned Names and Numbers
ICMP	Internet Control Message Protocol
ICS	Internet Connection Sharing/Industrial Control System
IDF	Intermediate Distribution Frame

IDS	Intrusion Detection System
IEEE	Institute of Electrical and Electronics Engineers
IGMP	Internet Group Message Protocol
IGP	Interior Gateway Protocol
IGRP	Interior Gateway Routing Protocol
IKE	Internet Key Exchange
IMAP4	Internet Message Access Protocol version 4
InterNIC	Internet Network Information Center
IoT	Internet of Things
IP	Internet Protocol
IPS	Intrusion Prevention System
IPSec	Internet Protocol Security
IPv4	Internet Protocol version 4
IPv6	Internet Protocol version 6
ISAKMP	Internet Security Association and Key Management Protocol
ISDN	Integrated Services Digital Network
IS-IS	Intermediate System to Intermediate System
ISP	Internet Service Provider
IT	Information Technology
ITS	Intelligent Transportation System
IV	Initialization Vector
Kbps	Kilobits per second
KVM	Keyboard Video Mouse
L2TP	Layer 2 Tunneling Protocol
LACP	Link Aggregation Control Protocol
LAN	Local Area Network
LC	Local Connector
LDAP	Lightweight Directory Access Protocol

LEC	Local Exchange Carrier
LED	Light Emitting Diode
LLC	Logical Link Control
LLDP	Link Layer Discovery Protocol
LSA	Link State Advertisements
LTE	Long Term Evolution
LWAPP	Light Weight Access Point Protocol
MaaS	Mobility as a Service
MAC	Media Access Control/Medium Access Control
MAN	Metropolitan Area Network
Mbps	Megabits per second
MBps	Megabytes per second
MDF	Main Distribution Frame
MDI	Media Dependent Interface
MDIX	Media Dependent Interface Crossover
MGCP	Media Gateway Control Protocol
MIB	Management Information Base
MIMO	Multiple Input, Multiple Output
MLA	Master License Agreement/ Multilateral Agreement
MMF	Multimode Fiber
MOA	Memorandum of Agreement
MOU	Memorandum of Understanding
MPLS	Multiprotocol Label Switching
MS-CHAP	Microsoft Challenge Handshake Authentication Protocol
MSA	Master Service Agreement
MSDS	Material Safety Data Sheet
MT-RJ	Mechanical Transfer-Registered Jack
MTU	Maximum Transmission Unit

MTTR	Mean Time To Recovery
MTBF	Mean Time Between Failures
MU-MIMO	Multiuser Multiple Input, Multiple Output
MX	Mail Exchanger
NAC	Network Access Control
NAS	Network Attached Storage
NAT	Network Address Translation
NCP	Network Control Protocol
NDR	Non-Delivery Receipt
NetBEUI	Network Basic Input/Output Extended User Interface
NetBIOS	Network Basic Input/Output System
NFC	Near Field Communication
NFS	Network File Service
NGFW	Next-Generation Firewall
NIC	Network Interface Card
NIDS	Network Intrusion Detection System
NIPS	Network Intrusion Prevention System
NIU	Network Interface Unit
nm	Nanometer
NNTP	Network News Transport Protocol
NTP	Network Time Protocol
OCSP	Online Certificate Status Protocol
OCx	Optical Carrier
OS	Operating System
OSI	Open Systems Interconnect
OSPF	Open Shortest Path First
OTDR	Optical Time Domain Reflectometer
OUI	Organizationally Unique Identifier

PaaS	Platform as a Service
PAN	Personal Area Network
PAP	Password Authentication Protocol
PAT	Port Address Translation
PC	Personal Computer
PCM	Phase-Change Memory
PDoS	Permanent Denial of Service
PDU	Protocol Data Unit
PGP	Pretty Good Privacy
PKI	Public Key Infrastructure
PoE	Power over Ethernet
POP	Post Office Protocol
POP3	Post Office Protocol version 3
POTS	Plain Old Telephone Service
PPP	Point-to-Point Protocol
PPPoE	Point-to-Point Protocol over Ethernet
PPTP	Point-to-Point Tunneling Protocol
PRI	Primary Rate Interface
PSK	Pre-Shared Key
PSTN	Public Switched Telephone Network
PTP	Point-to-Point
PTR	Pointer
PUA	Privileged User Agreement
PVC	Permanent Virtual Circuit
QoS	Quality of Service
QSFP	Quad Small Form-Factor Pluggable
RADIUS	Remote Authentication Dial-In User Service
RARP	Reverse Address Resolution Protocol

RAS	Remote Access Service
RDP	Remote Desktop Protocol
RF	Radio Frequency
RFI	Radio Frequency Interference
RFP	Request for Proposal
RG	Radio Guide
RIP	Routing Internet Protocol
RJ	Registered Jack
RPO	Recovery Point Objective
RSA	Rivest, Shamir, Adelman
RSH	Remote Shell
RSTP	Rapid Spanning Tree Protocol
RTO	Recovery Time Objective
RTP	Real-Time Protocol
RTSP	Real-Time Streaming Protocol
RTT	Round Trip Time or Real Transfer Time
SA	Security Association
SaaS	Software as a Service
SC	Standard Connector/Subscriber Connector
SCADA	Supervisory Control and Data Acquisition
SCP	Secure Copy Protocol
SDLC	Software Development Life Cycle
SDN	Software Defined Network
SDP	Session Description Protocol
SDSL	Symmetrical Digital Subscriber Line
SFP	Small Form-factor Pluggable
SFTP	Secure File Transfer Protocol
SGCP	Simple Gateway Control Protocol

SHA	Secure Hash Algorithm
SIEM	Security Information and Event Management
SIP	Session Initiation Protocol
SLA	Service Level Agreement
SLAAC	Stateless Address Auto Configuration
SLIP	Serial Line Internet Protocol
SMB	Server Message Block
SMF	Single-Mode Fiber
SMS	Short Message Service
SMTP	Simple Mail Transfer Protocol
SNAT Translation	Static Network Address Translation/Source Network Address
SNMP	Simple Network Management Protocol
SNTP	Simple Network Time Protocol
SOA	Start of Authority
SOHO	Small Office Home Office
SONET	Synchronous Optical Network
SOP	Standard Operating Procedure
SOW	Statement of Work
SPB	Shortest Path Bridging
SPI	Stateful Packet Inspection
SPS	Standby Power Supply
SSH	Secure Shell
SSID	Service Set Identifier
SSL	Secure Sockets Layer
ST	Straight Tip or Snap Twist
STP	Spanning Tree Protocol/Shielded Twisted Pair
SVC	Switched Virtual Circuit

SYSLOG	System Log
T1	Terrestrial Carrier Level 1
TA	Terminal Adaptor
TACACS	Terminal Access Control Access Control System
TACACS+	Terminal Access Control Access Control System+
TCP	Transmission Control Protocol
TCP/IP	Transmission Control Protocol/Internet Protocol
TDM	Time Division Multiplexing
TDR	Time Domain Reflectometer
Telco	Telecommunications Company
TFTP	Trivial File Transfer Protocol
TKIP	Temporal Key Integrity Protocol
TLS	Transport Layer Security
TMS	Transportation Management System
TOS	Type of Service
TPM	Trusted Platform Module
TTL	Time to Live
TTLS	Tunneled Transport Layer Security
UC	Unified Communications
UDP	User Datagram Protocol
UNC	Universal Naming Convention
UPC	Ultra Polished Connector
UPS	Uninterruptible Power Supply
URL	Uniform Resource Locator
USB	Universal Serial Bus
UTM	Unified Threat Management
UTP	Unshielded Twisted Pair
VDSL	Variable Digital Subscriber Line

VLAN	Virtual Local Area Network
VNC	Virtual Network Connection
VoIP	Voice over IP
VPN	Virtual Private Network
VRF	Virtual Routing Forwarding
VRRP	Virtual Router Redundancy Protocol
VTC	Video Teleconference
VTP	VLAN Trunk Protocol
WAF	Web Application Firewall
WAN	Wide Area Network
WAP	Wireless Application Protocol/ Wireless Access Point
WEP	Wired Equivalent Privacy
WLAN	Wireless Local Area Network
WMS	Warehouse Management System
WPA	WiFi Protected Access
WPS	WiFi Protected Setup
WWN	World Wide Name
XDSL	Extended Digital Subscriber Line
XML	eXtensible Markup Language
Zeroconf	Zero Configuration

References:

https://www.oreilly.com/library/view/comptia-network-n10-007/9780134866857/ch09.xhtml#ch09

https://www.oreilly.com/library/view/mike-meyers-comptia/9781260121193/ch3.xhtml#lev259

https://sourcedaddy.com/networking/ftp-sharing-and-vulnerabilities.html

https://www.speedguide.net/port.php?port=21

https://www.developer.com/tech/article.php/774121/FTP-Attacks.htm

https://sourcedaddy.com/networking/ftp-security.html

https://www.globalscape.com/blog/top-4-ftp-exploits-used-hackers

https://www.upguard.com/blog/biggest-threat-to-atm-security-is-misconfiguration

https://www.securityweek.com/serious-flaws-found-atms-german-bank

https://krebsonsecurity.com/2018/07/hackers-breached-virginia-bank-twice-in-eight-months-stole-2-4m/

https://krebsonsecurity.com/2018/08/indian-bank-hit-in-13-5m-cyberheist-after-fbi-atm-cashout-warning/

https://learning.oreilly.com/library/view/comptia-network-n10-007/9780134866857/ch09.xhtml

https://learning.oreilly.com/library/view/Mike+Meyers'+CompTIA+Network++Certification+Passport,+Sixth+Edition+(Exam+N10-007),+6th+Edition/9781260121193/ch3.xhtml#lev294

About Our Products

Other Network & Security related products from IPSpecialist LTD are:

- CCNA Routing & Switching Technology Workbook
- CCNA Security v2 Technology Workbook
- CCNA Service Provider Technology Workbook
- CCDA Technology Workbook
- CCDP Technology Workbook
- CCNP Route Technology Workbook
- CCNP Switch Technology Workbook
- CCNP Troubleshoot Technology Workbook
- CCNP Security SENSS Technology Workbook
- CCNP Security SIMOS Technology Workbook
- CCNP Security SITCS Technology Workbook
- CCNP Security SISAS Technology Workbook
- CompTIA Network+ Technology Workbook
- CompTIA Security+ v2 Technology Workbook
- Certified Information System Security Professional (CISSP) Technology Workbook
- CCNA CyberOps SECFND Technology Workbook
- Certified Block Chain Expert Technology Workbook
- Certified Cloud Security Professional (CCSP) Technology Workbook
- CompTIA Pentest Technology Workbook
- CompTIA A+ Core I (220-1001) Technology Workbook
- CompTIA A+ Core II (220-1002) Technology Workbook
- CompTIA CyberSecurity Analyst CySA+ Technology Workbook
- Certified Application Security Engineer | JAVA
- CompTIA Network+ v2 Technology Workbook

Upcoming products are:

- CCNA 200-301 Technology Workbook
- CCNP ENCOR Technology Workbook

Note from the Author:

Reviews are gold to authors! If you have enjoyed this book and helped you along certification, would you consider rating and reviewing it?

Link to Product Page:

Made in the USA
Coppell, TX
10 May 2024

32267819R00236